PRAISE FOR *CULTURAL INTELLIGENCE FOR MARKETERS*

"What makes Anastasia Kārkliņa Gabriel special is her ability to combine strategy with conviction. This book isn't just an intellectual exercise for her. It's a deeply rooted belief developed equally from on-the-ground activism and in-depth research. Anastasia pairs a grounded data-based approach with true pathos for the humans on the other side of the screen."
Rob Gaige, Head of Global Insights, Reddit

"In *Cultural Intelligence for Marketers*, Anastasia Kārkliņa Gabriel gifts us with a complete toolkit of concepts, questions, and language for effective, culturally fluent marketing. But the true brilliance of this book lies in how Dr. Gabriel models exactly what she means—not just in her writing, but in sharing her platform with brilliant yet underrepresented voices from across the industry. For marketers who aspire to both relevance and social responsibility, this book is for you."
Andrew Cohen, Group Strategy Director, Media.Monks

"Cool brands will no longer cut it in the plural and complex world we live in. Accountable brands just might. Dr. Gabriel shows and tells us how to weave social consciousness into the nearly impossible equation of ethical and responsible marketing. A must-read for anyone trying to make a real difference in how we create and communicate value for everyone."
Ted Weber Gola, Performance Creative Product Lead, Google

"Offers a critical perspective, urging us to stop evading our responsibilities and become more aware of our societal role. Dr. Gabriel's book is a necessary handbook for developing strategies inspired by culture, moving beyond the performative representations of diversity prevalent in our industry."
Sebastián Quiroga Cubides, Head of Strategy and Research, Sancho BBDO

"Anastasia Kārkliņa Gabriel offers a crisp, action-oriented blueprint for more conscious brand-building strategies. The book reads like a love letter to anyone in advertising who has at once intuitively understood the power of brands and also been widely underwhelmed by the way in which they have served the cultures from which they borrow."
Laura Frank, EVP Strategy Director, McCann New York

"While brands increasingly realize that they operate within culture, the materials at their disposal to learn how to do so responsibly, respectfully, and inspirationally are in short supply. Anastasia Kārkliņa Gabriel addresses this. An important and accessible read for anyone who wants to get better in this dynamic and fast-evolving field."
Andy Crysell, Founder, Crowd DNA

"If you want to see more people like you working in advertising and also in the advertising you make, this book might be the most important book you'll read in your life. You'll meet frameworks to help you push for change. You'll devour it, and then you'll probably hug it."
Mark Pollard, author of *Strategy is Your Words*

"Anastasia Kārkliņa Gabriel masterfully navigates the often overlooked and misunderstood ways that marketing both shapes—and is shaped by—culture. This groundbreaking work is a bold expedition into the heart of responsible brand marketing. Her insightful guidance illuminates the path towards a genuinely inclusive marketplace. Essential reading for modern marketers."
Joan Ball, Associate Professor of Marketing, Tobin College of Business, St. John's University, NY

"To ensure that our brands remain relevant and show up, we need new tools, approaches, and ways of thinking about culture so that we're more fluent and in tune with contemporary culture and audience expectations. The playbook to guide the way is *Cultural Intelligence for Marketers*. It helps to instill cultural fluency at the heart of brand management and should be required reading for anyone managing a brand today."
Dino Demopoulos, Chief Strategy Officer, GUT Toronto

"I suspect that many, if not most, marketers have yet to be exposed to the inextricable link between culture and consumption. That is why this book is an invaluable resource to inform, upskill, and empower brand leaders to be fit for their future. It makes cultural intelligence an articulable, appealing, and attainable imperative for marketers to meet the needs of the citizens they serve."
Samuel Monnie, SVP Revenue, Sustainable Brands, and co-host of *Across The Pond: Marketing Transformed* podcast

"Provides practical case studies and actionable frameworks, pulling from decades of past, present, and future wisdom. Part of what makes Anastasia Kārkliņa Gabriel's voice so contagious and affecting is her crystal clarity in seeing things both as they are and as they should be — a much-needed perspective for the times. If you're up to the task, this book is for you."
Nick Susi, Executive Director of Strategy, dotdotdash, and former Head of Strategy, Complex Collective

"Today, the players of industry are eager to tap into 'cultural intelligence' and, in this eagerness, often surface with a string of flippant trends or aesthetics instead of a critical orientation towards culture's layered modes of meaning. Deployed by Dr. Gabriel, cultural intelligence frameworks marry ethics and opportunity instead of positioning them as opposing goals of a zero-sum game. In aligning these interests, her book does a service to the field."
Mira Kopolovic, Global Director of Cultural Insights, We Are Social

Cultural Intelligence for Marketers

Building an Inclusive Marketing Strategy

Anastasia Kārkliņa Gabriel

KoganPage

First published in Great Britain and the United States in 2024 by Kogan Page Limited

2nd Floor, 45 Gee Street	8 W 38th Street, Suite 902	4737/23 Ansari Road
London	New York, NY 10018	Daryaganj
EC1V 3RS	USA	New Delhi 110002
United Kingdom		India

www.koganpage.com

Kogan Page books are printed on paper from sustainable forests.

ISBNs

Hardback   978 1 3986 1405 5
Paperback   978 1 3986 1403 1
Ebook   978 1 3986 1404 8

British Library Cataloguing-in-Publication Data

A CIP record for this book is available from the British Library.

Library of Congress Cataloging-in-Publication Data

Names: Gabriel, Anastasia Kārkliņa, author.
Title: Cultural intelligence for marketers : building an inclusive
   marketing strategy / Anastasia Kārkliņa Gabriel.
Description: London ; New York, NY : Kogan Page Inc., 2024. | Includes
   bibliographical references and index.
Identifiers: LCCN 2023054699 | ISBN 9781398614031 (paperback) | ISBN
   9781398614055 (hardback) | ISBN 9781398614048 (ebook)
Subjects: LCSH: Marketing.
Classification: LCC HF5415 .G235 2024 | DDC 658.8–dc23/eng/20231222
LC record available at https://lccn.loc.gov/2023054699

Typeset by Integra Software Services, Pondicherry
Print production managed by Jellyfish
Printed and bound by CPI Group (UK) Ltd, Croydon, CR0 4YY

CONTENTS

FOREWORD

For centuries, the global GDP was essentially zero. While commercial exchanges were indeed happening between buyers and sellers over this great span of time, the scale at which they occurred was minimal and the nature of these exchanges was largely utilitarian. People bought goods for practical purposes to get functional jobs done. And so was the case until the 16th century when Queen Elizabeth I had a grand idea that she would use consumption as a means of power (McCracken, 1990). This era is widely considered the golden age of England—a time of great expansion in the arts, education, and science in the country. Under her rule, Elizabethan England flourished, but not for everyone.

Her thinking was straightforward: Royalty would have everything, nobility would have less, and peasants would have nothing. Through this lens, nobility would be compelled to consume to maintain their status in the social hierarchy and proximity to royalty, while peasants would look up the social ladder knowing that their position in society was demarcated by their ability—or lack thereof—to consume. And such was the case until the early 18th century when Northern Europe experienced an increase in economic activity thanks to early manufacturing. Businesses in the region made a bit more money, so they paid their employees a bit more money, and these employees went out and spent more. As a result, more companies made a bit more money, and they too paid their employees more money, and they then went out and spent more. This economic activity catalyzed a cycle of consumption, which exploded at the end of the century with the advent of the Industrial Revolution. More companies hired more people to make more products that made more money for said companies by selling more things to more people. More, more. More.

So, what's the point of this history lesson? From its modern conception, consumption had almost nothing to do with functional value propositions and feature benefits. Instead, consumption was driven by social and psychological impulses—and so it is the same today. The brands and branded products we consume today have less to do with *what* they are and more to do with *who* we are.

But who are we? We are the identities to which we subscribe our self-hood. We are the narratives that we negotiate and construct with each other through our social interactions (Avery, 2010) that help us make sense of the world and how we fit into it. The multihyphenated nature of our identity makes for a complex, and often contradictory, intersectionality that constitutes who we are, demarcates the place(s) we occupy in the world, and aids our ability to find *our* people. As social animals, this is invaluable.

Not only does identity demarcate who we are, it also frames how we see the world. That is to say, because of who we are, we hold a certain set of beliefs and ideologies that make up our communal view of reality. For instance, is a cow leather, is it a deity, or is it dinner? Well, it's all three, depending on who you are and how you see the world. Things aren't the way they are, they are the way that we are, based on how we make meaning through the truths we hold about the world and the subsequent stories we tell ourselves about it.

We are who we are, and we translate the world accordingly—which is manifested in the ways by which we navigate the world. Our shared way of life—the artifacts we don, the behaviors we take on, and the language we use—are outward expressions of inward beliefs. And these expressions are communicated and socialized through shared works like literature, film, music, art, and branded products. The alchemy of these elements (identity, beliefs, shared way of life, and shared works) make up our culture, the system of conventions and expectations that delineates who we are and what people like us do.

Consumption is a byproduct of culture, oftentimes a vehicle by which we make our culture material. Culture influences our social needs which are in turn satisfied by consumption (De Mooij, 2001). It's inescapable. These are the same social and psychological impulses that drove consumption in Elizabethan England, and the same forces that catalyzed consumption during the Industrial Revolution and beyond. The result of which poses an imperative for today's marketers: If we are to influence consumption, we must understand culture and how to engage with it.

Much ink has been spilt exploring the relationship between culture and consumption. Scholars across myriad research disciplines have waxed poetic about the impact of culture on brand meaning, favorability, and choice. I, too, have contributed to the discourse in multiple modalities to strengthen our understanding of cultural consumption and extrapolate these dynamics to organization culture and society culture writ large. However, despite our acquisition and dissemination of knowledge on the matter, we have yet to equally invest ourselves in the rigorous interrogation of how to leverage our understanding of cultural consumption in a responsible way.

This kind of interrogation requires both an academic exercise and practical know-how. The academic component provides an examination of the social phenomena associated with marketing—as it pertains to identity, belonging, meaning, and the like—by utilizing a repertoire of cultural theory to deconstruct the invisible forces of consumer behavior that shape how we see the world and influence how we navigate through it. The practical component necessitates an ability to apply new perspectives to the right business context. The combination of the two provides the 1, 2 punch necessary to truly harness the power of culture and its influence. This requires a text to orientate leaders with the right theory and contextualize the uninitiated with the most apropos applications. *Cultural Intelligence for Marketers* is that text.

This is not a typical business book, and it shouldn't be. *Cultural Intelligence for Marketers* provides the frames we need to attune our understanding of contemporary marketing by accounting for the implicit and unintended consequences that result from brands that seek to harness the power of culture by engaging in it. Who wins? Who loses? Must it be a zero-sum game? This requires new perspectives for marketers and new tools to not only avoid potential public backlash but also, and perhaps more importantly, create a new operating system that considers humanity—not just "consumers"—when constructing strategies for how their brands go to market. To understand culture and ignore this imperative is tantamount to driving with a blindfold: You may be skilled, but your impaired vision can cause great harm to others as well as yourself.

This body of work removes the veil of opacity so that we can both see and be better as practitioners as well as citizens of the social world we cohabit. We can be better in business and in community. This raises the bar and the stakes for contemporary marketing, not just because of niceties but rather because this is where the world is going. Some may even argue that this is where we currently are today. You don't have to like it, but you'd be wise to understand it. Best of luck.

Dr. Marcus Collins
Marketing Professor at the Ross School of Business, University of Michigan
Best-selling author of For the Culture: The power behind what we buy,
what we do, and who we want to be
Former Head of Strategy at Wieden+Kennedy, New York

ACKNOWLEDGMENTS

In honor of my ancestors.
With deep gratitude to my teachers.
Owing to the generous love of so many friends.

At the annual convention of the National Women's Studies Association in 2018, I had the privilege of hearing Alice Walker talk about her mentor, Langston Hughes. "He disregarded my ignorance," she said, "which is what good teachers do." I knew exactly what that meant.

This book—my career, my training, my ideas, and my thinking—would not have been possible without my gracious teacher, trusted mentor, and cherished friend for over 10 years, Dr. Wahneema H. Lubiano. Ever since I was 19 years old, Dr. Lubiano patiently disregarded my ignorance and nurtured my capacity for critical thinking; she taught me that not knowing is but an opportunity to learn. That knowledge is, indeed, power.

Over the years, she bestowed upon me the greatest gift a student could receive; she not only taught me how to produce critical thought but also lovingly nurtured in me a deep sense of self-regard: An inner knowing that what I think and have to say matters.

It is my sincere hope that in using my training to make cultural studies more available and accessible to audiences outside of the academy who are looking for ways to cultivate critical consciousness in their everyday life and work, I will have used this gift in ways that will make her proud.

Introduction

A New Paradigm for Culturally Fluent Brands

Sometimes people say to me that cultural studies thinks culture is everything, but I don't think that at all. I think culture is very important; more than important, it's absolutely constitutive. But it's also one among other things—how could you not be also interested in capital, or war, and be alive today? Of course culture isn't everything. But culture is a dimension of everything. Every practice exists in the material world and simultaneously signifies, is the bearer of meaning and value. Everything both exists and is imagined. And if you want to play in the area where deep feelings are involved, which people hardly understand, you have to look at culture.

STUART HALL, IN CONVERSATION WITH BILL SCHWARZ

Every cultural shift has its tipping point, an origin story. Movements for radical social change that took root in the 1960s marked a palpable transformation in collective consciousness. The civil rights and the Black Power movements, the anti-war, second-wave feminism, and queer liberation movements re-energized the ongoing struggle to fulfill the promise of a more inclusive, multiracial democracy. This struggle for equity and justice not only challenged and changed the laws of the land. But it also began to rewrite unspoken cultural rules that have dictated social norms and behaviors for so long.

The struggle was not new, of course. The civil rights demands for equitable representation in media, which, decades later, would be echoed more loudly within the advertising industry, can be traced directly back to the early 20th century. The discourse on the role of identity in visual culture culminated during the Harlem Renaissance, with advertising being one of the "leading image-producing industries" held accountable for its role in racial stereotyping (Chambers, 2011). This period of activism paved the way for the inflection point that occurred in the mid-to-late 20th century, which marked a time when radically new ideas, long overdue legal rights, and progressive narratives finally began to take hold. And advertising was no exception.

In this era of change, the industry faced a critical moment. The advocacy of civil rights leaders inspired demands beyond race and ethnicity to encompass representation of gender in advertising. By 1978, the National Advertising Review Board (NARB) issued "a checklist of questions for advertisers and agency personnel to consider when creating or approving an advertisement" portraying women (Sivulka, 1998). Advertising agencies were advised to consult a checklist featured in Appendix A of the NARB report, titled "Guidelines developed by the National Advertising Review Board for the United States." Divided into four sections—destructive portrayals, negative appeals, constructive portrayals, and positive appeals—the checklist covered a range of harmful depictions. These included sexist stereotypes, belittling language, and creative ads portraying situations that "confirm the view that women are the property of men or are less important than men" (Sivulka, 1998). Among 23 bullet points, questions such as "Do my ads portray women as more neurotic than men?" or "Do my ads reflect the fact that girls may aspire to careers in business and the professions?" were presented for advertisers' consideration. This response from the NARB was hardly surprising, though. The pressure was on.

During this time of heightened social protest, feminists placed stickers saying "This ad insults women" on billboards, vandalized and rewrote ad taglines, and gave out so-called "Plastic Pig" awards to companies that continued to portray women in ways considered demeaning (Sivulka, 1998). As the *New York Times* reported in 1983, a feminist group, Women Against Pornography, considered "'any ad that reduces women to objects, to merely their sexual parts" to be pornographic and, thus, insulting to all women (Herman and Johnston, 1983). In 1983, the "award" went to Hanes, Cotler's Pants, Maidenform, Fidji Perfume as well as Dior for various ads depicting undressed women in subservient positions to men (Reilly et al., 1983). As the historical record shows, however, it wasn't all one-sided. Activists not only "zapped" brands who persisted in relying on sexist advertising but also looked to incentivize forward-thinking, culture-shaping brands that bravely tapped into more progressive narratives. During the award ceremonies hosted by Women Against Pornography, other advertisers were celebrated and rewarded by feminist activists for "their positive portrayal of women."

In 1985, for instance, during its fourth annual awards ceremony, the group honored brands with what they referred to as Ms. Liberty (Libby) awards. Among them was American Express, recognized for "one ad showing a Black businesswoman disembarking from a plane with a briefcase in one hand and a teddy bear in the other, and another ad showing male and female co-workers celebrating a woman's promotion." Toys To Grow On was also recognized for "an ad presenting a little girl in engineer's overalls calling instructions into a field telephone" as well as "United Negro College Fund for its television portrayal of a young Black woman's struggle to fulfill her dream of being a doctor." Much like today, this was a time of impassioned activism.

By then, the fight for inclusive representation had been going on for years. The women's liberation movement owed much to the foundation laid by the Black freedom struggle and the civil rights activities of the sixties, years earlier. It was the Civil Rights Movement that gave a platform to those who openly challenged blatantly racist, ethnocentric, and sexist stereotypes so rampant in the advertising industry at the time. During this period, criticism increased over portrayals of historically marginalized groups that were "considered stereotypical, limited, and in many cases derogatory" (Williams et al., 2015). Black leaders were the first to demand that marketers invest in a more accurate representation of cultural diversity in the United States.

The change was slow but the pressure was felt. In 1967, DDB was one of the first agencies to run a racially and ethnically diverse campaign, one of the first of its kind (Sivulka, 1998). William Bernbach, who founded DDB with James Edwin Doyle and Maxwell Dane, was the creative voice behind a campaign for Henry S. Levy and Sons, a major Brooklyn bakery, called Levy's for short. The campaign was a humorous play on "the Jewish rye," the bakery's most famous type of bread. The copy, which was intended to make the bakery "attractive to a wide range of potential customers," read, "You don't have to be Jewish to love Levy's" (Barthel, 1988). While William Taubin, a male copywriter at DDB, received credit at the time, the now-historic tagline was actually written by Judy Petras, a Jewish woman copywriter at the agency (Fox, 2014).

The ads were far from being culturally sensitive in their portrayals by present-day standards, but the campaign nevertheless featured Black, Asian, Italian, Chinese, and Native American models in ways never seen before. At the time, it was one of the first public ad campaigns to incorporate historically underrepresented groups and intentionally highlight the cultural and racial diversity of New York City. The campaign was ultimately highly successful and made Levy's the largest seller of rye bread in the city.

At the same time, attention to issues of cultural diversity in advertising was also given in academic circles. Two years after the DDB campaign for Levy's, a research study published by Dr. Harold H. Kassarjian (1969) hypothesized that the frequency of Black models, actors, and celebrities would have increased by 1965 as the advertiser "was unable to hide from his *social responsibility*." The opposite was found to be true.

Even in the late sixties, the public discourse and national media had already included widespread conversations about cultural representation in advertising. In response to his critics, one of whom argued that Kassarjian underestimated the progress of inclusion of Black people in advertising media, he responded: "Unfortunately, progress is still very slow, and we have very little to be proud of—the black model quite clearly is still a token..." (Kassarjian, 1971).

A token? Does that not sound familiar to concerns raised in the advertising industry today? Evidently, the conversations that marketers are confronted with today have been part of the industry's lexicon since at least the late sixties. All these conversations within academia, in activist circles, and in media focused on nothing other than the "social responsibility" of brands with respect to cultural issues, equitable representation, and inclusivity. It turns out that the discourse concerning inclusivity that marketers are now called to respond to is not all that new after all!

In fact, Professor Kassarjian began his research paper by specifically discussing how civil rights organizations, like the Congress for Racial Equity (CORE) and The National Association for the Advancement of Colored People (NAACP), "brought direct pressure upon advertisers" to increase the representation of Black Americans in advertising. In 1964, the *New York Times* reported the immense impact that civil rights organizing had already had on the advertising industry at that time:

Though 1963 produced handsome gains for most media, it also produced some thorny problems for advertisers. The most demanding stemmed from *the rising expectations of the [Black] community.*

Though advertisers have traditionally assumed that they could divorce themselves from the nation's social issues, the... revolution proved otherwise. [African-American] groups presented many leading advertisers with a difficult choice: Either use [African-Americans] in advertising and television programing or risk widespread... boycotts."

(Note: The author took the liberty of editing the quotation to replace outdated racial language.)

The pressure was on! In the fall of 1963, only a few weeks before the March on Washington, the American Association of Advertising Agencies held a special meeting attended by 102 advertisers from 56 agencies, during which the NAACP made demands for increased Black representation in general advertising, particularly on television. The Congress for Racial Equality (CORE), which was led by Clarence Delmonte Funnyé at the time, contacted advertisers one by one as well as calling advertiser meetings (Boyenton, 1965). Once, Funnyé stood on a street corner with several television sets and offered a dollar whenever a passerby saw a Black person on the screens. After six consecutive Saturdays, Funnyé had given away only 15 dollars in cash (Colby, 2012). As writer Tanner Colby notes, "Funnyé's stunt was a part of CORE's TV Image Campaign, an effort to pressure broadcasters into airing more, and more positive, images of black Americans on network television programs—and, just as importantly, in the advertisements that paid for them." The same year, Funnyé also wrote to the Coca-Cola Company's president at the time, Paul Austin, demanding that "African Americans appear in mainstream television and print advertisements for Coke" or face a boycott. While the company hesitated to run integrated ads, the first integrated television commercial finally aired in 1969, as was observed in Laura A. Hymson's doctoral research on Coca-Cola's cultural branding (2011).

A few years later, in 1970, the NAACP published the results of a study in the *New York Times*, which concluded that Black representation in TV ads was still minimal and fair representation of "televised programs and commercials [was] necessary to promote an image of racial equality" (Ferretti, 1970). Although progress was indeed painfully slow and minimal, in the following years, some changes occurred. Numerous racist brand characters, such as Frito Bandito, "Chinese Cherry," and "Injun Orange" were either discontinued or altered to eradicate visual elements that were outright stereotypical or insulting (Behnken and Smithers, 2015). The calls for cultural change evolved beyond racial and ethnic representation, and in the late 1970s, brands like Miller Lite, Coors Light, and Budweiser began placing ads in regional queer newspapers, with Absolut following suit in 1981 (Telford, 2023).

In hindsight, the industry was too slow to respond, adjusting to a shift in cultural values but ultimately offering only superficial concessions. Of course, just like in the present day, there were large segments of the industry that argued that advertising had no social obligation to historically marginalized people. There was a prevailing fear that inclusivity in advertising would "alienate" the white consumer.

It's important to recognize that inclusive representation back then was much like what some still to this day call a "controversial topic" in marketing and advertising. Over 50 years later! The demands for more diverse representation received pushback from the conservative segments of the industry and the public, who feared "alienating" white consumers; these concerns are still pervasive to this day.

We can trace many linguistic and cultural parallels between this past and our present. In an article first published in June 1965, journalism professor William H. Boyenton lamented the efforts of the Civil Rights Movement to "harness advertising for their own purposes" (Boyenton, 1965). Boyenton diagnosed a new direction in advertising. In addition to the three rules of business—advertising to people ready and willing to buy, using media to reach them, and making advertising that will win business—Boyenton wrote about "the novel fourth" dimension. It differed from "the old three" that "were concerned with profit only." This fourth dimension he called... "social purpose." Sounds familiar?

See, the study of cultural history is often dismissed as entirely irrelevant in business. But examining origin stories forces us to confront cultural knowledge that we will need to understand the present moment we inhabit. With this knowledge, we will be better equipped to shape the future of this industry. But what happens when we look back at marketing's cultural history? We can see much more clearly that even 50 years ago, marketers were not only aware of the need for cultural representation but were under active pressure from civil rights activists, feminists, and queer advocates to transform marketing into a more socially responsible practice. Much like today!

While conservative critics today argue that strategy and planning have been "tainted" or "corrupted" by new concepts like brand activism, inclusivity, or social responsibility that are irrelevant to business, the record of history is clear as day. The demand for more inclusive and socially responsible marketing is not as new as we dare to admit. The reality of evolving consumer expectations has now simply caught up with us, so much so that it can no longer be ignored. Understanding inclusive and socially responsible marketing as a novel phenomenon is not only a disservice to the marketing industry but is also profoundly and undeniably ahistorical.

Our society has thankfully seen significant social progress since the late 20th century. The voices of historically marginalized and excluded communities, like those who advocated against sexist and racist advertising several decades ago, have now moved from the margins closer to the center. The question that we are confronted with, then, is not *if* inclusivity has its place in marketing. Rather, the remaining question is, will we pay attention *now*? And as a popular saying goes: "If not us, who? And if not now, *when*?"

While advocates for inclusive marketing are still forced to tirelessly jump through all sorts of hoops to prove diversity's "business case," needless to say, the data-based evidence speaks for itself. The point here is this: The time is now, and our action is long overdue.

The cultural imperative for socially responsible marketing is self-evident, and its commercial impact has been well documented. Even before 2020, research showed that U.S. consumers of various backgrounds preferred diverse and inclusive ads. In August 2019, an Ipsos/Google study found that 69 percent of Black consumers are more likely to purchase from a brand whose advertising positively reflects their race or ethnicity (Google/Ipsos, 2019). Of LGBTQ consumers in the United States, 71 percent are more likely to "trust a brand with advertising that authentically represents a variety of sexual orientations." Since then, abundant research has only confirmed these findings, and younger generations now demand increasingly more from brands. Microsoft Advertising found that 76 percent of Gen Z are more likely to support brands that are authentic in their advertising (DePalma, 2020). On top of existing consumer expectations, we now also know that Gen Z will be the last generation with a white majority in the United States, according to a study by William Frey at the Brookings Institute (Helmore, 2023). According to a more recent survey by Amazon Ads and Environics Research (2022), 67 percent of U.S. consumers believe it is important for brands to promote diversity and inclusion, while 7 in 10 say that "DEI is important when choosing a brand to purchase from." And in sparks & honey's Responsible Marketing Index 2023, 81 percent of consumers surveyed by the consultancy agreed that brands and businesses have a role to play in addressing social issues that affect their customers. Inclusivity, cultural representation, and social responsibility are the future of marketing strategy. Marketers can either embrace these things and step into this future now or scramble around when it arrives. The choice is ours.

After all, this is precisely what happened in 2020. When Mr. George Floyd, described in his obituary (2020) as a "gentle giant" who brightened every room "with his contagious laughter and broad smile," was mercilessly murdered by the police in Minneapolis, protests of historic magnitude erupted across the United States and around the globe. When, much like during the era of the Civil Rights Movement, brands came under scrutiny, marketers no longer had any other choice but to respond. Some of us have been waiting for this moment all along.

By then, I had been involved in the racial and social justice movements as an activist and political organizer long before the hashtag #BlackLivesMatter was coined by Alicia Garza and later popularized along with the movement's co-founders Patrisse Cullors and Opal Tometi. For 10 years, I was proudly and humbly trained by the most brilliant thinkers in the Black radical and intellectual tradition, when undergoing my doctoral training. After 2016, I was honored to organize alongside other grassroots activists to put our bodies on the line to resist the resurgence of right-wing extremism and overt white supremacy across the country by means of democratic peaceful assembly and non-violent direct action. Until that groundbreaking summer of world-wide protests, grassroots activists like us had been relegated to the periphery and treated as too "radical" or unreasonable by mainstream society. Now, it felt like a historic time, a breaking point. And it surely was.

Finally, brands started recognizing how important understanding culture is. In the next few years, I would go on to consult on cultural strategy for iconic brands like Nike, Disney, Ulta Beauty, Samsung, American Express, Hinge, Fujifilm, eBay, and others. I was privileged to be sought out by ad agencies, market research, and innovation consultancies from across the United States, Canada, and the United Kingdom. Clients now looked to more advanced analytical insight into issues of cultural change. It became impossible to avoid social and political issues. Understanding activist movements that have been historically overlooked became a business imperative. Today, developing cultural knowledge and leveraging critical analysis of power and oppression are integral prerequisites for achieving cultural relevance in the world of brands.

And it surely starts with expanding our horizons. As conscious marketers committed to leveraging marketing and media for social good, the urgency to broaden what I term "our point of reference" couldn't be higher. Marketing colleagues who realize the significance of understanding culture in marketing today routinely ask me how to break out of the business bubble: How can I learn more? How do I expand my worldview? Only recently, I received a message on social media from a marketer asking if I could put together a reading list of socially conscious books and resources. Marketers who recognize that culture is central to the future of marketing yearn to learn and expand their point of reference in the world. And they are on to something. This curiosity isn't merely an intellectual exercise for personal edification; it's a strategic imperative for business, especially in an industry often limited by its own geographical and cultural gaps in awareness, knowledge, and the practice of inclusivity in the workplace.

For one, perspectives at agencies and in-house are frequently confined to the perspectives of those in large metropolitan cities like New York City, London, or Los Angeles. And yet, we must remember: Culture is equally lived, experienced, and shaped elsewhere. It is often lived in radically different ways from what we know to be familiar. To understand culture, to know how to leverage cultural conversations, and how to make a meaningful impact on both business and society, the industry needs to broaden its cultural worldview. This means engaging with perspectives from activist communities, critical humanities, cultural theory, and historical knowledge. It seemingly has little to do with immediate business needs, but seeking out and immersing yourself in these bodies of knowledge will equip you with insights needed to execute more culturally fluent marketing in the long run. This book aims to do just that.

Not only because doing so benefits the brand clients, although that is certainly true. But because brands have an enormous influence on culture. Brands not only respond to and reflect modern-day culture; the messaging consumers receive through marketing media actively shapes cultural norms, ideas, and values that constitute what British Jamaican cultural theorist Stuart Hall called our collective "common sense." Hall defined "common sense" as that which "feels as if it has always been there" (Hall, 1977). And what is marketing if not a collection of culturally resonant narratives disseminated in the form of strategic messaging in a way that moves people? In drawing on these familiar cultural stories, marketing media either affirms, defies, or re-interprets this "common sense" sense of how things are or how things should be. What we see represented in marketing media (and, therefore, normalized in our culture) further shapes what is acceptable in society, who is accepted, what is desired, who is desirable, and so on.

After all, so much of successful marketing is just effective cultural storytelling about who we are and what we care about. As Dr. Marcus Collins notes in *For the Culture*, these systems of meaning around us "act as vehicles that transport meaning from a culturally constituted world in which we live to the brands that we consume and later adopt as part of our own cultural practices" (Collins, 2023). It's surely no coincidence that representation in marketing so vividly mimics and reflects broader social norms; the world as we know it is our point of reference, and if we are not intentional and conscious of our impact, we will simply reproduce stories around us without thinking much about it. And if advertising is, indeed, a "strong persuader and a reflector of our culture," then marketers have not only the power but also the responsibility to provide a means by which inclusion of historically marginalized people can be achieved "in the mainstream of life" (Cohen, 1970).

This is precisely why all those years ago, civil rights organizers and feminist activists felt so impassioned about demanding better representation from the industry. They understood back then what we, too, so unmistakably understand now: The status quo is no longer an option.

That's why *Cultural Intelligence for Marketers* exists. To provide a new point of reference for understanding how to understand and leverage the power of culture in brand marketing. This book will begin with a foundational chapter on brands' role in culture. I will introduce you to a more innovative and hopefully inspiring way of thinking about culture and brands together, which I hope will invite you to see your work as a marketer in a more empowering light. Following that, we'll dive right in. I will introduce you to the 4Cs of cultural marketing as I conceptualize the most important pillars: Culture, communications, critical consciousness, and community. Each chapter will cover one of the four elements in depth and detail. You will have an opportunity to delve into the nuances of brand accountability and community co-creation. You will learn how to move away from calling anything and everything "intersectional" for the sake of it to actually putting intersectionality into practice. We will also cover how to develop a critical lens to decode cultural movements, social issues, and cultural texts. Throughout these pages, you will also have an opportunity to learn from some of the most talented and brightest voices in inclusive marketing and cultural fluency. The chapters in this book will feature insights and perspectives in the form of one-on-one interviews with experts who walk the talk in their everyday lives as marketers with an unapologetic, bold, and innovative culture-forward approach to business and social change.

As I mentioned, the marketing world can be a bubble of its own. It will hopefully soon become clear why it is so important that we strive to broaden the diversity of our thinking and lived experiences in this field by deconstructing things like power, access, and privilege. For one, we must actively subvert who is typically considered an "expert" in the industry and share our platform whenever possible. Intentionally, then, the experts interviewed and featured throughout the book are women and genderqueer industry leaders who are Black, immigrant, neurodiverse, and otherwise coming from historically underrepresented backgrounds in the industry. This choice is entirely purposeful.

As you will soon discover, one of the premises of this book is that deepening our engagement with culture means that we also need to develop our understanding of power. Who has it, and who has historically been denied it? Who is most commonly featured and given a platform to be an authority on a subject matter? How can we share access to being in the spotlight, which we earn due to our talents and hard work as well as our privilege? Multiple truths can co-exist at once.

For this reason, I am most honored to share the space on these pages with these bold, visionary voices. I am certain that as a reader, you will find even deeper meaning, inspiration, and tactical advice in the insights about culture, marketing, and industry trends they have so generously shared throughout the following chapters.

If you are a current or aspiring marketing leader and are eager to learn how to make your work more inclusive, socially responsible, and culturally intelligent, this book was written for you. In *Cultural Intelligence for Marketers*, you will learn more about the power brands hold in shaping cultural norms, values, and expectations and, most importantly, how to yield this power responsibly. This book does not aim to challenge, disrespect, or dismiss the conventional wisdom of business strategy or the art of planning. But it is not an introductory read about glossary terms like diversity and inclusion, either. Rather, I hope this book leaves you with a fresh new perspective on leveraging culture in marketing in a way that boldly challenges performativity and superficiality in our industry. As the history record shows, the current approach not only does not work but holds us back from genuine progress. The time to get it right is now, so let's get to work.

In Conversation with Dr. Harold H. Kassarjian

Dr. Harold H. Kassarjian is Professor Emeritus of Marketing at the UCLA Anderson School of Management. Dr. Kassarjian received his doctorate in social psychology from UCLA and began his career with a survey research firm with clients such as the New York Times, Los Angeles Times, *radio and TV stations, and traditional marketing firms. He has had visiting professor appointments at Illinois, Penn State, Denmark, Mexico, Portugal, Armenia, and at the Federal Trade Commission. Dr. Kassarjian has taught courses in consumer behavior, marketing, marketing research, mass communications, statistics, psychology, and social psychology. His consulting appointments have ranged from governmental and regulatory agencies to private industry—often as an expert witness on marketing research and consumer behavior topics. His seminal content analysis study, "The Negro and American Advertising, 1946–1965," was published in the* Journal of Marketing Research *in 1969. It was one of the first studies in marketing that sought to analyze Black representation in advertising over time.*

AKG: Dr. Kassarjian, I am honored to have this special opportunity to talk to you. What a privilege to share this time with you, and what a unique opportunity for our readers, too, to read the words of someone who was one of our predecessors and pioneers in this line of work. The readers should know that you published one of the first studies on the representation of Black Americans in advertising over 50 years ago. In 1969, to be exact. Your study used content analysis to analyze the frequency of Black models and actors featured in ads between 1945 and 1969. I can't help but think how the first Black Studies program in the United States was only established at San Francisco State University in 1968. Surely, this was not a popular topic of research in the academy at that time. What prompted you to invest in this research?

HK: The conversation about this topic emerged from the Civil Rights Movement. At that time, so much media attention was focused on the role of African Americans, the place of African Americans in society, and so on. Everybody had an opinion! Especially about how Black Americans have been treated and represented in advertising. I thought to myself, "but we don't have any data!" I decided I would go ahead and get data on the issue and see what the actual changes have been. In fact, have there even been significant changes up to the Civil Rights Movement days at all? Has any progress been made? I continued that work up to 1979.

AKG: What did you discover in your research over this time period?

HK: Nothing dramatic, just what you would expect... By '73, the number of Black people in ads had increased only slightly. And by '79, it had increased dramatically, except that... Black Americans were not being represented in any sort of realistic middle-class roles in ads. Black Americans were represented as the big shots, so to speak. They were pigeonholed into roles of high visibility but narrow scope, portrayed as heroes, football players, and entertainers. That kind of nuanced, everyday representation was glaringly absent. They were not represented as the everyday middle-class person. That kind of representation was sorely lacking. You didn't see Black men portrayed in realistic everyday roles back then [in '69], and despite supposed progress, you didn't see them in '79 either.

AKG: You discovered in your 1969 study that by the mid-1960s the numbers of Black people in ads had actually decreased compared to 1956. "The advertiser," you wrote, "was unable to hide from his social responsibility," yet still feared what you called "consumer reprisal." I pause and linger on these words while reading this because these exact words might as well be written in one of the industry publications in 2023. What was it like to do that research at the time? Did you work on your own? What kind of reaction did you receive in response to your research?

HK: I've always been on my own. Once the research was published, the college showed some interest. The media showed a great deal of interest. I received an awful lot of media exposure at the time. My colleagues were interested—that is, those who were interested in social issues and questions related to social policy. But the average consumer researcher, however, wasn't too interested in this kind of work. The typical consumer researcher was more interested in how the consumer behaves and why. Not so much... what is the right way to behave? What is a good way to behave, or what is the correct way to behave for your own benefit?

AKG: In the 1960s, there was mounting pressure to improve the representation of Black Americans in advertising. As you noted in the article, the civil rights leaders believed that adequately representing Black Americans in conventional middle-class settings would help rewrite harmful racial stereotypes in culture. Much like now, the civil rights leaders believed that advertising could reshape cultural narratives and advance the cause of inclusivity. What was the response to that sort of thinking specifically within the marketing industry at the time?

HK: The civil rights movement was pushing for more and more inclusion of African Americans. No surprise! The industry, on the other hand, being as conservative as it is... I don't mean politically conservative, but business conservative—well, politically too, I suppose! There was a significant concern about what would happen if you had a Black and a white person in the same ad together. That was their main concern. What will the effect be on African Americans, and what might the effect be on whites at the time? There wasn't much data, but little by little, a few studies came out.

AKG: It's sobering to think about this from the vantage point of the present, considering in the last 10 years, I can count a couple of times when there was a negative response to a cereal ad and another retail ad featuring an interracial couple. Of course, so much of the hatred is now targeted at the representation of people from LGBTQ+ communities. But what did the studies find at that time?

HK: A few studies showed that when you had a Black person in the ad, African Americans preferred it and preferred that product. As one would expect, it was very positive for Black people to see other Black people in advertising; as consumers, they reacted positively toward it. Now the question was, how would whites react to the kind of products that we were talking about? Little by little, a few studies came out here and there that showed that when you asked whites and tested the effect on whites of seeing a Black person in the ad, it actually had no effect on whites at all. So, with Black consumers, it had a positive effect. With whites, it didn't matter. That is, the industry was entirely wrong in being concerned that there would be a backlash! The studies were not many and not big, but it didn't matter at the time. I was, at that time, very interested in content analysis, so I was interested in asking: What are the facts, and what is the case with data? Now, then, the question was what about all-Black ads, all-white ads, or mixed-race ads? Black ads again had very little effect on whites. They just didn't give a damn! Whites just didn't give a damn. That's where we stood.

AKG: This resonates with the present moment. An abundance of studies has been published on the positive effect that diversity in advertising has on consumer preferences. And yet, there is still a constant need to defend what we call "the business case" for inclusive marketing. This fear of backlash continues to exist, despite all this data that we now have in our hands.

HK: But it was just the beginning, you know. The conversation evolved. In the late '60s and early '70s, that's when these concerns came up. Should Black and white people in ads even be standing apart? Could they be touching? Could they be caressing each other? Could they be kissing? Could they be hugging? You know, these are all issues at that time. In almost all of the ads we saw at the time, there was a separation between the two.

AKG: Advertising reflected the social norms of that time.

HK: That's right. For instance, you did not get Black and white people touching, especially not in any sexual or affectionate way, whether that's caressing or even a kiss. The belief that there would be a backlash was pretty strong. It just wasn't touched.

AKG: In hindsight, we are not surprised to hear that, knowing the context of the Jim Crow era and the struggle against racial segregation leading up to the late 1960s and 1970s. And yet, even now, the industry continues to have near-identical conversations about how "controversial" it might be for brands to engage with issues of race, gender, and particularly sexuality and gender expression. It is not lost on me that you began that particular journal article by writing—and I quote—"It has become almost axiomatic to claim that mass media of communication, and advertising as a subset, reflect the culture and society in which they exist." Would you please elaborate for our readers about this relationship between advertising and culture and the role of what you referred to even in 1969 as "the social responsibility of advertisers"? That is so powerful to read 54 years later as I write this book.

HK: I don't know if my opinion has changed since that time. We have always believed that advertising both reflects the culture and also drives the culture. We are affected by advertising, not just by the kind of shoes we wear, but by the things we think about and do. I think it was just as strong then as it is now. In fact, maybe stronger today because now there is so much impinging on the consumer from so many sources. Advertising has been diluted a bit. At that time, advertising was a major information source, where we got information on how one behaves, how one dresses, and everything else. Yes, it reflected the culture, but it also pushed that reflection forward… pushed it forward. You weren't going to get equality issues [represented in advertising] before then, but once the public discussions started, it had an effect.

When we talked about equality in those days, it meant "African Americans" or maybe other ethnic minorities, too. It did not mean women. Women were to be in a home, but they were not expected to become Secretary of State or run for Vice President. That was not a role for a woman, according to the views at that time. That was just not considered. It was just too far out, in left field, so equality at that particular point in time did not mean gender equality. It meant "minority." The conversation about gender in advertising did not come into effect until the late '70s or early '80s when we started thinking about gender. But not at this time, not at the time of the Civil Rights movement.

AKG: In our earlier correspondence, however, you wrote to me that you went on to publish some work about women's representation in advertising as well.

HK: It was what interested me at the time. The study I did later was on the role of women in the comic strips in Sunday's comics. How were women treated there? How did that get started? As a first-year graduate student, I started collecting the Sunday comics in the *Los Angeles Times* and the *Examiner*. In those days, the comic pages were maybe 16 pages long. In those days, it was a lot. There were a lot of strips, so I just collected them. Every Sunday, I would get the newspaper, take out the comics, and put them in a box. Soon, it became more boxes and soon after, my garage was pretty full of boxes. It must have been in the '80s or the late '70s that I started thinking, it's time to pull my comics out and look at the issues of the day. What were the issues of the day? The role of African Americans, the role of women, the role of Asian Americans, and the role of other minorities. That's in fact what I did. I did a regular full-blown content analysis from the time I was a student to that point in time. I had 46 years worth of material. It was not a random sample by any means. But it was the best I could do. It was the best I had. And what did we find? With Asian Americans and other minorities, it was impossible to do the study. There weren't any! You might find one person, but Asian Americans and African Americans dropped out of comics. But women did not. Women were treated very interestingly in the comics. They were all superwomen. There were no plain old everyday women. They had primarily two roles. One was the helpless little thing that the superhero had to save. You got a little bit of that. But the majority were superwomen. There was the character of Brenda Starr, the reporter, who was brilliant at everything she did. There was Wonder Woman. It was the same way that African Americans were being treated in advertising, as supermen or big shots, so to speak. Football players or entertainers. If you had a Black person, it was some type of hero-like character. If you had a woman, it was a superwoman. So again, there was nothing equal there. They were not in an equal role in terms of realistic everyday portrayals.

AKG: As a researcher and a scholar but also perhaps as a consumer in your daily life, was there a particular point in time during those years where you may have noticed a change in the industry? Was there ever a tipping point that signaled progress?

HK: There were no tipping points. It was very slow.

AKG: Will the role of culture and social issues always be a part of marketing and advertising? I ask this because the book I am writing asks, how do we think about these issues? How do we really understand inclusion and the history of diversity in advertising so that we can become more culturally intelligent as marketers? Do you think it's something that is just part of what it means to be an advertiser, always to be watching culture and the kind of consumer expectations in regard to social issues?

HK: Advertisers care about these issues but they don't want to go too far. They don't want backlash; they don't want to upset their potential market. Historically, marketers have been very conservative but might include some things here and there. The more modern ones—the more gutty ones—do include it. And when they do, we notice it because advertisers are generally so conservative. Again, not politically conservative but in terms of their approach. But it's all the same... advertising reflects culture. It's helping push it along but it's also reflecting it. When we are truly ready for interracial marriage, we are going to see more frequent portrayals of interracial marriage in ads or magazines. Seeing these images is what's going to help push culture along. Same with the total equality of women in society. It's the same. It'll come up in an ad when the time is right, but the fact that it's in the ad in the first place will help it along. Advertising will help move culture along.

AKG: There's a kind of reciprocal relationship here. Advertising reflects culture but also helps move the culture forward. Earlier, you highlighted research from the '60s that showed how Black audiences responded more favorably to ads featuring Black models or actors. Now, I've been looking over contemporary studies that indicate similarly that audiences are actively seeking brands that present more diverse models and scenarios that truly represent the diversity of our society in all its complexity. It's intriguing to me to observe how, over the span of 50 years, this sentiment persists and perhaps has even intensified now.

HK: I hadn't thought about that. But you know, you're right. You're right. That explains why we're seeing way more minorities on television. The audience is expecting it. Audiences want it because that's an indication of more inclusiveness. I like that! Your book is going to be pretty interesting.

AKG: I would love to send you a copy when it's out.

HK: I was going to say! As soon as I hear about it, I'm going to buy that copy.

AKG: Thank you, Dr. Kassarjian. Thank you for your work. It is the honor of my career to be in conversation with you.

I extend my most sincere gratitude to Dr. Harold H. Kassarjian for his time and thoughtful attention. It's a privilege to have the opportunity to document and preserve the insights of those who pioneered this work long before many of us even considered it. Without the work of our predecessors, we would lack both the foundation and the inspiration to confront the challenges of today. Their dedication and commitment to critical inquiry serve as both a cautionary tale and an enduring source of wisdom. These legacies offer vital lessons as we navigate the present we've inherited. As you begin this book, I wish to uplift and honor the insights of civil rights advocates, activists, and marketing leaders who took it upon themselves to ask the difficult questions when it was least popular. Their example should inspire us to carry the torch.

1

Redefining Brand Success: The Essentials of Cultural Fluency

WHAT TO EXPECT

In this chapter, we will cover the knowledge essential for understanding culture and driving inclusive, conscious, and responsible marketing outputs. Before we dive deeper into the elements of cultural intelligence in the next chapters, let's align on the fundamentals that will shape our understanding of cultural innovation and inclusivity in marketing. Above all, we need to establish why we even need to spend so much time thinking about the relationship between culture and brands. Below, we will seek answers to the following questions:

- Why do marketers need to understand the relationship between brands and culture?
- What influence do brands have on shaping culture?
- What do we mean by cultural intelligence?
- Why is social awareness essential for cultural intelligence?
- What makes a brand genuinely culturally fluent?

Reality Check: Getting Real About What's Not Working

There is a purpose behind why we began the introduction to this book by delving into the historical origins of inclusive representation, or lack thereof, in marketing and advertising. The point, I hope, should be obvious by now. The discourse on inclusive marketing that the marketing and advertising industry has been engaged in since 2020 is hardly new. It is a conversation that began at least 50 years ago. I hope it will become clear that much can be uncovered and learned when we apply a critical lens to understanding the interplay between culture, history, and social change over time.

For one, it offers us a sobering mirror into what was, and what still is. The realities of the past do not have to be daunting, however. Knowledge is power, and knowing the mistakes of the past doesn't have to immobilize us in despair. On the contrary, being conscientious and attentive to the efforts of those who, in hindsight, were on the right side of history can inspire us to make similar choices today. As marketers, we have an opportunity in our hands to choose differently and more wisely this time around.

There is no point in sugarcoating it, though. For over 50 years, the progress has been painstakingly, unbearably slow. In a private interview, I asked Professor Harold Kassarjian what the tipping points were in the struggle for more inclusive representation in advertising, and his answer was short and precise. It cut through a moment of silence that followed. "There were no tipping points," he told me. "It was very slow." Even that honest acknowledgment alone felt important to hold space for. Moving forward requires the bravery of looking back. We have the opportunity to take stock of the present in light of the past—and approach it with honesty, integrity, decency, and courage.

I first heard of this "formula" when I heard philosopher Dr. Cornel West speak at a university campus. Drawing on the ideas of iconic Black sociologist W.E.B. Du Bois, Dr. West has maintained that if we are to confront the ethical challenges of our time bravely, what we need the most are qualities like honesty, integrity, decency, and courage. What can we learn from the past when we embody these qualities in our work? What can it reveal to us about the reality of our present day? At the very least, we might conclude that, in light of the industry's history, the practice of inclusive and socially conscious marketing must begin with honesty and a commitment to sustainable change.

This "formula" grounds how I will talk about conscious marketing practices in this book. For too long, the ethics of marketing and its power in culture and society have been, if not completely avoided in the industry, then certainly sufficiently overlooked. This is no way to build brands that use this power responsibly.

In marketing, we often applaud brands that are daring and innovative. We admire their bold viewpoints and strong stances. But how often do we pause to appreciate that brands are ultimately run by ordinary people? It's these people behind the brands who have accepted the challenge of being bold, courageous, and self-aware in confronting their own biases and mistakes.

In this book, you, too, are invited to ask difficult questions, engage in uncomfortable conversations, and commit to ongoing continued education that is so essential if more brand-driven businesses are to become more conscientious of their impact. The courage and innovation we admire in brands start with the people behind them. People like us.

From this vantage point, every marketing strategy, every campaign, and every creative ad is *an opportunity* to make a meaningful impact, not only on the business but on society at large. To achieve this, we need to establish practices, processes, and expectations that don't merely encourage social responsibility and critical consciousness in marketing outputs. Instead, these values should be normalized as standard expectations within the industry.

Embracing uncompromising honesty as a cornerstone of ethical marketing demands leadership that is both visionary and empowered to make informed, intentional decisions within their organizations and teams. To truly disrupt the historical tendencies to sideline demands for inclusion, we must take on an honest evaluation of present-day challenges and barriers.

DEFINING THE TERMS: WHAT IS CULTURAL FLUENCY?

I define cultural fluency here as the brand's capability to engage in culture with resonance, integrity, and measurable impact by consciously using media to shape cultural conversations. For brand-driven businesses, this means not only aligning and resonating with historically excluded consumer segments but also developing the foresight to be at the forefront of, and even anticipate, the continuous and real-time shifts and evolutions in culture and leverage them for commercial advantage and social good. Cultural fluency, then, denotes proficiency in putting the insights acquired through the practice of cultural intelligence into practice and scaling them across the entire business function. Culturally fluent brands invest in the practice of cultural intelligence as the foundation upon which a brand's cultural fluency is built. Cultural fluency is what is achieved when brands engage in the ongoing process of learning to track culture and leverage cultural knowledge for commercial success and social good. It is the difference between brands that simply exist within a culture and those that become an integral and valued part of the emergent cultural conversation.

Let's start by openly dissecting the challenges confronting brands today. Increasingly, customers have evolving expectations of brands to demonstrate fluency in issues of culture and identity. And yet, brands still too frequently fail to connect with audiences who expect not only "inclusive" representation in campaigns and ads but also a greater overall cultural fluency in how issues of diversity, equity, and inclusion are taken on and addressed. Here are some of the most common ways in which brands fall short of meeting these expectations:

- Presenting stories that implicitly or explicitly rely on stereotypes or only offer a single perspective that fails to challenge the status quo.
- Using tokenism by occasionally featuring models from underrepresented backgrounds to appear diverse while not truly emphasizing inclusivity.
- Implementing superficial gestures that fail to acknowledge past harms or create meaningful improvements.
- Making promises of social impact that brands are either unable or unwilling to keep.
- Creating campaigns that may seem diverse but still inherently have ingrained colorism, unrealistic beauty standards, or they center models or customers from dominant groups.
- Appropriating from marginalized communities without involving real people in the process or compensating them for their contributions.
- Failing to understand the complexities of how various forms of oppression along the lines of race, gender, class, etc. intersect and producing overly simplistic or even harmful outputs.
- Perpetuating outdated narratives that uphold binary notions of gender or don't recognize evolved gender dynamics in family, childrearing, lifestyle, sport, or health.
- Casting models from underrepresented backgrounds in creative, but not actually making products and services accessible to customers of various abilities, body sizes, skin tones, etc.

- Waiting for a crisis to occur before taking action rather than being consistently proactive in promoting inclusivity and social responsibility.

Without honest introspection and actual commitment to integrity in how marketers execute marketing strategies, any attempt at so-called "inclusivity" will remain superficial and, at best, performative. Inclusive representation cannot thrive on superficial attempts at "performing" commitment to change, or out of a surface-level understanding of culture, people, and communities that have been historically underrepresented, overlooked, and underserved. It requires precision that can only be achieved through thoughtful research, openness to new approaches, and diversity of thought.

The lack of diversity in hiring and retention isn't the only issue here, though, although it's a significant one. Brands make missteps due to a lack of investment in cultural training and media literacy regarding questions of culture, identity, representation, ideology, and power, which are impossible to avoid in today's cultural landscape.

These last three elements—representation, ideology, and power—will figure heavily into the content of the next few chapters. Thinking critically about representation, power dynamics, and historical inequities is the key to executing a socially conscious marketing strategy. In practice, this means developing and using analytical tools you will learn in this book, such as critical analysis and textual interpretation, to thoroughly understand how oppressive systems manifest in representation within marketing and beyond. Armed with this knowledge, we can proactively identify bias and single-story narratives, and work to counter harmful dominant narratives, stereotypes, and assumptions in strategic outputs. To drive both commercial success and social impact, marketers must possess the skills to decipher cultural nuances, know how to navigate complexities and contradictions, and then leverage these cultural insights to drive innovative solutions to the status quo. And it all begins with understanding how culture works and the role that brands play in it.

The Imperative of Cultural Literacy: A New Competitive Edge

Let's start with a foundational premise. Culture is omnipresent. Culture touches *everything*, and I don't mean this as an exaggeration. Culture is how we make sense of and give meaning to the world around us, how we organize social relations, and how we decide what's valuable to us. Cultural theorist Stuart Hall teaches us that through spoken and unspoken protocols that communicate accepted practices, norms, and values, society constructs "a dominant cultural order" that generates "preferred meanings" (Procter, 2004). In simple terms, this means that culture is an extraordinarily powerful driver in shaping and guiding the way society operates. It defines what is considered "normal" and socially acceptable while determining what is undesirable or abnormal. In this sense, culture is not a rigid concept that can be contained, nor is it limited to a specific language or a tradition of a particular group of people. Rather, culture is a much more complex and dynamic system of meanings, practices, and different forms of representation that influence and are influenced by a set of social, political, economic, and historical forces.

Culture is simply "a version of reality" that we inhabit. I like to think of culture as a force that is always in motion; it is perpetually subject to change and reconfiguration as different fractions of society compete over meaning or their own interpretation of "truth." Most obviously, we see this manifest in the increasing polarization and fragmentation of society. As dominant groups vie for their interpretation of "truth," the result is often a contentious landscape where public opinion becomes more divided than unified. Take, for instance, the ongoing debates around the so-called "woke" culture, neo-fascist attacks on diversity and inclusion programs, public schools, and the banning of books. Not to mention the assault on reproductive rights and the dignity of trans, non-binary, and queer people. These issues highlight how disparate segments of society are in a continual struggle to define cultural norms and values, vying to assert their own interpretation of what is "true" or "right." This impacts virtually every dimension of our lives, from family structures and gender roles to expectations around personal appearance and even access to public spaces or educational and career opportunities.

Culture, then, is hardly a backdrop to our lives. It's not just the environment or the community we are raised in, with its traditions and rituals. It is an entire ideological lens through which we come to accept things as natural or "how things should be." Culture is so powerful precisely because its hold on us is often invisible.

Beyond the obvious markers of culture like language, traditions, food, and culturally specific attire, from the beginning of our lives, culture shapes how we see the world and how we relate to each other within it. By operating on the level of what cultural theorists have called "ideology," culture molds our beliefs about what is right or wrong, what is beautiful, what is valuable, and what is sacred. It shapes our perceptions of reality, working to influence our choices, desires, and reactions. And in this way, culture shapes every facet of our everyday lives. It sets the parameters for acceptable discourse and behavior, serving as the backdrop against which various social dynamics play out.

But how does this intricate web of culture relate to marketing strategy? The answer lies in one word: Media. Cultural messaging is disseminated through various mediums—religion, news, politics, and so on—but it is mass media, like popular culture, entertainment, and advertising, that holds immense power over public perception and societal norms. For instance, consider how obvious and outdated cultural norms of the past decades seem today just by looking at vintage ads. These ads didn't just market products; they marketed values, aspirations, lifestyle, and ideals, revealing the dominant ideologies of their time.

It would be a mistake to think that today's marketers are not influenced by, or influential in shaping, dominant cultural beliefs and norms today. Just as old ads give us insights into the past, today's marketing and advertising campaigns are both a mirror and a driver of society's present-day values. And so, then, to effectively engage with contemporary audiences that are increasingly conscious of this fact, brands must develop a kind of fluency in navigating culture. Put simply, brands have a responsibility to be aware of the societal narratives they contribute to and potentially change.

This is hardly a new idea. "It has become almost axiomatic to claim," UCLA Marketing Professor Harold Kassarjian observed all the way back in 1969, "that mass media of communication, *and advertising as a subset*, reflect the culture and society in which they exist" (Kassarjian, 1969). When I asked him to clarify the role of culture in marketing, Kassarjian insisted once again that even 50 years ago, culture and advertising could not possibly be thought of as separate from each other. Throughout history, brands have both uncritically reproduced culture by reflecting it and shaped culture by disseminating visuals, messaging, and narratives that further ingrained these ideas in it. Understanding the bidirectional relationships that brands have to culture—meaning understanding how brands reflect and simultaneously shape culture—is the key to building a culturally intelligent strategy.

Here are the key points to remember as we proceed further into the practical aspects of understanding how culture and brands work in relationship to each other:

1 Marketing is a form of mass media, much like pop culture or entertainment.

2 Brands disseminate meaning that reflects present-day culture.

3 Brands are both commercial entities and influential cultural actors.

In the age of technological innovation and digitization, advertising and marketing wield enormous influence. As a form of mass media, brand marketing has become immensely influential in shaping our perceptions and societal norms. Some scholars argue that mass media is more influential than other cultural institutions like education, religion, or even our families of origin (Williams et al., 2004).

The first tenet of cultural intelligence for marketers is recognizing the significant influence that brand-driven businesses wield in today's culture and media landscape. As such, conscious marketers must rid themselves of the notion that some brands are "just" marketing a product. Even marketing something as seemingly straightforward as a mayonnaise brand taps into cultural codes surrounding family relations, gender dynamics, household rituals, and so on. If anything, the offensively sexist tropes of "go make him a sandwich" or "women belong in the kitchen" were, in part, codified and normalized in food advertising. These ads often reinforced traditional gender roles, portraying women as responsible for household duties such as meal preparation while men were depicted as the primary breadwinners. Understanding this power equips brand leaders to use media and technology more responsibly, ensuring that marketing strategies are not merely commercially successful but also conscientious about their influence on society and culture.

Marketing as Cultural Output: Transforming How We Market

Brands are in the business of transferring strategic messages to audiences with the intention of influencing their behaviors and perceptions. Being implicated in the process of media production and consumption, brand marketing is inescapably a part of what we call "meaning-making" in a culture. How could it not be? As marketers, we are not only putting products or services in front of the audiences. No, we package these products and services within narratives that are emotionally resonant and appealing. After all, that's what strategy ultimately is—storytelling that is strategic in a way that it uses emotional resonance to achieve specific outcomes. Whether increasing brand awareness at the top of the funnel or driving low-funnel purchase behaviors, marketing strategy aims to incite behavior in response to specific stimuli.

Whether the goal is boosting brand awareness or driving sales, marketing strategies are crafted to elicit specific behaviors using cultural narratives around us. Marketing taps into the underlying cultural "ideology" that shapes people's wants, desires, and values, using insights into cultural patterns and human behavior to craft narratives that resonate. Here, "ideology" isn't referring to political affiliations but rather to the unwritten rules and shared beliefs that guide our actions and decisions. Because brands don't merely sell products. Brands sell aspiration.

Just think about what most globally successful brands have in common. From Nike and Apple to Disney, Chevrolet, and Chanel, brand narratives encapsulate some kind of ideological meaning that resonates with us, whether it's the age-old desire for social status, the appeal of innovation, the nostalgic allure of tradition, the fulfillment of athletic achievement, or a longing to recover a sense of magic in our lives. As Holt and Cameron (2012) demonstrate in their seminal book *Cultural Strategy*, the most iconic and successful brands tap into cultural ideologies that not only resonate deeply with societal values and operating beliefs at the time but excavate new emergent narratives that speak to our deepest desires. These brands are irresistible to us precisely because they pay attention to cultural disruptions and harness these shifts in real time to innovate and deliver a better ideology when there is a demand for it within the culture. Holt and Cameron call these moments of "ideological opportunity," which, as they write, "provide one of the most fertile grounds for market innovation." Culture is embedded into the DNA of most successful brands out there.

What all of this points to is that brands are deeply symbolic; brands are cultural containers imbued with meaning, much like religious symbols or totems. As Marita Sturken and Lisa Cartwright note in *Practices of Looking* (2001), if religions used language and imagery throughout human history to convey "religious myths, church doctrines, and historical dramas," then brands do essentially the same in today's saturated mass media landscape. In her TED Talk titled "How symbols and brands shape our humanity," Debbie Millman explores a similar idea when she says, "Our greatest innovations aren't brands providing a different form or a different flavor of our favorite snack. Our greatest innovations are the creation of brands that can make a difference in our lives and reflect the kind of world that we want to live in."

In today's culture, Nike's "swoosh" logo or Apple's iconic apple silhouette are hardly just visual designs on a blank screen or a cardboard package. Similar to deeply meaningful religious symbols that have created groups of loyal followers through history, brands are complex and sophisticated repositories of meaning that use cultural codes, or what cultural theorist Roland Barthes called "myths," to represent something much more meaningful than the material essence of a product offering.

Brands are inseparable from culture, and so brand marketing is not only a strategic business activity but in itself an irrevocably cultural output. Much like religious symbols or totems, brands encapsulate a set of associations that consumers form while engaging with mass media. To truly leverage culture in ways that are not only commercially successful but socially conscious and inclusive, we must understand how to use this influence responsibly. And it starts with truly embracing the idea that brands are cultural agents.

Brands as Cultural Agents: A New Marketing Paradigm

Through much of modern-day history, brands have—often irresponsibly—capitalized on cultural shifts, adapting cultural narratives for the benefit of the business and circulating cultural messaging through marketing and advertising communications. One way to start transforming this is to intentionally reframe how we think about brands and think of them as *cultural agents*. Here are only a few examples of many that show us just how powerful the influence of brands is within culture:

- For a long time, the color pink was commonly associated with boys, while blue was considered more suitable for girls. However, after World War II, gender roles in the United States became more rigid, as men returning from the war reclaimed jobs, which resulted in pushing more women back into the domestic sphere. During this time, retail brands began to color-code children's clothes, with blue becoming associated with boys due to its connection with the uniforms of soldiers. On the other hand, pink took on more delicate and feminine connotations. In the 1950s, advertising campaigns started promoting pink as a color exclusively meant for girls. The influence of advertising on culture has been so significant that now we often assume that girls wearing pink and boys wearing blue is somehow a natural thing (Zalis, 2022).

- Cigarette brands used to advertise their products with slogans like, "More doctors smoke Camels than any other cigarettes," and smoking was often portrayed as glamorous (Sivulka, 1998). During the women's liberation movement, Virginia Slims took advantage of this cultural moment and launched a campaign with a tagline that said, "You've come a long way, baby." This campaign associated smoking with women's independence and empowerment. One of the ad's copies read: "It took Marjorie Taylor

25 years to gather the courage to smoke in front of her husband. It took Mr. Taylor 25 seconds to pack his wife's bags." The ads encouraged women to break the rules by picking up smoking, seeing it as a symbol of feminist emancipation and a way to claim their break from patriarchal expectations (Craig, 1999).

- Not that long ago, buying water in a plastic bottle was irrelevant, seen as unnecessary or a luxury. In the late 1970s and 1980s, brands like Perrier introduced the idea of purity, promoting bottled water as a pure, natural alternative to tap water. As environmental degradation worsened, this became more relevant. Brands capitalized on that. Ads used images of pristine mountain springs and untouched water sources, creating a perception that bottled water was superior. Later, bottled water ads leaned into codes of health and active lifestyle, with brands like Evian and Fiji strategically using visuals of active, health-conscious, and youthful people. Of course, to this day, bottled water is essential to health and safety in economically marginalized communities that are subjected to environmental racism and, thus, exposed to health hazards through dangerous water sources. However, bottled water has, nevertheless, become an unquestionable part of modern-day living in economically advantaged communities where tap water is either safe to drink or otherwise could be easily filtered.

In recent years, brands like Mattel, Camel, Old Spice, Victoria's Secret, Always, Abercrombie & Fitch, and Axe serve as contemporary examples of how brands can unconsciously perpetuate stereotypes and cultural norms that are now recognized as objectively harmful. Over time, their messaging has played a role in shaping societal views, including those related to gender norms, beauty standards, and desires, primarily through their products and advertising campaigns. Looking back, it becomes evident that too many brands of the past often conveyed exclusionary messages without even realizing it. Some promoted ideals centered around white, thin, and conventionally attractive bodies, while others perpetuated narratives that sexualized women and objectified their bodies in advertisements. However, eventually, many of these brands had to become more attuned to cultural shifts, as the changing reality became apparent. The lesson here is evident: Brands that don't take time to understand and align with evolving cultural values will eventually have to change their brand identity. The only issue is that by the time they do so, it may be too late.

CASE STUDY
The Cultural Evolution of Victoria's Secret and Axe

Victoria's Secret was once a brand known for its ultra-thin and tall models that emphasized female sexuality and its desirability (Bennett, 2015; Smith, 2002). In 2016, Mallory Schlossberg wrote an article in *Business Insider* titled "Victoria's Secret is ignoring a massive shift in the lingerie industry, and it could be costing it tons of money." Schlossberg pointed out that, with the lingerie industry undergoing a massive cultural shift toward body acceptance and self-love, "this new attitude from consumers threatens everything that Victoria's Secret's marketing is known for." While brands like Aerie pioneered the movement by abandoning Photoshop brushing in 2014, in an interview with Refinery29, an anonymous photoshopper for Victoria's Secret was reported claiming that models of a bigger size did not sell the brand's products well (Miller, 2016). Fast-forward almost 10 years. In order to lead and dominate the market, eminent lingerie brands and startups like Rihanna's Savage x Fenty, Abby Morgan's Cuup, and Kim Kardashian's Skims paid closer attention to cultural evolution and changing consumer values and were size-inclusive from the start. Smaller but more inclusive rivals began to take part of the market share, becoming a substantial threat to business. And because cultural evolution is inescapable, brands that have previously perpetuated unrealistic body standards have had to scramble to catch up.

In 2021, in an essay titled "Victoria's Secret swaps angels for 'what women want.' Will they buy it?" the *New York Times* reported the brand attempting "the most extreme brand turnaround in recent memory"(Friedman and Maheshwari, 2021). By featuring seven women "famous for their achievements and not their proportions," including soccer star Megan Rapinoe, 17-year-old Chinese-American freestyle skier Eileen Gu, and inclusivity advocate Paloma Elsesser, the brand, the authors argued, attempted to "redefine the version of 'sexy'" that the brand "represents (and sells) to the masses." Since then, Victoria's Secret has evolved into a brand attempting to reflect contemporary values that resonate more strongly with modern-day women, after a multi-year hiatus, during which the brand attempted to reposition its brand image and messaging. According to the reporting by the Associated Press (D'Innocenzio, 2023), Victoria's Secret has undergone a "complete overhaul" by celebrating different body sizes in "The Victoria's Secret World Tour." The brand dropped its infamous "Angels" and replaced them with a group of women with different body types, disabilities, and skin tones, including a model with vitiligo.

Similarly, a brand like AXE underwent its own transformation. Known for its men's grooming products, the brand was known for promoting a singular and often unrealistic ideal of male desirability. Their marketing often depicted men becoming irresistible to scores of women after applying the AXE deodorant (McManis, 2007). With the emergence of cultural movements challenging toxic masculinity and normalizing vulnerability in men, brands like AXE that drew on stereotypical narratives of masculinity quickly became seen as out of touch. In 2016, AXE launched the "Find Your Magic" campaign that encouraged men to embrace their individuality, normalizing the idea that there's no one way to be a "man." The ad included a model in a wheelchair as well as a gender-queer person voguing, a style of dance originating from Black and Latino queer ballroom culture and frequently performed by drag queens. By 2021, the brand released a new "The New Axe Effect" commercial that featured a quirky, full-figured young Black man with glasses and an endearing smile. This was a total break from previous campaigns in the advertising industry that emphasized men's sex appeal as that which is desirable while objectifying and sexualizing women in the process.

In both cases, evolving in response to cultural shifts was unavoidable if the brand wanted to sustain itself. Failing to adapt promptly can result in negative business outcomes, loss of market share, and a decrease in customer base. Brands that remain stagnant risk becoming obsolete or irrelevant. But cultural relevance is not just about avoiding pitfalls. It's about being in an ongoing process of locating new opportunities within culture; it's about innovation. Brands that adapt can tap into new markets, identify new consumer segments, and secure brand loyalty in the long term while transforming society for the better.

Master Cultural Literacy, Master the Market

In today's competitive marketplace, cultural literacy is not just a preference anymore, it has become a necessary advantage. Rather than playing catch-up with cultural shifts, brands that leverage cultural knowledge stay ahead of the game by anticipating and shaping such shifts. But this isn't something that just happens.

If we understand cultural strategy as the practice of understanding signals, trends, patterns, and movements in culture and then using this knowledge to achieve specific business outcomes, then we must develop skills, frameworks, and a common language to get there. The industry is in urgent need of a new paradigm that centralizes and prioritizes cultural knowledge and critical thinking in the core of inclusive and culture-driving marketing. Our approach to culturally intelligent, innovative, and inclusive brand marketing must actually place both cultural knowledge and critical thinking front and center of our practice.

And yet, an undeniable paradox still exists within the industry. It is surprising that despite the growing importance of cultural marketing, still too few organizations seriously invest in truly preparing brand managers and strategists for the era of cultural marketing of tomorrow. As inclusive marketing strategist Lola Bakare (2023) asks with precision and a necessary sense of urgency, "How many of the top ad schools even offer a course on inclusive marketing, marketing responsibly or anything along those lines, much less require one?" Most existing avenues for professional training that marketers, planners, and creatives have access to hardly ever mandate continued education in media literacy, studies of identity-based perspectives, or even prevention of internalized bias. And in the worst-case scenarios, these aspects of culture-oriented learning are seen as entirely irrelevant to brand marketing. Somehow, we still think we can get away with it. But as Bakare so powerfully underlines, "… if we truly want to move past the perils of mediocrity, cultural literacy is anything but inconsequential—it's the key to clearing the exponentially ascending bar that will define the creative excellence every brand's success will demand." In other words, if we want to evolve, something has to give.

It might be assumed that cultural literacy matters for well-known, purpose-driven brands like Unilever, Dove, Ben & Jerry's, Nike, or Patagonia. These brands place social purpose and community impact at the heart of their engagement with cultural communities and contemporary trends. But reducing the uses of cultural literacy solely to purpose-driven marketing is a mistake. No brand is immune to perpetuating stereotypes or unwittingly reinforcing harmful narratives in their pursuit of relevance in the marketplace. In this sense, cultural literacy surpasses mere strategy—it stands as an essential prerequisite for any brand going to market in a diverse consumer landscape.

Procter & Gamble's understanding of the broader significance of cultural literacy in brand marketing merits consideration. In an article titled "Marketing with cultural intelligence for growth and good" published in *Forbes*, Gillian Oakenfull (2021) explains how P&G has adopted a "self-awareness of the influence of one's own culture on one's thinking, attitudes, and behavior." In the article, Oakenfull highlights how P&G has taken an intentionally proactive approach to avoid making *avoidable* errors when marketing to historically marginalized and underrepresented audiences. To prevent any risks and paying for preventable mistakes, the company has invested heavily in enhancing its cultural capabilities. Even as the company aims to create a workforce that mirrors the demographic diversity of its audience, *Forbes* reports, the leadership sees external inputs as indispensable to fill in gaps in knowledge and awareness. To make up for any internal limitations in cultural insight, P&G take a proactive approach. The company turns to expert advice, direction, and perspectives from culturally diverse panels of social media influencers and researchers with specific expertise in cultural issues (Oakenfull, 2021).

Cultural literacy isn't an attribute that brands can simply retrofit. Being proactive pays off in the long term. In today's marketing landscape, agencies and in-house teams face immense pressure. Brands need more than memorable campaigns; brands of tomorrow need a sharp cultural edge. To stand out and thrive in an increasingly socially aware marketplace, brands must embrace the new era of brand marketing, where understanding culture isn't optional; it's essential. Contemporary marketing is in dire need of new ideas, approaches, and strategies to combat persistent issues such as cultural appropriation, enduring inequities, and the pervasive absence of genuine inclusion. More than ever, learnings from critical humanities (cultural studies, media theory, and critical race, gender, and sexuality studies) are urgently needed in the marketing world. Enter cultural intelligence, a new paradigm for navigating culture in the world of brands.

Cracking the Code: What is Cultural Intelligence?

Originally, cultural intelligence was coined to refer to an individual's capabilities to adapt when interacting with others from different cultural regions (Earley and Ang, 2003). Researchers P. Christopher Earley and Soon Ang introduced the concept in their human resources and business management book *Cultural Intelligence: Individual interactions across cultures*, published by Stanford University Press in 2003, and it was later further popularized by Linn Van Dyne. The concept focused on individuals' ability to interact and adapt their views and behaviors cross-culturally. Coined at the turn of the century amidst rapid globalization, the concept of cultural intelligence responded to increased interconnectedness that affected technology, business, travel, and commerce (Ang et al., 2011). By focusing on adaptability across cultural contexts, researchers bridged the gap between IQ (cognitive intelligence) and EQ (emotional intelligence) to respond to these new realities. Since then, the term has gained traction within cultural analytics and marketing strategy. However, there's no consistent understanding of how it applies to marketing beyond cross-cultural management.

Within academic circles in marketing, the term has been understood almost identically as "the ability to function effectively in different cultural contexts" or, in other words, "a specific form of intelligence focused on an individual's ability to handle intercultural situations" (Oakenfull, 2021). This definition focuses on skills marketers can develop to become adaptable to "difference." On the other hand, insights analysts and creative leaders at Ipsos define cultural intelligence as ways in which "brands and communication travel across cultures" (Debia et al., 2022). Still, other marketing leaders have even talked about cultural intelligence in marketing as the ability to "reach multiple cultures" at once or to put "diverse" consumers at the center of the mainstream (Embry, 2023; Evans, 2023). Still, numerous other industry publications I have reviewed for this book use the term "cultural intelligence" without a clear definition at all.

So, which one is it? Definitions matter. Without them, we risk losing our analytical precision. Simply adopting concepts from other fields without proper alignment is ultimately unproductive, as it remains unclear whether we are working toward the same objectives. For instance, some of the definitions I shared with you above rarely, if ever, center questions of equity, justice, and inclusion, which are so central to executing cultural strategy in a socially conscious and ethically sound way. This approach is misguided. After all, under a capitalist system, brand-driven businesses are anything but neutral when it comes to engaging with culture and people. There is an inherent power imbalance at play: Brands do not just need to understand people for the sake of being empathetic but to influence behavior and drive specific commercial outcomes. It is, therefore, necessary that we redefine cultural intelligence in the context of marketing to include brands' social responsibility to consumers and a critical perspective on how brands have historically appropriated elements of culture for the sake of profit. Having a shared definition will enable practitioners to work toward common objectives with a more socially conscious and ethically sound perspective on cultural strategy.

CONSIDER THIS

Working within the context of capitalist structures requires that conscious marketers begin to understand brands' role in society not only through the lens of culture but also power, history, and oppression.

In a capitalist system, brand-driven businesses hold immense socio-economic power within consumer culture, including a monopoly on capital. Brands are not people, and approaches to cultural fluency that focus exclusively on the brand's capacity for "empathy" or "cultural sensitivity" often overlook questions of accountability, harm reduction, power imbalance, as well as appropriation and extraction of cultural artifacts from marginalized communities. Awareness of history, power, and inequitable practices is crucial in socially conscious marketing. An approach to culture that focuses on "understanding differences" but does not address questions of power and systemic inequities within the industry only further fails current and budding marketers who are eager to level up their marketing strategies and work toward a more equitable and inclusive future of marketing.

Now that we have established a common ground, I would like to share my original model for understanding cultural intelligence. This model embraces a more critical approach to culture and brands. It does not overlook the power that brands have historically held when transmitting messages to customers through mass media and shaping culture in the process, and it is intentionally and unapologetically attentive to issues of justice, power, and equity in the context of brand marketing.

Cultural intelligence is not one skill that can be mastered. It is not limited to understanding a particular consumer group either. Cultural intelligence involves tracking patterns in culture using a critical and socially conscious lens. I define **cultural intelligence** as an ongoing practice of analyzing movements, trends, and social forces, evaluating their cultural significance and commercial implications to achieve strategic outcomes that both drive business forward and transform culture for the better. This means not only being able to successfully resonate with specific audiences, as that is only a fraction of what cultural intelligence can do. Cultural intelligence enables brands to develop a critical outlook and foresight to be at the front and ahead of culture as it shifts and evolves in real time. Because the terms we develop and use need to speak to relevant contexts, I am defining the term "cultural intelligence" in a distinct and specialized manner specific to marketing; it is unrelated to its original coinage in another field.

Cultural intelligence brings together cultural insight, strategy, and innovation to help brands unlock the power of cultural fluency over time. **Cultural fluency** refers to a brand's overall ability to understand and strategically navigate culture that can only be acquired, developed, and harnessed through the ongoing practice of analyzing cultural patterns (cultural intelligence). It is what ultimately enables the brand to effectively engage in culture with integrity and a sense of responsibility toward the business and society across all business functions. If cultural intelligence is the ongoing practice of decoding and leveraging cultural data, then we can understand cultural fluency as the brand's overarching capacity to mobilize these advanced cultural insights to infuse cultural awareness and social consciousness into its strategies, innovations, and business operations. In other words, cultural fluency is a business capability acquired through the ongoing practice of decoding culture that over time can begin to inform business processes and mechanisms beyond brand strategy as such. This distinction helps brands clarify the path forward and teases out the tactical function that cultural intelligence plays in business strategy.

Culture, Strategy, and Innovation

Culturally intelligent brands that attain cultural fluency within the marketplace not only effectively target specific consumer segments and respond to existing cultural conversations, they embrace their role as cultural agents to shape and drive culture forward. These brands learn to responsibly harness cultural knowledge to amplify relevant cultural movements and create meaningful impact, all while driving growth, differentiation, and loyalty. When cultural knowledge and foresight, strategic planning, and innovative thinking are synthesized to work together, they form a framework that I've captured in the Culture-Strategy-Innovation (CSI) model below (as illustrated in Figure 1.1). Take a moment and look at Figure 1.1, a visual representation of the CSI framework, which explains the core elements of cultural intelligence.

The framework has three main pillars: Culture, strategy, and innovation. These pillars are set against a larger schema, which I term critical social consciousness. This refers to the intentional awareness of how our ideas, processes, outputs, and practices affect people, the planet, and the future of society at large. The framework is fueled by four "forces" that work to pressure-test the work on all sides: Equity, inclusion, impact, and accountability.

By combining data-driven cultural insights, strategy, and innovation in a deliberate and continuous manner and then pressure-testing them against ethical values, brands can begin to harness cultural intelligence in a manner that leverages cultural data for business advantage while also reducing harm and promoting equity and inclusion.

FIGURE 1.1 The Pillars of Cultural Intelligence: Culture-Strategy-Innovation

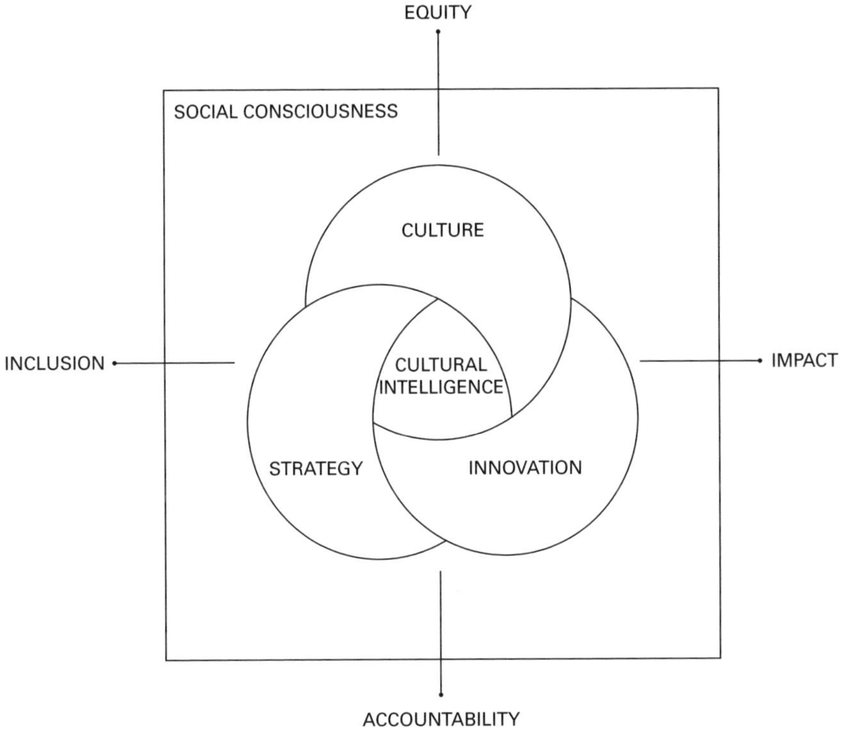

An original framework by Dr. Anastasia Kārkliņa Gabriel © 2023. Reproduction or use without permission is prohibited.

The Elements of the Framework

What does this mean in more practical terms? Let's break it down one by one:

- Understanding **culture** requires going beyond "awareness" of differences. Cultural analysis helps brands develop the capabilities needed to decode social behaviors, subcultures, cultural movements, and trends, understand dominant and emergent undercurrents driving them, and strategically connect the brand to relevant elements of culture. This process can draw on various methodologies, including cultural analysis, semiotics, trend spotting, foresight, qualitative research, data analytics, artificial intelligence, social listening, expert interviews, etc. First and foremost, however, it depends on marketers' understanding of culture as a system of meaning, which we will delve into in the next few chapters.

- **Strategy** makes cultural knowledge actionable. Planning is what helps brands identify effective ways of making a commercial impact by aligning the brand with culture. It is what activates and connects cultural knowledge to strategic objectives that a brand needs to meet in order to reach its target audiences, win new business, and sustain itself in the long run. Without strategy, cultural insights, no matter how advanced, are just a piece of well-researched knowledge, no matter how superb. Strategy is a way of determining what's right for the brand and what isn't. It is strategic decision making that brands need in order to apply insights in such a way that drives actual tangible change, commercially and socially.

- **Innovation** is another irreplaceable piece that often gets overlooked in inclusive marketing. In most simple terms, innovation is the introduction of something new. To be at the forefront of the cultural zeitgeist in ways that are effective, relevant, and memorable, brands have to embrace innovative, out-of-the-box thinking. Any brand that seeks to tell better, more inclusive stories or take on a relevant social issue to drive brand differentiation and social impact is ultimately innovating against the dominant culture. Brands that deploy cultural intelligence always already innovate against the status quo; they are innovators of culture and brand by virtue of harnessing cultural knowledge to identify spaces of opportunity.

- Surrounding this visual model are the elements that act as pressing forces to ensure the **ethical integrity** of the work: Inclusion, equity, impact, and accountability. Like forces of gravity, ethical considerations ground and anchor each side of the model. This is to signify that there is never a time when social consciousness is not part of cultural intelligence as a practice of intentional, conscientious engagement with culture, people, and society. Relegating these ethical principles only to "culture" is a common mistake that brands make when assuming that these questions are only relevant to this one space. Instead, social consciousness is conceptualized here as a sharp multi-focal lens that continually refocuses the entire model, ensuring that every component—cultural analysis, research processes, casting, planning, creative, or design—is approached with an intentional awareness of inclusion, equity, impact, and accountability.

CONSIDER THIS: WHAT IS CRITICAL CONSCIOUSNESS?

Coined by Brazilian educator Paulo Freire in the 1960s and taken from the Portuguese word *conscientizadora*, the term "critical consciousness" refers to "a state of in-depth understanding about the world and resulting freedom from oppression." I use this umbrella term to speak about equity and inclusion in this book because of its roots in grassroots educational and activist circles. This helps balance out ways in which corporate discourse has co-opted these concepts, which, in some contexts, have lost their original meaning. In his seminal books *Pedagogy of the Oppressed* and *Education for Critical Consciousness*, Dr. Freire explained critical consciousness as a way for learners to question the realities of their social and historical conditions. Freire (1985) called this a way of continually "reading the world." For Freire, critical consciousness was not just a state of awareness but a transformative process that empowers individuals to recognize, challenge, and change the oppressive structures and narratives around them. It requires a deep recognition of and reckoning with systemic inequities and the cultural and social constructs that sustain them. In a marketing context, this means not merely acknowledging the existence of diverse audiences and trying to "understand" them but using one's relationship to the work to actively challenge and dismantle harmful stereotypes, biases, and practices within advertising narratives and broader marketing efforts. In this sense, critical consciousness is a call to action: An opportunity to commit to being part of systemic change on an ongoing basis rather than choosing the easy route of perpetuating the status quo.

As you can see in this framing, cultural intelligence is not used in the same original context of human resources or cross-cultural communication; rather, the term is used in a different context here to speak specifically to the role of advanced cultural insight in strategic planning and inclusive marketing. This reframing moves us beyond adopted definitions of cultural intelligence that do not sufficiently capture the nuances and complexities of cultural marketing as a whole. This provides a more comprehensive outlook on impactful, culturally fluent brand marketing that moves marketers beyond consumer research alone.

The Anatomy of a "Culturally Fluent" Brand

How does the CSI model translate into practice? Below is an evaluation list that captures the essence of the CSI model in the form of practices, values, and questions that characterize a "culturally intelligent" brand. Use it to evaluate your current client work or reflect on how you might want to approach your work going forward.

CHECKLIST: CRITICAL EVALUATION

- Has the brand developed the capabilities to decode cultural shifts, emergent trends, and the evolution of cultural values and consumer attitudes on an ongoing basis?

- Is the brand proactively cultivating foresight regarding the future of culture and its consequential role within a specific vertical or category?

- Has the brand identified an approach for tapping into emergent cultural movements, subcultures, or narratives as spaces of innovation and category-defining opportunity?

- Does the brand utilize comprehensive methodologies to capture dominant and emergent drivers behind cultural movements relevant to the brand?

- How are the brand's strategic initiatives tailored to represent, amplify, and resonate with historically overlooked consumer segments?

- How does the brand assess and determine which cultural movements align the most with its identity and strategic goals?

- How dedicated is the brand to ensuring its culture-driven campaigns uphold principles of diverse, inclusive, and counter-dominant storytelling?

- What tangible commercial and social impacts have been achieved through the brand's culturally informed campaigns and initiatives?

- What mechanisms does the brand employ to ensure accountability, especially when a cultural initiative doesn't hit the mark or misfires?

- How consistently are ethical considerations and equity-based standards embedded throughout the brand's marketing processes, from initial research to campaign execution?

No vision can be effectively actualized without a foundational knowledge of core principles, ideas, and concepts within a practice. In order to begin actualizing this approach to cultural intelligence, you will need to draw on analytical skills and social awareness that will help you decode culture and then apply thinking rooted in principles of social consciousness to your outputs. Making the CSI model actionable requires the foundational pillars upon which it stands—culture, communication, critical consciousness, and community. By focusing on each of the 4Cs, you will be able to activate knowledge that will help you learn to decode culture and leverage cultural insights to achieve cultural relevance in a socially responsible way.

Think of the 4Cs as the foundational building blocks. They provide the core understanding required to start building an inclusive strategy. In essence, the 4Cs are not just preliminary concepts but integral elements of what it means to learn to think about culture through a critical lens.

With this in mind, the rest of the book is divided into four main parts to help you do just that. Each will offer an opportunity to rethink how you approach analysis of culture, provide you with activities and exercises to reflect and question, teach you how to identify bias and gaps in awareness, and offer new ways to think critically about brand purpose, impact, and accountability. This iterative approach ensures that you're not just imitating inclusivity but embedding it into your everyday decision making.

In Conversation with Rachel Lowenstein

Rachel Lowenstein is the Global Head of Inclusive Innovation at Mindshare, leading strategy and innovation for how brands use marketing, media, and technology to reshape society for good. She has worked with global brands such as Unilever and Booking.com to be more intentional in marketing. Recently, Rachel co-created the Impact Index with support from WPP's Racial Equity Fund, a tool that analyzes the impact of media on marginalized communities and helps brands shift their investments away from harmful content. Additionally, she recently led research on the state of bodily autonomy in the United States and the role of the private sector in protecting bodily autonomy rights. She is passionate about the possibilities of media for social impact while considering the ethics of how we use technology.

AKG: Rachel, thank you for your time. In this chapter, I discuss the relationship that brands have to culture. As a marketing practitioner, what has compelled you to do the work of connecting brands to culture and social issues?

RL: I professionally grew up at my agency, seeing the outsized impact the private sector can and does have on culture. Increasingly, I became frustrated that the idea of inclusive marketing should be sidelined to CSR or charity efforts—as if brands and agencies don't have an impact on real people with every decision we make (intended or not). For example, the impact the ad industry has on journalism or platform policies for monetization or content moderation that disproportionately punish women, queer and trans people, and BIPOC. Whether we like it or not, brands and agencies have massive responsibility on material issues surrounding social justice, climate change, and an increasingly toxic media ecosystem.

I was, and remain, absolutely certain that the future of brands and agencies needs to include experts on social issues as much as it does on where the futurists are taking their bets on all the shiny objects around data, the metaverse, web 3. I channeled that frustration into action and created the Global Inclusive Innovation group to help our clients use media, marketing, and tech for social good in line with their business objectives.

It's a lazy myth that you can't contribute to society and grow your brand—look at Barbie being a massive financial success for Mattel and Warner Bros while creating a plotline where the antagonist is literally the patriarchy. As a consultative unit charged with helping our clients critically and creatively think about the potential of marketing for good, we work with brands in a fluid way. Sometimes we're brought in as disruptors on strategy, other times as ideators on campaigns. My favorite, and I find the most fruitful, way that clients benefit from working with us is through thought leadership inspiring new ways of thinking.

Mindshare's positioning is predicated on Good Growth, ensuring that brand growth is enduring, sustainable, and diversified. Not a flash in the pan and contributing to the many issues that short-termism has inflicted on businesses and society. Inclusive Innovation is a critical factor in the agency's overall positioning.

AKG: I want to follow up on the value of innovation. Why is innovation specifically such an important element, and how do you define "inclusive innovation"?

RL: My background is in "traditional" marketing innovation—so I love this question. Our industry is obsessed with chasing shiny objects—sometimes those shiny objects are critical to the future of media and culture (the iPhone), sometimes they're fun things that we should embrace purely for the novelty (AR), and sometimes they're things like the metaverse where every brand in 2022 thought they were screwed if they didn't have a metaverse strategy (surprise: They probably didn't need one).

Inclusive innovation recognizes that the sparkly, fun things in our industry can be valuable, but innovating for the belonging of historically marginalized people has massive potential. Look at Rihanna's entire business model—Fenty Beauty and Fenty Lingerie were created as a gap to how beauty has been so exclusionary that innovating for inclusion has made RiRi a billionaire.

We seem to put a lot of attention on chasing the latest/greatest innovation for vanity when innovation for humanity is sorely lacking.

AKG: Are there examples of inclusive innovation that you could share with our readers?

RL: I have two examples from work that we've done. The first is a tool we created with socialcontext, which is a startup from the University of Colorado Boulder professors, and our client Tyson Foods, who patronized the project. It's called the Impact Index. My colleague Jared Greene and I were immensely frustrated by the pervasively racist rhetoric being monetized by media publishers during the 2020 Black Lives Matter protests. As the world's largest global media agency, we knew that we had a responsibility on this issue. Jared and I spent almost two years concepting and searching for a partner who could help us build a tool that would analyze editorial content, use academic research and expertise to decide how that content was depicting the Black community (positive, neutral, negative, toxic) and then provide an analysis on an article level of how that partner ranked so we could make more informed media investment decisions. We call it a human safety tool—not a brand safety tool. It's intended to be more nuanced than what traditional brand safety can provide.

If a brand has made very public statements about racial equity and supporting BLM, aligning those values to how they spend their ad dollars isn't just a moral imperative but a reputational one as well. Jared and I chose socialcontext to work with us because they're academics first, technologists second, being experts in online abuse, disinformation, and more. Tyson was able to leverage the tool to increase their campaign performance AND shift funds toward positive impact partners. We were recently awarded WPP's Racial Equity Fund to iterate the tool further— our goal is to use it as widely as possible to make more intentional investment decisions.

The second piece of work is a campaign we launched at Cannes Lions this year called #AutisticOutLoud. Autistic representation in media is abysmal—almost all mainstream media about the disability is stereotypical or reinforces harmful, outdated ideas. As a late-diagnosed autistic woman, this was something I knew we could change as well. We created an idea for our client Hiki, an app for the autistic community to find relationships and friendships, to create the first-ever large-scale, mainstream project to shift autistic representation in media. We partnered with Getty Images and tasked diverse autistic creators to take self-portraits of themselves. The images live on Getty Images and Unsplash. We've had brands like Google and IBM pledge to use the images in their own advertising.

AKG: Topics like disability and especially neuroinclusion are typically relegated to the conversation about equity in the workplace; it's not something many brands have touched otherwise. Speaking of innovation and uncharted spaces of opportunity, what role can brands play in overlooked issues such as this?

RL: You're correct that the conversation on neuroinclusion is hyper-focused on workplace dynamics, but I would add that we've barely even scratched the surface on fixing that issue. Almost 80 percent of autistic folks are under or unemployed, largely because workplaces are inaccessible and exclusionary to autistic and/or neurodivergent people. Disability seems to be an area of DE&I that is overlooked. As someone who is disabled, I think it's part ignorance, part fear of doing it wrong, and part a pervasive savior complex that we've seen in media and advertising where disabled people are spoken over/for. It's why #AutisticOutLoud was, sadly, so revolutionary. There are very few examples of autistic people making creative decisions or representing themselves on mainstream stages.

Brands can play a significant role in disability inclusion and more specifically, neuroinclusion. Most of the things I talk about with brands aren't expensive, intensive, or even revolutionary. For example, I consulted with Google on The Neu Project, which is a guide for making professional events more neuroinclusive. Some of the recommendations we have in there are really simple stuff, like sending an agenda, adjusting lighting, or having clear instructions in materials. Going back to my earlier point, brands can get caught up in having the latest shiny thing but getting the basics on inclusivity right is 1) more impactful in every sense, and 2) not as complex as some marketers might think. It's just about having the right experts on your team—which is a whole other conversation about the lack of disabled talent in our industry.

AKG: Some brand leaders might genuinely want to make an impact but can often feel hesitant or even fearful of a backlash. What is the role of risk in inclusive innovation?

RL: I have a lot to say on this topic. First, doing good doesn't have to be a big statement—in fact, a lot of the work we've done with brands has been quieter moves. Changes to how they're spending their ad dollars. New partnerships with diverse media. How they use brand safety technology, which has historically provided challenges to already marginalized people. What audiences they're targeting. For brands who are very risk averse, we actually like to talk about growth through the lens of diversifying their audiences. You simply will not grow as a brand if you're speaking to the same people or without nuance to cultural realities.

Second, many decisions a brand makes are going to come with risk, and if there aren't risks involved in their marketing, I'm not sure how long they'll be in business.

The brands who have had the very worst backlash had half-baked efforts. If inclusive marketing isn't a priority for you, then don't make it a hyper-visible effort to consumers. If you want to do something incremental, then have the right experts in the room who can help you decide the right positioning, the potential backlash, and your subsequent response. Because the reality we're seeing now of brands backing away entirely from Pride, women's rights, and more will hurt brands in the long run by being so fickle to very sizable audiences.

2

Unlocking the 4Cs
of Cultural Intelligence

WHAT TO EXPECT

As we pivot from our discussion on the inherent link between culture and brands, let's delve deeper into the building blocks of culturally intelligent marketing. In the preceding chapter, we have identified why cultural literacy is so imperative in today's rapidly evolving marketplace. We examined why brands have to integrate cultural insight, strategy, and innovation to enable cultural intelligence. Armed with this understanding, we will now move on to why each of the 4Cs—Culture, Communication, Critical Consciousness, and Community—is so indispensable to crafting a culturally incisive and socially responsible marketing strategy. In this chapter, we won't only cover various areas of cultural knowledge but also go through several activities designed to sharpen your analytical skills. You'll be prompted to question assumptions and identify gaps in thinking. We will explore the following questions in the next few pages:

- What does each pillar refer to, and how does it apply in practice?
- What kind of values underlie the principles of cultural intelligence?
- What are the main concepts that will help me analyze culture?
- How do we define consumer and cultural "truths"?
- How do we question assumptions and analyze cultural ideology?
- What framework to use to analyze cultural movements?

Culture isn't a static list of attributes we can simply tick off. It's a dynamic, complex force that requires a similarly agile approach to understand and leverage fully. This chapter aims to be more than just an instructional guide or a checklist; it's designed to enhance your analytical skills and deepen your understanding of the subject. We don't merely want to "know" culture; we aim to engage with it critically every step of the way. This involves scrutinizing our own biases and preconceptions, asking tough questions, and then questioning assumptions that might be hiding in our answers.

To be successful as conscious marketers in this complex cultural landscape, our tactics and strategies must be as fluid and adaptive as culture itself. Stagnation is antithetical to cultural fluency. The goal here isn't to reach a final understanding of culture, but to develop an ongoing, critical dialogue with it—a dialogue that evolves as culture does. As marketers, we must embrace and embody the same fluidity and flexibility. Culture is always evolving, and to keep up, we must too.

In the section below, we will go over each pillar, unpack what it means, and how it relates to the marketing processes. If you find these notions abstract at first, don't worry, as each chapter will capture them in-depth and you will soon learn the necessary tools to activate them in practice.

Unlocking the 4Cs: Tools for Advanced Cultural Insight

Culture

We've established that understanding culture is crucial. You hear it everywhere though: "Let's tap into the culture." "This is a cultural moment." But what does culture mean? The term has become a buzzword, thrown around in client meetings and on the largest stages. The term itself has been diluted to near ambiguity. There has yet to be a wider consensus on its precise definition.

Too often, in inclusive marketing, culture is reduced to a set of group traits or differences that make us human. But in a marketing context, it is critical for marketers to recognize that culture is far more than a set of distinctions between groups of people, such as their language, traditions, or common practices. While these elements are certainly constitutive of culture, they don't capture its full scope.

Let's get clear. Culture is a dynamic, ever-evolving meaning-system that facilitates how meaning is disseminated through various channels—from language and media to visual culture, artifacts, and arts. This process is called representation. But just like the notion of culture is too often simplified in marketing, representation can't be reduced to the question of *who* is represented (in an ad, campaign, or an initiative) either.

Think about cultural representation this way. Everything communicates meaning; it's an unspoken language we all share. Think about how the color red represents passion. A fist in the air represents racial pride and people's power. Two fingers raised up like a letter "V" signify a call to peace. A white rectangle on a red background means "stop." A pink ribbon is universally recognized as a symbol for breast cancer awareness. A rainbow flag is a universally accepted symbol of LGBTQ+ pride. This isn't something you read in a book; you just know.

Representation is how meaning is produced and exchanged in culture through the use of language, signs, and images. No one needs to explain why a rose symbolizes love or why a bitten apple is now associated with one of the largest tech brands in the world. A person wearing a cross signals to the world their religious identity, while a person wearing a sweatshirt with a Nike swoosh is also communicating a particular belonging to an in-group. We don't recognize these instances as examples of how signs in culture communicate *ideology* in the same way that we would recognize that a person displaying a religious symbol is signaling an ideology to others.

At the core, however, both are engaged in the same process of representation that transmits meaning—and a particular ideology, whether it's a lifestyle, subculture, or cult. In this way, culture is formed by a network of codes and conventions that are received and interpreted by others, enabling shared understanding and a collective sense of identity in the process.

No wonder that cults or hate groups create symbols and insignia to signal allegiance to others. Symbols are powerful in that way. We, too, signal our affiliations and even our individual identities through the brands we endorse, the music we engage with, the language we use, and the social and political causes we support. These seemingly mundane choices function as cultural signifiers, telling others who we are—or at least, who we aspire to be. This is how we come to understand ourselves within the larger sociocultural matrix: by using symbols and signs to signal our identity, beliefs, and ideologies to those around us.

Brands, too, are bearers of meaning always already implicated in cultural ideology. Symbols, codes, rituals, and artifacts that appear in marketing communications through language (whether visual, verbal, or auditory) transmit implicit or otherwise implied messaging to audiences. As marketers,

FIGURE 2.1 The 4Cs of Cultural Intelligence

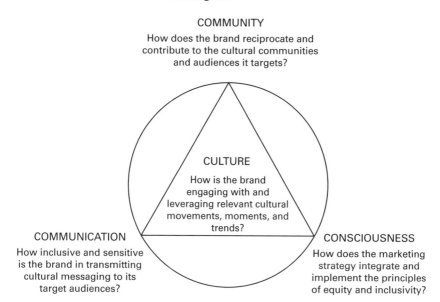

Original framework by Dr. Anastasia Kārkliņa Gabriel © 2023. Reproduction or use without permission is prohibited.

our task is not only to deliver these messages but to understand how these messages are encoded with meaning. And we need to understand how audiences might decode them based on their cultural backgrounds, identities, worldviews, and experiences. For example, picture any brand campaign that went wrong. It likely failed because marketers did not anticipate how the messaging would be decoded and received by audiences. The brand didn't have the awareness of how one thing can signify multiple meanings across contexts, nuances, and different audiences. What the brand thought was well-intentioned ended up being ill-received or even harmful because the mechanism of cultural representation was not fully understood.

Once marketers understand, however, how messages are encoded through representation, we can do a much better job at anticipating different interpretations. With this knowledge, marketers can design outputs that are not only emotionally resonant but also culturally sensitive.

When we are aware of how cultural messaging works, inclusivity can finally become an integral aspect of brand messaging rather than an afterthought. A marketer's job isn't merely to stitch cultural awareness into brand messaging as a last-minute add-on. The real work begins early by embedding a cultural lens right at the start of your process even as the brief is still being formulated. The next time someone in your marketing meeting suggests tapping into "culture," push for clarity and consider:

- Diving deep into the cultural undercurrents, power structures, and historical narratives that not only shape your target audience's worldview but also shape the culture within which your brand exists.

- Understanding deeper symbolism or meaning that a specific topic, ritual, or perspective might have for your audiences, accounting for overlooked or historically marginalized perspectives.

- Evaluating dominant cultural narratives to ensure that your brand's messaging doesn't unintentionally contribute to harmful or stereotypical portrayals or perpetuate unintended messaging.

So, the question we will explore in the next chapter, devoted to this entire topic, isn't just "What is culture?" but rather "How can we learn to view culture more critically and act on this cultural knowledge?" That's not a peripheral concern in inclusive marketing. It's the core issue that sets the tone for everything that follows.

Communication

Communication isn't just a footnote in the practice of cultural intelligence either; it's a central pillar. If representation answers how meaning is constructed and conveyed through language, images, and media, then communication explains how it is transmitted and received by audiences. The mechanism of communication isn't just about relaying a message; it's about how that message will be interpreted, dissected, and ultimately integrated into culture.

In this sense, communication transcends the simple exchange between sender and receiver, encompassing the medium and the expansive social backdrop in which this exchange unfolds. Understanding how communication works in culture helps clarify how messages in media are not just sent out by the producers of media (in this case, marketers) in one direction, but also shaped by the audience's own interpretation of that message within a larger societal context. This matters for the practice of cultural intelligence in inclusive marketing because it ultimately clarifies the process by which brands transmit messages to their audiences and why, so often, brands' attempts at being culturally fluent and inclusive in their messaging are not received in the way the brand had intended.

In a marketing context, understanding these complexities adds a critical layer of depth to how brands communicate with audiences. Focusing on brand communications as that which is implicated in broader cultural processes, with all their cultural, ideological, and structural factors, helps brands prepare for how their messages might be interpreted. Developing culturally intelligent communications, then, means considering the power dynamics, norms, and values that influence how marketers communicate with audiences and, in turn, how these audiences interpret and interact with marketing communications. Ultimately, cultural fluency in marketing depends on marketers, planners, and creatives becoming aware and contentious about the influential impact that marketing messaging and brand stories have on the receiving audiences and society at large.

The role of communication in cultural intelligence is not just tactical; for brands, it's existential. It asks us to reconsider not just how we talk to customers, consumers, and wider audiences, but what we're really saying— what values, ideologies, and cultural assumptions are embedded in brand messages transmitted to the audiences? And how are these received, negotiated, or even resisted by different segments of the public?

So, if we're talking about culturally intelligent communication, we're really talking about a two-way street. On one end, brands project messages to audiences. On the other, audiences receive, interpret, and often reshape these messages based on their own cultural perspectives. The task, then, isn't just to "speak" but to predict how that speech will be "heard."

When we delve into the domain of communication in the practice of cultural intelligence, we're not just fine-tuning our messaging; we're reckoning with its cultural gravity. Once brands understand the culture within which they exist, brands need to wrestle with the ethical imperatives of their messaging within that culture. And that isn't a tangential concern; it's a foundational one, a core issue that can make or break the cultural resonance of a messaging strategy. This anticipatory step is critical: It's where inclusive communications either succeed or fail.

The stakes of communication go beyond whether brand messaging is effective. Communication cuts to the heart of how a brand situates itself within broader cultural narratives. Does the brand amplify underrepresented perspectives and innovate against culture, or does it inadvertently perpetuate stereotypes and incomplete stories? Crafting inclusive and culturally intelligent brand communications means that marketers need to:

- Ensure that in marketing communications, the brand is using inclusive and culturally sensitive language, imagery, and creative (e.g., using gender-inclusive language, avoiding outdated terminology, ensuring diversity, etc.).

- Scrutinize the use of cultural symbols, language, rituals, imagery, and other cultural artifacts in your marketing content to ensure it is not appropriative and is intentionally considerate of cultural perspectives that have been historically overlooked.

- Understand and leverage the theory of "audience reception" to anticipate feedback and prevent negative PR and unnecessary scrutiny of brand and marketing narratives (more on this in Chapter 4!)

Continuous innovation in data analytics provides an unprecedented opportunity to level up culturally intelligent communications. Harnessing insights from consumer behavior, social listening tools, and real-time analytics enables marketers to adapt and tailor brand messaging to reflect the cultural conversation. Ultimately, this is about asking: How is the brand using the power of media and technology in society to really listen to audiences and communicate in a way that is positive and inclusive, and that elevates and amplifies needed perspectives that often have been historically overlooked?

The purpose of culturally intelligent communication isn't just resonating with target audiences in culture—it's an ongoing dialogue with culture itself. It calls us to ask not only how we are talking to diverse audiences but how we are likely going to be heard. What impact does a brand's communication have in culture? And are we willing to listen in return? It's these critical considerations that make a brand truly culturally fluent.

Critical consciousness

This brings us to the third pillar: Critical consciousness. Critical consciousness is the ongoing practice in cultural intelligence. Grounded in the critical interrogation of power dynamics, biases, and systemic inequalities that orchestrate our social realities, critical consciousness teaches us to discern the oppressive mechanisms that underline culture. But the invitation for marketers to adopt a critical lens on power and equity extends further; it asks us to translate observations into transformative action. Scholars and researchers (Diemer et al., 2017) identify three main components to critical consciousness:

1 Critical reflection

2 Political efficacy

3 Critical action

Critical consciousness, which is deeply rooted in fields like cultural theory and liberatory pedagogy, intersects with marketing in a significant way:

1 For marketers deeply committed to driving change, **critical reflection** is a continual process of evaluating how a brand exists in the world with respect to equity, sustainability, and inclusion. Given the immense influence that brands command in culture, the responsibility rests squarely on the shoulders of inclusive marketers to consider whether marketing strategies either reinforce or proactively challenge dominant systems.

2 When we talk about **political efficacy** in the realm of marketing, understanding one's ability to bring about change is paramount to using the power of brands for good. At its core, it's about recognizing and seizing your brand's power to enact genuine social change. Sure, your brand can resonate with a particular cultural moment or subculture, but can it go a step further to produce a product, an offering, or a campaign that advances equity, inclusivity, and sustainability? Brands are not just spectators; brands are simultaneously commercial actors and cultural intermediaries.

3 As for **critical action**, forget empty promises and performative gestures. If the brand is claiming to be about inclusivity, equity, and sustainability, then the actions must match the rhetoric. The imperative is clear: Don't just say it, do it. The marketplace is littered with examples of brands called out for performative activism or for failing to deliver on promises. Brands' commitment has to translate into decisive actions that make a discernible impact. A focus on critical action reminds brands of the importance of undertaking tangible efforts in culture. The modern brand has an opportunity—and I would argue, an obligation—to be a transformative cultural force. This is about more than performative gestures or nebulous commitments to "corporate social responsibility." We're talking about a deep-seated shift in how brands engage with culture, customers, and stakeholders alike.

By cultivating critical consciousness as individuals, marketers can challenge conventional wisdom and surface hidden assumptions, leading to more inclusive and equitable marketing strategies. This process involves fostering self-awareness, embracing curiosity, and developing empathy to understand and appreciate diverse perspectives and experiences. By prioritizing critical thinking and actively questioning assumptions, biases, and power dynamics, the industry can create more inclusive, equitable, and culturally intelligent campaigns that resonate with diverse audiences, still advance commercial objectives, and contribute to positive social change. In practice, incorporating critical consciousness into your marketing strategy looks like this:

- Conducting proactive internal audits to identify potential biases or harmful narratives in your marketing practices, such as audience targeting, message development, and content creation.

- Engaging in regular reflection, dialogue, and training to foster self-awareness, empathy, and a commitment to social responsibility within your marketing team.

- Actively seeking out and incorporating diverse perspectives and experiences into your marketing content, ensuring it reflects and respects the cultural context of your target audience(s).

- Taking critical action that is most compatible with the brand, whether explicitly engaging in purpose-driven campaigns or simply integrating inclusivity into brand storytelling and content.

Community

Far too often, brands market to certain communities but simultaneously engage in cultural extraction—for profit. When a commercial entity weaponizes its influence through the exploitation of cultural knowledge, it establishes its dominance in a marketplace at the expense of marginalized voices. It's no longer tenable for brands to merely appropriate cultural narratives; such practices are rightly seen as exploitative and disconnected from the communities they purport to engage with. Instead, brands of tomorrow must pivot toward a co-creative ethos—a mutual exchange where value isn't simply taken but also returned.

Instead of this one-sided extraction, brands should aim for a symbiotic relationship where cultural value is not just appropriated but respected, valued, and compensated. Only then can brands genuinely contribute to acting responsibly and advancing equity and inclusion through meaningful community engagement. In a landscape that increasingly scrutinizes performativity, this isn't just good ethics—it's also good business.

By making a tangible impact and pursuing initiatives to contribute resources to communities the brand engages with, we can move away from extraction and tap into co-creation—a cycle of value creation and value sharing. Embedding community and accountability into marketing processes requires marketers to:

- Engage in active listening and dialogue with the communities you serve to understand their needs, values, and cultural norms.

- Use this information to tailor your marketing messages to resonate with your audience genuinely.

- Partner with community organizations, influencers, creatives, organizers, and leaders to amplify your reach and include perspectives on how the brand can make a positive impact.

- Collaborate with trusted community members who can help build trust and legitimacy with your target audience.

- Create opportunities for your audience to actively participate in your marketing campaigns.

- Seek to invest financial resources or direct a portion of profits to sustain existing community-led efforts rather than only positioning the brand and its product as the solution.

Marketers of the future will recognize the 4Cs not as mere footnotes to marketing initiatives but as foundational elements of the marketing practice that inform everyday decision making—from research and planning to creative ideation and tactical execution.

From Thought to Action: Developing Cultural Insights

For too long, we've underplayed the value of critical consciousness and marketing strategy. We've allowed brands to remain passive, to benefit from tapping into cultural movements, trends, marginalized communities, and subcultures without contributing to them. New solutions need to be grounded in culturally informed innovation. As socially conscious marketers, we have an opportunity to experiment and apply new interdisciplinary perspectives to our work. In an ever-changing marketplace, standing still is hardly an option; we must be proactive in evolving our strategies, approaches, and ways of thinking to remain relevant, imaginative, innovative, and impactful. But there's another layer to this, too.

I want to draw your attention to how each principle of cultural fluency is more than just a concept—it holds us accountable to take real, actionable steps. Critical thinking must eventually lead to critical action, and that's how we know that we have developed and integrated a *practice* of socially responsible and conscious marketing. Whether we're talking about using our work to counter stereotypes we see in today's media, reflecting on past inequalities and using media to amplify underrepresented voices and causes, or looking toward the future to strategizing more inclusive outcomes, each tenet demands that we ground the impact of our work in something tangible.

Sustainable change won't materialize through lip service or performative gestures. Being ready to take bold, big swings is what drives genuine transformation. Playing it safe might offer short-term gains, but taking calculated, strategic yet courageous risks is what lands brands at the forefront of culture—and top of mind for consumers.

None of this, however, means much if we don't change how we fundamentally think about culture and how we mine it for insights. Critical thinking is not just an intellectual exercise, but a transformative practice that invites us to reassess, question, and expand our frameworks for understanding the world. So as we delve deeper and deeper into discussing the practical implications of cultural intelligence, let's bear in mind that our approach is not merely about implementing new tactics; it's about adopting a more nuanced outlook. In the next section, we'll go over how to arrive at more advanced thinking about culture, and it starts with abandoning the oversimplified idea that is so prevalent in market research and planning: The search for a one-size-fits-all human "truth."

Rethinking Cultural Research

As marketers who are genuinely committed to ensuring that marketing strategy is authentic and inclusive, it is our responsibility to question how we think. Essential to cultural intelligence is our ability to understand that meaning is not fixed but rather is always evolving and shifting depending on the context. Yet as marketers we commonly talk about an insight as one universal discovery about people's lived experiences, preferences, attitudes, and desires. But if culture is more fluid and dynamic than we might have previously assumed, then there might be more than one "truth" that exists at any point in time.

Traditionally, marketers have treated insights as singular "truths" that apply universally across a specific category, customer base, or even broader cultural trends. This perspective often boils down complex social phenomena into digestible, but incomplete soundbites that may not capture the nuance of human experience or social dynamics influenced by experiences of oppression, marginalization, and historic inequities. This single-angle approach misses an important consideration: Truth is subjective. And who is most often left out? People who have been historically marginalized and overlooked in media, culture, and in marketing and advertising, too, of course.

Our capacity to unearth advanced cultural insights is proportional to our ability to generate multiple truths and see the insight from different vantage points. This requires that we learn to step outside of ourselves by recognizing our biases and gaps in knowledge, lived experiences, and cultural awareness. I am not at all suggesting to you here that marketers entirely abandon the notion of landing on a consumer or cultural truth. No, in fact, unearthing meaningful and actionable insight is so central to building an effective strategy. What we need to acknowledge, however, is that what we find truthful can often reflect the dominant culture's perceptions *unless* we proactively and intentionally work to uncover perspectives that might have otherwise been overlooked.

In this sense, the search for a singular "truth" can actually stifle the rich potential for understanding that comes with a more critically conscious approach to cultural analysis that actively looks to center perspectives of women, Black people and people of color, neurodivergent people, people with disabilities, and people from LGBTQIA+ communities. Neglecting to incorporate this lens into cultural analysis and insight generation inadvertently perpetuates existing power imbalances, biases, and stereotypes by upholding a single point of view as the normative standard.

This willingness to step and see outside of us is the key element to the practice of cultural intelligence and conscious marketing more broadly, of course. Before we can become competent in cultural analysis, we need to be willing to assume a commitment to be incessant about asking: What's missing here? What else might be flying under the radar? What else might be going on? Culture is always evolving, and our knowledge must evolve along with it, which requires introspection, humility, and critical attention to "ways in" to an issue or a topic that is otherwise easily overlooked. The most common mistake you could make in the process of unearthing and leveraging cultural insights in developing your strategy is assuming that the cultural "truth" unearthed without further probing is universal to the human experience.

In order to unlock the potential of cultural intelligence, marketing and brand strategists need to seriously consider how our perspectives, lived experiences, and gaps and limitations in knowledge might skew the truth by centering subjectivities of those who share our point of view on the world as well as our own lived experiences. The 4Cs model offers an intervention in conventional ways of thinking, to ask:

- What is the truth?
- Who defines what is seen as truthful?

- What impact does our identity and lived experience have on insight generation? In what ways can bias and gaps in cultural awareness be unspoken parts of insights generation?
- How do we ensure that underrepresented perspectives are not only visible but actively guide our thinking and insights process?

Cultural innovation in marketing strategy depends on our ability to unearth an insight that surprises, delights, or shocks. An insight is a discovery of a new meaning. When brands make mistakes in embedding inclusivity in the marketing strategy, it is not simply because marketing teams lack insight. Highly likely, the insight that was formulated and accepted as a cultural or consumer "truth" and embedded within what was supposed to be an "inclusive" marketing strategy was either incomplete, culturally insensitive, or unintentionally overlooked other truths that exist outside the scope of marketers' awareness (whether experiential or intellectual). Point is, unless we are consciously and intentionally thinking of centering overlooked points of view, it is easy to slip into our own biases.

And so as you begin your process, make it a habit to pause to consider not only opposed or clashing perspectives but those that contain hidden nuances, inconsistencies, and subtleties. The first lesson to the study of culture is that rarely is there one single narrative for any cultural issue. Whether you are in the beginning stage of market research or developing marketing communications, start to develop the habit of routinely asking yourself these questions:

- What do I think I know, and how do I know that it is true?
- Is there another way to look at this issue, audience, or cultural topic?
- What is the other side of this issue that I might not have considered?
- Have any biases, stereotypes, or assumptions come into play here?
- Whom does this perspective benefit? Whom does this perspective undermine?
- What if I were to assume that the opposite is true? What tensions does that bring to the surface?
- How can this perspective be criticized from another viewpoint?
- Who might say that their perspective hasn't been considered? What would they say?

- Whom have I consulted who has either direct expertise and/or lived experience to validate my interpretation? Have I involved other voices in this process?

Engaging in this simple exercise at the beginning of your research process is not only how your brand can avoid spending millions of dollars on marketing that under-delivers or on managing public response to backlash, but how you can anticipate and prepare for backlash in advance. After conducting and analyzing research and aligning your findings with your objectives, you will eventually decide on the exact angle to pursue. This is also a helpful exercise to anticipate any reactions, repercussions, or feedback.

When it comes to executing conscious and socially responsible marketing, critical thinking isn't optional. Dismissing critical thinking (and action!) costs revenue, new business, and immense possibilities for future innovation. Consider that most brands that have made mistakes in engaging with contemporary culture or taking on issues of equity and justice in ways that were immediately criticized could have prevented the eventual failure by ensuring that the cultural issue was considered from several angles, thus anticipating the popular backlash.

Embedding a culture of questioning in your strategic process is how you can assess risk and strategically prepare for it. Start questioning early and do it repeatedly. That kind of analytical adaptability should be seen as necessary for the practice of cultural intelligence, period! Contrary to popular belief, so little of our work as changemakers in marketing is actually about mastering a particular topic or understanding the totality of experiences of one "multicultural" audience segment or another. We can't know everything, but we can practice to thoughtfully question information, beliefs, and assumptions that we come across.

The 4Cs model of cultural intelligence is less about offering you a specific checklist and more about developing analytical tools rooted in critical thinking that you can put into practice, no matter time, place, client, or context. The practical use and, most importantly, the impact that applying these 4Cs and key tenants ultimately can have will depend on the ability to spot assumptions and apply a critical lens to the thinking of others as much as our own. And that's exactly what we'll cover next.

ACTIVITY: STRATEGIC QUESTIONING FOR CULTURAL PROFICIENCY

A brand-driven business wants to run a campaign to reach younger consumers by positioning the brand as culturally relevant. The team has decided to pursue a campaign that reclaims the word "allyship" by centering the idea that to be an ally means to act, not just talk. The first few research and brainstorming sessions with the in-house brand team have generated several ideas, including an initial hypothesis that stood out to the team the most: Allyship is about speaking up and leaning into uncomfortable situations. The team decides to proceed in this direction and run several consumer focus groups in-house to get at a deeper insight to inform campaign strategy.

Team members post on their personal social media and across professional groups on LinkedIn to recruit consumers for two focus groups (15 each). The team is committed to recruiting a diverse group of participants but the timelines are tight and so the project falls short of recruiting those who identify as Black and Latine.

The research team asks participants to share the last time they remember experiencing a conflict about racial justice issue and choosing to lean in to learn as an ally, instead of getting defensive. The discussions seem to go well, and there isn't all that much disagreement, besides a few people from marginalized backgrounds who talk about the importance of psychological safety and mental wellness, so speaking up isn't always in their own best interest. However, the team evolves insights into a strategic cultural territory titled "Embrace the Uncomfortable."

Pause and reflect on what could be challenging about this approach to research. How could the team have executed it differently? What gaps in awareness and biases might be affecting not only the research results here but also the research design itself? In what ways, if any, does the approach to research reflect the dominant perspective on allyship? Let's keep thinking here. How does this research approach consider the perspectives of those who have been historically marginalized? Does it? Is the concept of allyship explored by the team to be truly inclusive of multiple lived experiences, from those who use their privilege to act as allies vs. those who are marginalized by oppressive systems? What about what it means to be on the receiving end of discomfort due to being subjected to prejudice, not just witnessing it? In what ways, if any, does the idea of allyship as it was undertaken in this project place lived experiences of those from socially dominant groups at the center? Finally, what might a more culturally sensitive, mindful, and inclusive process look like? By the way, while I added fictional elements and changed essential details, this example is based on a real-life story.

In subsequent chapters, we will dive significantly deeper into the application of each of these questions and others. For now, keep them in mind as you transition from one chapter to the next. There are no right or wrong answers here—only a deliberate commitment to curiosity, attention, and critical thinking! Embrace it as a practice of learning and the necessary process of constantly improving and evolving your insights.

Challenging Assumptions: A Prerequisite for Cultural Innovation

In cultural fluency, unexamined assumptions are your invisible adversaries. The hidden biases or gaps in awareness can implicitly dictate choices, from creative decisions to strategic directions, in ways that inadvertently perpetuate cultural stereotypes or simply miss the mark. Culturally fluent marketing demands that we engage in a serious interrogation of assumptions as we encounter them, a practice that goes beyond consumer research or tracking market trends. By rigorously probing our preconceptions, we can arrive at a more nuanced and sophisticated understanding of our target demographics, the cultural ecosystems they navigate, and the contexts within which your brand exists.

Below you will find a list of common misconceptions about contemporary culture and the role of brands within it. Each misconception shared here is supplemented with examples of quotes that capture beliefs about culture that have plagued the marketing and advertising industries. But times are changing, and so each example is followed by suggestions on how to begin to address and undo common misconceptions.

Common misconceptions

ACTIVITY: RETHINKING CULTURE

TABLE 2.1 The Art of Questioning: Learning to Probe Assumptions

Outdated Assumptions	How to Probe Assumptions
"Legacy is the cornerstone of our brand. We have always been successful in this market by drawing on this nostalgia, so we don't need to adapt our messaging to current culture."	How has the meaning of legacy itself changed since the brand was founded in 1974? In what ways, if any, has nostalgia come to mean something else to the younger generation? Are there aspects of this nostalgic past that today's consumers might find concerning?
"We've already researched this minority community extensively, so we can tweak our findings from three years ago since we already know exactly how our target audience will respond."	What histories, perspectives, and forms of thinking have created wide-held assumptions that marginalized communities are monolithic? How might have the events, social issues, or trends over the last three years shaped or evolved the perspectives of your target community? What opportunities might the brand be missing by not tapping into new cultural narratives to unlock even more widespread success?
"Cultural shifts might happen, but at the core we all share the same core beliefs and values—family, peace, wellbeing, and aspirations for success. We should tap into these safe emotional registers."	In what ways are cultural values shaped by experiences of dominant groups? How differently might audiences from historically underrepresented groups experience cultural values, such as family, community, or peace? What factors might be at play in subjectivities of people who have experienced systemic marginalization vs. those who have not? Have these factors been accounted for?

Take a moment to examine Table 2.1 and consider how critically minded questions can be employed to reveal assumptions, misconceptions, and stereotypes, while making space for curiosity and further investigation.

Refer to Table 2.2 below to practice the same process of critical interrogation. Think about the following misconceptions about culture and how you would respond to assumptions that might be made in marketing. While you might immediately spot what might be missing from the narrative, challenge yourself to think like a cultural analyst. Deepen your questioning to account not only for cultural change but also for the time period and social norms, perspectives, subjectivities, and values that, historically speaking, have not always been at the center.

TABLE 2.2 What is Culture? Interrogating Common Misconceptions

Culture is a Monolithic Entity That Unites Groups of People
"Our messaging has always worked with moms, so why change what's not broken?"
"This is interesting but subcultures or microcultures are irrelevant to our target audience, so researching niche trends would be a waste of time."
"Our product solves a universal need, so if we focus too much on representing niche cultural differences, we will alienate our audience."
Culture is Only Determined by Geography
"Unity is a core American value. These are polarizing times, and we want to be the brand to remind people of the importance of unity as Americans. Let's play it safe and use this creative angle, since it will resonate with everyone."
"Our product will be a hit in Asian markets, since our creative strategy really speaks to the cultural values of the East."
Culture is Only Determined by Race/Ethnicity/Gender
"What does 'the Black community' think about this issue?"
"Since we are primarily targeting makeup users who are women, our strategy should focus on the 'female' experience."
"If we want to resonate with the Latinx community, we should do all of our campaign communications exclusively in Spanish."

Once you have thought about or written down your questions, consider going over these assumptions once again to probe your own assumptions. Did you miss anything? This practice of self-reflexivity is central to critical analysis, which is irreplaceable in the practice of cultural intelligence.

Below is a general checklist of questions that you can refer to whenever you need to probe an unexamined belief and or train your team in the process of applying critical analysis:

- How has the meaning of the concept changed over time?
- What social forces have contributed to the adoption or rejection of this concept?
- In what ways might different people interpret this concept differently based on their own experiences and backgrounds?
- What are the implications of this assumption for different groups of people?
- Are there any historical or cultural factors that might be influencing the way this assumption is being made (by me or others)?
- How do ideologies and identity formations in culture (race, gender, sexuality, class, disability, etc.) influence perspectives on this concept or idea?
- What assumptions are being made about power and privilege in this situation?
- How do institutional structures and policies shape the interpretation or application of this idea?
- What ethical considerations arise from the concept? Who wins and who loses?

Learning to question your assumptions will help you spot issues in research, strategy, or creative outputs before they turn into problems. It might be worthwhile to dive further into the different types of questions you can ask in your practice of questioning, including open-ended, probing, clarifying, reflective, and evaluative questions.

Open-ended questions encourage discussion while probing questions explore a topic on a deeper level. Clarifying questions seek to define specific terms or concepts. Reflective questions encourage self-reflection, and evaluative questions assess the impact. As you can see here, you can tackle an idea, an assumption, or a concept from all sorts of levels.

By being aware of our very human tendency to make assumptions or take things for granted and then using a variety of these questioning techniques to challenge them, we only gain a more comprehensive understanding of a problem or an issue long before it turns into a business liability.

Questioning isn't about being wrong or admitting a mistake per se. It's about leveling up the approach and refining the nuance of insights we have the opportunity to uncover. Asking the right kinds of questions is a winning strategy, not just for avoiding missteps but also for uncovering opportunities that might otherwise go unnoticed.

In Conversation with Reema Mitra

Reema Mitra, *Vice President of Strategy, is an award-winning, seasoned strategist with a passion for shaping the future of businesses. With a background in strategic planning and a keen eye for innovation, she has been a driving force behind the success of numerous organizations. Reema brings over 15 years of experience in the world of strategy and business development, beginning her journey at renowned PR firm, Weber Shandwick, where she honed her strategic skills while working on high-impact projects for Unilever.*

Reema is instrumental in charting the course for the companies she works with, leading initiatives that have propelled them to new heights. Throughout her career, Reema has been recognized for her outstanding contributions and has been awarded at the Cannes Lions for her contribution to the Dove Real Beauty Campaign. Her educational background includes a master's degree in Innovation from Goldsmiths University. Her primary aspiration is to continue shaping the strategic landscape of organizations, fostering growth, and driving innovation while making a lasting impact.

AKG: In this chapter, we discuss the significance of questioning, pushing back against the status quo, and crafting new brand narratives. You worked on accounts that integrated culture-defining ideas long before "inclusivity" was a popular buzzword. How did you get started in this space?

RM: I've been in marketing for 15 years now, working in-house and at agencies like Huge, DDB, Edelman, Isobar, PHD, and most recently EssenceMedia.Com. I've also worked at a company called TodayTix in-house, as well as Better.com, a unicorn mortgage startup, on a freelance basis. I've had varied experiences across the board. Some clients I've worked on include Ikea, Dove, Google, and Unilever. I've had a wide breadth of client experience, which has been amazing. But what I'm most passionate about are purpose-driven narratives. I love working on brands that have some kind of higher mission or purpose, a higher order that they're hoping to bring to the world. Brands that look to better the community, better human beings, better our society—these are brands I care about the most.

AKG: The pillars of cultural intelligence all point in one direction: Building brands that are intentionally more socially conscious and impactful in culture. Some critics have said that brand purpose and the focus on inclusivity in marketing are diluting the original tradition of planning. How do you see the role of social good in marketing?

RM: Truth is, people hate ads. They don't like being advertised to. People are smart these days. Your traditional planning toward creatives in TV ads, out-of-home ads, and email marketing ads isn't as effective anymore. Why are purpose-driven brands important? Why is the narrative so important? There've been numerous studies that suggest consumers prefer brands with good embedded in their ethos; brands that are trying to better society. Whether it's giving back, sustainability, or something like Dove's self-esteem project. There's evidence that people prefer those brands. Purchasing power is power. People demonstrate that through the brand choices they make.

AKG: You've worked on brands that used media for good before it was popular. What was it like working on these bold and brave projects back then?

RM: The Dove project dates back to maybe 2000 or the early 2000s with Edelman working on it. I recall meeting up with a supervisor when I was onboarded to the brand. When launching this brand, the team realized real beauty was a space no one was addressing, so they aimed to approach it differently. Dove began as a beauty bar, and its primary claim was its moisturizing capability. A significant percentage of the product was more a moisturizer than a cleanser. From there, it evolved into the Real Beauty initiative. The PR professionals knew some might question Dove's role in the real beauty discussion, hence, they backed the campaign with actual self-esteem workshops and the self-esteem fund, investing corporate dollars to give the campaign further depth. Dove has since been a trendsetter, not only contributing financially but also sparking essential dialogues about topics like airbrushing, body image, and even supporting doulas for Black women who may not receive adequate medical care during pregnancy. And campaigns like the Real Beauty Sketches made a significant cultural impact. It's an iconic brand. It's done so much good in the world in terms of the types of conversations it's opened, which I think is just as important as actually giving back to society. It didn't only hit on what was wrong with the world. It was inviting us to challenge our own beliefs around what is beautiful as opposed to just pointing out the toxicity in the world. Today, Dove directly addresses broader issues like patriarchy and white supremacy. Dove is going after those things directly! They've been able to do a lot of this work from a place of igniting those conversations and being at the forefront of wanting to push the boundaries further. The brand has consistently been bold and courageous.

AKG: Many of us want to do bolder and more daring work. Yet singular incidents of consumer backlash and subsequent news cycles and never-ending click baits around these spectacles fuel some apprehension. What might you say to a marketer eager to make the work more inclusive but who fears taking on a risk?

RM: That is such a good question, because it's a question you ask yourself every day when you show up to work. What is actually going to make a difference in the world and what's going to keep the brand competitive? Taking risks is exactly like what this game is about. Part of being a strong marketer is saying to yourself, what is happening in the world? Whether I'm selling a shoe, beer, or soap, how can these things actually make their way into culture? How can we find ways to become part of what's happening out in the world? There are a lot of skeptics around that because there are people who think culture- and purpose-driven narratives don't sell products. But if we look at the world's most famous brands, they've all taken risks.

If you look at what Nike did with Kaepernick or what Red Bull did a couple of years ago with getting into sports and soccer when not many Americans were watching soccer at the time. These types of big swings are what gets you to be memorable. It's what gets you in the history books. It's what gets you in the minds of consumers! Ultimately, *that is your job*—to make the brand top of mind. If you're not taking risks, if you're not thinking about culture, if you're not thinking about how you can borrow from a culture without appropriating it... these are things that make a marketer a marketer.

AKG: What a powerful reminder. What do you do to question your assumptions about the world and practice unearthing more robust and inclusive insights?

RM: How I stay plugged into culture as a marketer is important. I get inspired by so many different things because I'm living my life. I think that if you're not out there in the world engaging with the world and what's going on with it, then you really don't have a whole lot to come into the cultural conversation with.

As an example, my partner's a big D&D player, which stands for Dungeons and Dragons. He loves it, and he's super nerdy about it. What I found out was there was a YouTube gameplay of D&D called Critical Role. It was a channel that came out and it was so popular that Amazon made a cartoon based on this game. Watching culture transcend itself like this is so fascinating to me. I would have never known that if I didn't have that context. I really wouldn't think much of it. I wouldn't think it was a big deal. I wouldn't think it was a big community, but it's massive. It's also an inclusive game. That's what makes it so popular as well, that people can play it on their computers or people can play it in person. Without having that knowledge or being out in the world, that could have been a missed insight on my part. To me, it's important to engage in the world around you.

Broad awareness is the way to go. Being inclusive is a way to do that. It's a way to invite people in. It's a way to get them to say that this is for you as well. It just makes good marketing sense.

When I was at TodayTix we wrote the mission statement which said, "Find a seat for everyone." It was not just marketing to theater nerds and people who love theater but also people who had never seen a show in their life and were waiting their whole lives to see one. It was about inviting people in who are not your typical white audience that goes to see those shows. It was about making theater as inclusive as possible because that's the goal of the company: Selling cheap theater tickets to make it accessible for anyone who wants to see it. Working on that was a significant part of my career, and I think one that was very notable because of the work that we did to bring theater access to as many people as possible. Being inclusive means that you are inviting the most people in and offering for them to enjoy the brand, be a part of the brand, participate in the brand, and sometimes even make the brand. Some of the best brand innovation has come from people speaking up and saying, "This is not for me" or "It didn't feel like this was my experience with your brand."

AKG: Some marketers still worry though, "Will this alienate my core?" What do you say to that?

RM: I remember how briefs for African American or Asian American audiences would always come as ancillary to the actual "main brief." But I always say, if you build a system for the most marginalized or the most vulnerable in that system, the whole system benefits. It's much better to take that point of view and talk to the people who are historically excluded from your brand marketing because it actually makes the marketing stronger for everyone else.

AKG: You spent significant time studying innovation as part of your graduate training at Goldsmiths. What do you think it means for a brand to truly innovate in a culture in a way that takes into account human truths that have historically been overlooked or treated as less relevant?

RM: Cultural insights are what drives those types of innovations. For instance, Rare Beauty have created their products so that people who are differently abled or don't have much mobility in their hands can open their products much more easily. Selena Gomez has her own disabilities and that's baked into her brand. That's a packaging innovation right there. When you integrate cultural insights and what people actually need out of something, you're able to build something better and something more that benefits the entire system a little bit better.

3

Culture:
Building the Foundation for an
Inclusive Marketing Strategy

WHAT TO EXPECT

In a fast-accelerating cultural landscape, identifying emerging market trends, developing an inclusive brand, and achieving culturally meaningful differentiation require marketers to stay abreast of contemporary cultural shifts and deeply understand their origins. In this chapter, we will delve into the basics of conducting research, collecting, and interpreting data with greater precision and rigor, covering the following questions:

- What essential concepts from cultural studies are useful to the marketer's toolbox?

- What tools of cultural analysis can help marketers better understand representation?

- How should marketers frame more effective research questions to decode culture?

- How can marketers decode cultural texts and map cultural movements?

The ability to "read" culture doesn't necessarily require advanced training and is accessible to anyone: It only requires a patient "reader" of culture who is attentive and perceptive to the constant evolution of cultural meaning. Let's dive in.

Decoding Culture for Competitive Advantage

Everyone has the capacity necessary to decode culture. Although it might not seem so yet, you are already completely proficient in this skill, whether you know it or not. See, all social life is organized by cultural cues and norms that we pick up, learn, and rehearse. As social actors, we navigate our daily lives, deciphering meaning and following social protocols, often without giving it a second thought.

The decision to shake hands or bow in a business meeting, the tone you choose to use in an email to a manager, or the calculated assuredness in your voice during a client call—these actions are guided by culturally constructed norms of formality, professionalism, and decorum. As you go through your day, you are already constantly receiving, analyzing, and behaving according to established cultural protocols. This cultural knowledge is so innate to you that you don't have to think about it twice.

Think about the last time you attended a formal event. You probably knew intuitively how to dress, interact with others, introduce yourself, socialize, how to use cutlery at each meal, and even when to applaud. You could have also been navigating complex, socially constructed expectations linked to your assigned or perceived gender, race or ethnicity, ability, or body size—markers that often unfairly delineate how one "should" act or appear to others. These expectations extend beyond just attire to comportment, speech patterns, and even the level of assertiveness or deference you display. These rules are unspoken, but we know them so well. Should you decide to deviate from these expectations, chances are you'd be hyper-aware of your conscious choice not to conform, aware that your nonconformity could be a subject of scrutiny, criticism, or even punishment. There were no instructions offered to you for this when you arrived. You simply knew.

Your implicit ability to understand cultural codes around you directly results from your own cultural knowledge—the ability to read, interpret, and respond to cultural cues surrounding you. This is a skill we begin to intuitively master as soon as we start communicating and interacting with the world as children. From an early age, we are schooled in the subtle arts of social signaling and behavioral conformity. Whether it's observing our caregivers, mimicking peers, or being explicitly taught what is "right" and "wrong," we absorb these cultural instructions—and they become part of us.

As we mature into adults, these lessons don't just stay with us; they become ingrained mechanisms of how we operate and what we expect of ourselves and others. The clothes we deem appropriate, the language we consider respectful, the rituals we observe—all have their roots in those formative years. Unless we are consciously aware of how culture operates in our lives, we then reinforce these norms with those around us either explicitly or implicitly, thereby perpetuating the very social architecture we ourselves inhabit daily.

I want to invite you to start thinking about culture in this way. Not as something that you need to learn to analyze solely as a marketer or a brand manager but as a kind of cultural "software" that you're already running on, often in the background. Understanding culture in this way begins by learning how to identify the implicit scripts, norms, and values that are already influencing your perceptions, decisions, and interactions. Why? By decoding our own cultural programming, we unlock the capacity to start viewing the world more critically: We soon realize that everything we touch is implicated in a broader cultural ecosystem rich with meanings that we are continually shaping and being shaped by.

Culture is not this one thing or the other; it's a totality. Building on cultural theorist Raymond Williams' concept of culture as a community's "whole way of life," Stuart Hall (2016) aptly defined culture as "experience

FIGURE 3.1 Culture: A Way of Life

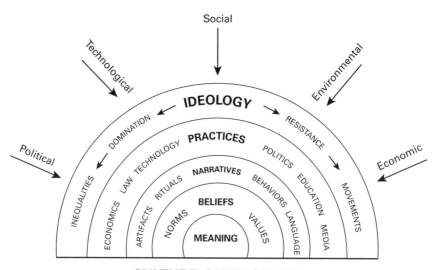

CULTURE: A WAY OF LIFE

Original framework by Dr. Anastasia Kārkliņa Gabriel © 2023. Reproduction without permission is prohibited.

lived, experience interpreted, experience defined." Because culture is a "whole way of life," Hall noted, cultural analysis is a way to "discover shared ideas and forms of communication." Hall maintained that culture is a space of "negotiation" or, more specifically, a site of "interpretative struggle."

What does this mean? Culture is always a competition of meaning: What is good and sacred to us, who belongs and who doesn't, and what (and who) is acceptable and welcome. At the core of culture are symbols that we use to construct meaning and to mark and communicate our beliefs, values, and norms. What we value, worship, and believe in gets expressed through practices, behaviors, and rituals that we partake in to signal our belonging to others. Cultural practices, rituals, and artifacts, in turn, constitute knowledge systems that shape respective institutions, media forms, and paradigms that we use to relate, categorize, socialize, and govern. All of this makes up ideology, a lens through which we understand and make meaning of the world.

Ideology is a push-and-pull of competing interpretations of the world; some ideologies dominate, while others resist. Think here of the push-and-pull of patriarchal and feminist ideologies that shape everything from knowledge systems and institutions to everyday rituals, protocols, and codes of conduct but offer different frameworks for living. As an entire way of life, culture is necessarily shaped, molded, and defined under the forces of political, economic, environmental, and social pressures. Figure 3.1 shows a conceptual interpretation of this ecosystem. For centuries, humans have adapted to their environment by erecting social systems to make sense of a complex, ever-changing world. Culture is an exercise in persuasion: *This* is the way to live.

What is marketing if not a focused exercise in shaping perception by strategically tapping into cultural ideologies of what is acceptable, valuable, worthy, or aspirational? Here comes the main implication of why this way of thinking about culture matters for building an inclusive marketing strategy. The challenge facing marketers is that these cultural codes and behavior patterns become so deeply rooted in our social structure that we often fail to recognize them. They're both invisible and omnipresent, continuously shaping how we see the world. These cultural codes are the backdrop to our everyday lives, ever-present but rarely acknowledged. The challenge, and indeed the opportunity, comes in learning to decode these often "invisible" norms so that we can become more conscious of how harmful ideas, bias, or oppressive norms can unintentionally creep into the messaging that brands disseminate into the world as themselves producers of mass media.

Cultural analysis, then, is simply a more formal process of consciously and intentionally engaging in a critical interrogation of cultural norms, protocols, and institutions that many of us are already engaged in as thinking individuals navigating the complexities of our society. And here's the catch: You can't become an inclusive marketer unless you learn to interrogate these codes, understand their implications, and start thinking more critically about the kind of messaging that brands put out into the culture.

In marketing, turning a critical eye on taken-for-granted aspects of cultural life is an opportunity to move away from superficial or even harmful or stereotypical storytelling and toward culturally relevant and representative narratives. Below are some of the ways that cultural analysis can be effectively deployed in advertising and marketing, giving marketers the ability to:

- uncover the ideologies and cultural tensions fueling trends relevant to the brand;
- recognize how power dynamics and inequities intersect with cultural and social issues that are relevant to the brand, category, or the product;
- discern the symbolic meanings behind cultural artifacts for accurate and culturally sensitive use in creative storytelling;
- scrutinize campaigns to ensure they are devoid of cultural stereotypes, outdated tropes, and damaging narratives;
- align a brand's strategy with emergent cultural movements to pinpoint avenues for growth and engagement.

Before diving into the practical applications of cultural analysis in marketing, it's essential to familiarize ourselves with fundamental terms that encapsulate the dynamics of culture. Let's focus on two pivotal concepts— representation and ideology. These ideas will serve as cornerstones in your practice of cultural intelligence. Understanding how to identify "ideology"— the hidden messages—within various forms of representation will become crucial for crafting more inclusive and socially conscious outputs.

How Culture Works: Key Concepts to Know

Representation

In marketing and advertising, representation is often assumed to be a simple concept that refers to how things or people are shown or depicted in the media or other forms of communication. To improve representation in marketing, brands typically cast a more diverse group of models or actors to signal that they value inclusivity. In other cases, representation is understood as the need to cast research participants from historically underrepresented groups. None of this is wrong. These practices should be actively encouraged, practiced, and defended as crucial to culturally intelligent marketing. However, this understanding of representation remains incomplete, which prevents marketers who genuinely want to be more inclusive and socially responsible from taking their work to the next level.

Let's unpack what representation means. To represent means to describe or depict something. But it also means to symbolize or signify. Representation is not simply about the appearance of something—about how things look to us or who is included. Representation conveys meaning in culture. It is a complex process that determines how cultural practices, objects, and symbols are constructed and signified through visual, verbal, or gestural language.

On a basic level, representation is never simply about how something looks. It is about what something means on a level of cultural ideology—not only literally ("lipstick is a beauty product") but also ideologically ("wearing lipstick is what only women do"). In this way, all communications carry concealed meaning that is communicated and conveyed through representation.

This understanding is especially relevant to image-generating industries like marketing and advertising. Take, for example, the notorious ad campaigns from the mid-20th century that perpetuated racial stereotypes, depicting Black people in demeaning or subservient roles. These ads weren't just "of their time"; they actively *represented* and *reinforced* the societal prejudices, racist beliefs, and power imbalances of that era. Similarly, portrayals of women in advertising often confined them to domestic roles, subtly reinforcing the notion that a woman's place was in the home. When we see an advertisement featuring a person of a particular race, gender, sexuality, class, or ability, we're not just seeing a visual image; we're also encountering a set of assumptions, stories, and power dynamics that the image brings with it.

This is why, when a well-known retail brand used a Black child to model a hoodie that read "coolest monkey in the jungle," it struck a nerve and caused an uproar. When another retailer put out a campaign where a "little school" boy wearing a t-shirt with Albert Einstein on it was portrayed next to a girl who was called "the social butterfly" and "the talk of the playground," the brand was slammed for blatant sexism. In these instances, the brands weren't just selling clothes; they were unintentionally perpetuating harmful cultural narratives.

The "coolest monkey in the jungle" hoodie didn't just happen in a vacuum; it invoked centuries of racial stereotyping and derogatory language that have been used to dehumanize Black people. Similarly, the Einstein "genius" boy next to the "social butterfly" girl wasn't just an innocent design choice; it reinforced traditional gender roles and expectations limiting boys and girls, and those who don't conform to binary gender expectations. These examples illuminate a central point here: Marketing doesn't just reflect culture; it shapes and perpetuates it. When marketers fail to critically interrogate the cultural ideologies brands are tapping into, the result can be outright harmful—and hurtful.

With this in mind, we can begin to recognize how representation is not neutral or objective but is influenced by various factors such as power dynamics, social hierarchies, and ideological perspectives. This is why an understanding of cultural representation as a form of ideology—those deeper, often invisible scripts that guide our behavior and expectations—is essential. It's key to creating marketing campaigns that are not only successful but also conscientious.

For this reason, too, semiotics, or the study of signs and symbols, is fundamental to brand marketing—more on this a little later in this chapter! Understanding that representation is not only about who is represented but what cultural meaning is being reinforced or reproduced is crucial for recognizing the power dynamics and social implications of images, messages, and symbols being communicated to consumers. By analyzing the cultural ideology behind representation, marketers can ensure that brand messaging aligns with consumer perspectives and values, actively challenging outdated ideologies and promoting new, more inclusive stories about who we are.

Ideology

As you might have noticed, I couldn't avoid explaining representation without invoking the term "ideology." This is because by communicating meaning into the world, representation reproduces cultural ideologies of one kind or the other; there is no avoiding that. Ideology is often seen as a political concept more appropriately taken up by politicians, researchers, and activists. But this is not what we mean here. As it is understood in cultural studies, the concept of ideology offers a different perspective, one that is much more valuable for marketers who are striving to become more conscious and inclusive. In this context, ideology refers to the lens through which we view the world, a form of cognitive mapping that orders and makes sense of the complex realities we inhabit.

At a basic level, ideology is any system of beliefs, values, and assumptions that shape how we see the world and interpret information. Ideologies are often invisible or taken for granted, but they are powerful forces that influence our perceptions, behaviors, and choices through the process of representation. Like all forms of media, marketing messages can either reinforce dominant ideologies or interrupt, negotiate, or challenge them.

Consider how, historically, marketing within the fragrance industry relied heavily on gendered stereotypes, particularly when it came to selling perfume. In these scenarios, women often appeared in roles subservient to men, commonly depicted in a sexualized manner. Ads from previous eras often showcased women—frequently barely dressed or captured in provocative poses—in positions subordinate to fully clothed men. These campaigns aimed to tap into cultural themes of romance, sensuality, and luxury, but in doing so, they not only reflected but also perpetuated sexist ideologies.

Fast-forward to today, where pro-feminist ideologies have moved from the periphery to the center of cultural discourse. In line with this shift, contemporary fragrance marketing increasingly embraces narratives of self-love, independence, and women's empowerment. Campaigns that once sexualized or objectified women are becoming obsolete. The point is, by promoting targeted messaging through marketing campaigns, brands always already implicitly endorse and reinforce certain ideologies or, in other words, a set of ideas, beliefs, and values that shape how we understand and interact with the world.

For marketers, the key takeaway is this: Ideology is often conceptualized as repressive—a way to enforce conformity—but it can also be enabling, allowing new possibilities for communication and engagement. An inclusive brand can offer its audiences an ideological alternative to consider, negotiate, or even adopt: This is what Dove did with its Rare Beauty campaign, what Fenty x Savage achieved with its size-inclusive lingerie, and what Gillette accomplished with its culture-defining trans-inclusive storytelling.

These brands offered audiences an ideological alternative to consider, negotiate, or even adopt—one that their target audiences could not only identify with but also rally behind. Consumer preferences increasingly hinge not just on what a product does but on what choosing that product says about the consumer's own ideological positioning in an increasingly polarized society. Brands are, thus, in the business of spreading ideas and value-based narratives, which is to say, brands are in the business of ideology.

What's hard about this, however, is that ideologies don't necessarily operate at the level of articulated thought or discourse, which makes them
difficult to spot. Ideology is often submerged in everyday practices, embodied in images, or codified in seemingly banal everyday choices—like the
symbolism in an ad or the seemingly innocent dialogue in a commercial.

Take marketers who produced sexist advertising in the fragrance category 10, 20, or 30 years ago: They did so because this was the industry
standard at the time, a reflection of the prevailing ideological norms. This
doesn't absolve them of responsibility but contextualizes their choices
within a broader cultural framework where such portrayals were not only
accepted but also expected. Had they taken the time to interrogate culture
through the lens of ideology, they might have acted differently. Still,
the prevailing standards were less a result of individual decisions than they
were a manifestation of systemic norms, ones that hadn't yet been broadly
questioned or deconstructed. And here's the uncomfortable truth: We are in
no way unlike the advertisers of the past. We too operate within our own
cultural matrix, inevitably reproducing what we consider to be "normal" at
this moment in time.

Today, a new wave of conscious marketing calls for us to not only identify but also dismantle the hidden biases and subtext that may be subtly
woven into our campaigns. This starts by learning how to decode ideology.

ACTIVITY: LEARN TO DECODE IDEOLOGY

In a meticulously crafted advertising campaign, a hypothetical luxury watch
brand reveals a collection of visually stunning images. One shot stands out: A
white, aesthetically pleasing model is pictured at ease on a yacht against the
backdrop of stunning blue water. She lounges center-frame in a bikini while
reclining on a deck chair. Holding a champagne flute in her hand and with her
back conspicuously arched to emphasize her body's curvature, she glances
aimlessly to the side. On her wrist rests an exquisite luxury watch, catching the
sunlight with a bright shimmer.

Directly behind her, a tall man in a well-tailored suit grips her shoulder
tightly, his own watch prominently displayed. The rest of the background is
filled with two groups of equally attractive, impeccably dressed friends—diverse
in ethnicity and gender—engaging in conversation while also enjoying the
luxuries aboard. In the distance, one group of women is giggling and taking
selfies. A group of men is pouring drinks in the corner; two men shake hands.

The bright imagery creates an aura of exclusivity and carefreeness. The copy
reads, "Time Well Spent: Luxury Living, Unapologetically Yours."

How to Decode:

- Who appears in the ad, and who is noticeably absent? What do these choices reveal about perceived social standing and roles?

- What underlying beliefs and values emerge when you consider all these signs collectively? What message does the ad transmit about what constitutes success, happiness, or social prestige?

- How might this ad resonate differently with diverse audience segments? What are the potential pitfalls or benefits of these divergent interpretations?

- How does the interpretation of racial dynamics shift if the male model behind the female protagonist is of a different race than her? What additional layers of complexity are introduced when considering intersections of race, gender, and masculinity?

- Who in the ad appears to have agency or control, and who does not? What does this reveal about underlying assumptions related to power dynamics?

- Could such an ad ever feature a woman instead of a man gripping the main figure's shoulder? Why or why not?

- What could be done to make this ad more inclusive? Are there alternative narratives or different visuals that could be used?

A Possible Interpretation of Ideology

At first glance, the advertisement projects an air of inclusivity: A group of friends, diverse in ethnicity and gender, luxuriating on a yacht. However, the central figure—a thin, white model—sits at the confluence of multiple axes of privilege: Race, body type, and presumably, economic status. Despite the apparent diversity of her companions, their positioning as peripheral figures only serves to reinforce her centrality. One possible audience reception is to conclude that luxury, success, and beauty are still most authentically embodied in a figure that conforms to established Western ideals.

Moreover, by making whiteness central and positioning other ethnicities at the periphery, the advertisement inadvertently reproduces racial hierarchies. Although ethnic diversity is shown, it's framed as secondary to the central white experience, thereby elevating whiteness as a kind of "norm" against which other identities are defined. Their presence appears designed to signal that this brand is "for everyone," yet their peripheral positioning suggests that they are framed as accessories to the central character's lifestyle—a life that consumers should aspire to emulate. Similarly, the looming figure of a man behind the central woman adds another layer of complexity. In contrast, the visuals of men shaking hands in the background reinforce traditional gender roles where male figures wield influence and control.

Cultural ideology is often less apparent and takes some critical attention to bring to the surface. I have made some of the details here more apparent for the sake of explaining as clearly as I can what you would normally focus on when decoding an image: Identity markers; the composition and arrangements; visual symbolism; contextual clues; and the interplay of these elements. Remember—when decoding ideology, you are in an active search of what we might think of as "subtext." In other words, you're not merely observing what's explicitly presented but delving into the layers beneath. The task is to unearth the unspoken messages, implicit biases, and hidden meanings that lie beneath the surface of the text as it appears.

How to Frame Effective Research Questions

Decoding ideology should be an integral step accompanying your research and data collection process. It won't always manifest as a direct analysis of a specific campaign—that's where we started, as I find it to be the most practical and accessible way to illustrate and teach this analytical approach. Nonetheless, this critical thinking style will prove valuable to you right from the moment you receive the brief. Consider it less as a rigid, step-by-step method and more as a method of inquiry, guiding your attention and helping you identify key points to probe and question. The practice of "decoding ideology" is simply your willingness to go beyond the obvious to ask: What else might be happening here?

When beginning research into culture, it might be tempting to follow the advice that is too frequently circulated and accepted as given in marketing: Find a brand-relevant "human truth." But as we discussed in the previous chapter, what we commonly regard as the universal "truth" is often, if anything, subjective and influenced by dominant perspectives, biases, and lived experiences—unless they are actively interrogated and questioned. This is where decoding ideology becomes essential early on: It's imperative to prioritize critical thinking regarding inclusivity and diversity from the beginning.

Once again, this isn't meant to suggest that a human truth doesn't exist. Indeed, many lived experiences encompass universal elements; however, these universal aspects can coexist alongside a multitude of diverse perspectives and interpretations. Our initial step, however, should always encompass an honest examination of our assumptions, rooted in our own perspectives and experience, when approaching a topic. We then should craft research questions intentionally structured to embrace the potential for multiple truths to emerge.

Let's explore the two projects below as practical demonstrations of how incorporating ideology and representation can be seamlessly woven into the process right from the beginning of any cultural research process.

CASE STUDY
The New Era of Beauty

Imagine your retail client wants to craft a compelling brand narrative for heightened cultural relevance. The aim is to drive brand awareness at the top of the funnel and position the brand as a significant contributor to the ongoing cultural conversation about diversity, particularly within the beauty category. Before we get to define your research questions, it is worth asking a few preliminary questions as follows:

- What do most people tend to believe about beauty in our society?

- How do people's assumptions or preconceptions influence the way our culture perceives, engages with, and reinforces ideas of beauty and the standards linked to it?

- Are there ongoing criticisms, ideological debates, or social tensions related to the concept of beauty within this market and across target audiences?

- Considering factors like politics, social dynamics, and contemporary matters, what are the conflicting "truths" on what beauty signifies to different people?

- How do my own beliefs align or conflict with these various perspectives? How might my preconceptions influence the way I perceive, engage with, and reinforce ideas of beauty and beauty standards?

These questions, while not exhaustive, prompt us to embrace a more critical perspective. In this context, "critical" doesn't denote a negative or dismissive stance. It is not a mere exercise in asking questions for the sake of asking questions either. Instead, this approach offers a means to examine cultural norms, concepts, and our own thought processes more deeply instead of simply rushing into gathering evidence about what a specific group might feel about a given topic. It lays the foundation for comprehensive cultural analysis that reaches beyond superficial observations.

With this in mind, you would want to proceed by allowing this process to help shape further research questions that can help unearth more meaningful cultural insights for your consideration. Refer to Table 3.1 to steer your process and focus on the questions that align most closely with your specific brief.

TABLE 3.1 Designing an Equity-Conscious Approach to Research

Focus of Investigation	Sample Research Questions
Definition	• How is the concept of beauty currently perceived and practiced within our target culture? • What specific practices, ideas, and behaviors are encompassed within the realm of beauty in this culture? • Are there well-established narratives that define the meaning of beauty in this cultural context? • What are the prevalent behaviors linked to beauty practices within this culture? • Are there particular symbols, rituals, or practices associated with beauty, and where are these practices commonly observed or conducted?
Origin	• What are the historical and earlier known perceptions of beauty within this culture? • How have these historical perceptions of beauty been influenced by or contrasted with other cultural or societal concepts, such as class, race, and more? • In what ways has the meaning of beauty evolved and been negotiated over time within this culture? Which social groups have been most affected by these transformations, and what kinds of groups have historically been excluded from prevailing beauty standards?
Evolution	• How has the notion of beauty evolved over different periods of time within this culture? • Can we identify significant historical or social events that have had a substantial impact on the concept of beauty and how it is practiced in this culture? • In what ways do economic, gender, racial, or age-related factors intersect with, influence, or reshape prevailing beauty perceptions? • Are there specific cultural artifacts, such as media, popular culture, literature, art, or historical documents, that offer deeper insights into the evolution of beauty ideals within this culture?

(continued)

TABLE 3.1 (Continued)

Focus of Investigation	Sample Research Questions
Tensions	• What are the contrasting and conflicting narratives surrounding beauty within this culture? Who are the key stakeholders involved, and who benefits from these narratives? Conversely, who is excluded or marginalized by them? • How do these tensions manifest in society? In what ways are these conflicting narratives of beauty navigated and negotiated by individuals? • Are there emerging trends or narratives that challenge traditional notions of beauty? Who is driving these new perspectives, and who stands to benefit from them? What novel ideas are being generated and propagated within this cultural context?
Ideology	• How do underlying ideologies related to gender, race, sexuality, and class shape the concept of beauty within this culture? How has this interplay evolved over different periods of time? • In what ways have these ideologies transformed to either conform to or challenge prevailing societal norms and power structures? How has the overarching concept of beauty evolved as an ideology itself? • To what extent is beauty interconnected with other ideological constructs, such as notions of success, morality, attraction, health, wellness, or wealth? How do these intersect with and influence the cultural perceptions of beauty? • How is beauty portrayed and represented in various forms of media, popular culture, and politics within this culture? What role does media and politics play in shaping beauty ideals?

This doesn't suggest that your research process should be solely centered on addressing every possible question from this list or beyond. You can refer to this list for inspiration or when you're uncertain if you've covered all aspects. An essential aspect of this exercise is recognizing the research priorities, which should align with your client's specific brief and business goals.

CASE STUDY
The Future of Sports

Let's examine another hypothetical scenario, which, similar to the one discussed earlier, is drawn from previous consulting work. Imagine that a prominent client in the apparel industry aims to set their brand apart and position it as a leader in shaping the future of athletic lifestyle. We will use this scenario to illustrate the types of questions you might pose, supplementing the approach detailed in the preceding section.

The difference in this example is that this client has made it clear that their objective is to innovate a new space within the category, while the client from the previous example was interested in finding a culturally relevant "way in" to the current cultural conversation.

Interpreting this new directive, we are led to shift our focus from making sense of present cultural narratives and their origins, genealogies, and evolution to forecasting possible futures for athletic lifestyles. This calls for an adjustment in our approach to setting research questions, and so the questions we ask at the beginning of our research must reflect this change in focus.

Instead of mapping out the current discourse on sports and athletics and tracing its origins, we will set out to interrogate existing signals that reveal future directions, which could include questions we outlined for the previous case study but would otherwise primarily focus on innovation and the impact of social transformation on the future:

- What sociocultural, technological, economic, or environmental factors have the potential to reshape our understanding of athletic lifestyle in the next 5–20 years?

- How might shifts in sociocultural dynamics across various domains like sports, wellness, fashion, health, and movements for greater inclusivity and accessibility indicate a transformation in the future of sports and athletic lifestyles? Who are the key beneficiaries in these potential scenarios?

- In what ways might changes in urban planning and living spaces influence how sports are conducted, practiced, and enjoyed in the future?

- How could shifts in media consumption and the entertainment industry impact the way sports are consumed and experienced in the future? Who stands to gain from these changes?

- Do these anticipated cultural shifts marginalize, exclude, sideline, or overlook particular lived experiences and perspectives in any way? If so, how can we address these issues to ensure inclusivity in the future of athletic lifestyles?

The questions you formulate at the outset of cultural analysis will depend on the client's brief and, more precisely, their target audience, category, business challenges, and commercial objectives. It's important to emphasize that both sets of questions, despite the shift in focus, continue to encompass inquiries related to power, marginalization, and equity. As we delved into the foundations of cultural intelligence in the introductory chapter, critical consciousness—with a focus on inclusion, equity, accountability, and impact—remains a constant "force" that applies critical pressure on the process to ensure the strategy is genuinely inclusive.

Too frequently, integrating critical consciousness is restricted to marketing strategies that explicitly engage with topics of social and racial justice, diversity, equity, sustainability, and accessibility—for example, when it comes to explicit social impact campaigns. This is not a winning strategy. Instead, it stands as a missed opportunity in a rapidly evolving cultural landscape, where an integrated cultural fluency practice within the marketing strategy is no longer simply a "nice-to-have." Regardless of whether inclusivity is an explicit focus in the brief, an upfront focus on issues of equity, inclusivity, and accessibility is paramount to conscious marketers moving away from performativity to critical action. This approach will more effectively reveal any potential pitfalls, unconscious biases, or gaps in cultural understanding.

Cultural Research: Leveraging Advanced Insights

Now that we have explored how to formulate research questions, let's place these questions within the context of cultural analysis and data collection. Cultural analysts, strategists, and marketers rely on a wide range of qualitative, quantitative, and mixed-method approaches to data collection. These methodologies range from qualitative interviews, focus groups, and ethnographical fieldwork to surveys, social listening, and, more recently, natural language processing technologies. Since marketing professionals are typically already acquainted with approaches to market and consumer research, I won't dwell on detailed explanations of these methods here. Here, we will focus on cultural analysis.

Cultural analysis, as a form of data collection and critical interpretation of the social world, relies on analytical capabilities that draw heavily on secondary desk research. This makes it a useful, practical choice for marketing teams, whether at agencies, client-side, or in-house. In addition to understanding the evolution of consumer culture through the lens of consumer needs, wants, problems, and desires, cultural analysis—being one of the primary tools of cultural intelligence—draws heavily on the interpretation of popular culture, media, entertainment, arts, technology, and politics.

Yet the method of cultural excavation remains conspicuously underutilized within marketing departments. Based on years of observation, I attribute this oversight partly to marketing's historical focus on directly surveying consumers about their needs, preferences, and aspirations—a concentration that is unquestionably valid. But while consumer research remains indispensable, it omits a critical nuance.

Any insights about consumer culture or target audience become only more revealing and meaningful when they are contextualized within the context of the culture that consumers inhabit. This is because culture shapes consumer behavior as much as consumer behavior shapes culture. But most consumers don't have the training to analyze culture in a manner that integrates their personal experiences within the context of wider cultural shifts. In other words, they can talk to you about their experiences but they usually can't and shouldn't be expected to arrive at more advanced insights into parallels and connections to culture writ large. As a result, the onus falls upon us—as marketers, researchers, and strategists—to discern how consumer insights derived from focus groups, interviews, or surveys intersect with broader cultural currents. These currents can either be mirrored in consumer narratives or exist in a dynamic tension with them. It's on us to figure that out.

To achieve this, a deeper, more nuanced understanding of culture is imperative. What I offer next is an invitation to reimagine culture as a collection of what we will call "texts." In this context, a text is a collection of signs that convey meaning. It can be anything from social media conversations and memes to advertising campaigns and news headlines—each is a microcosm of cultural currents that are shaping culture in real time.

Such a perspective encourages us to think about culture on a deeper level, beyond fleeting trends or surface-level observations masquerading as insights. It's at this juncture that the most insightful learnings often emerge, rooted in advanced insights into the cultural fabric that brands inhabit.

Collecting and Analyzing Cultural Texts

Most of us, at one point or another in our schooling, were likely asked to analyze a text. As students, we might have analyzed characters in a novel, examined the main themes in a short story, or discussed either the use of symbolism in a poem or a history-defining speech. Rarely, however, do we think about the critical reading and thinking skills we practiced in our middle-school classroom as relevant to our professional practice as marketers, let alone applicable in culture marketing. And yet, this is precisely where conscious marketers should begin.

Mastering cultural analysis as a methodology begins with learning to perceive and "read" culture as a constellation of "texts" that are available for our critical interpretation. A text, in this sense, is understood as any form of cultural expression or artifact that conveys meaning and can be interpreted (or as we often say, "decoded") by others; this could be written works, advertisements, clothing, or other everyday items. This is precisely where the concepts of representation and ideology come together; if representation is a process of communicating meaning and ideology is the underlying system of beliefs and values that shapes it, then texts are the final output. Texts encapsulate cultural meaning.

We recognize cultural texts as repositories of meaning when analyzing written forms like novels, poems, speeches, or historical documents. These texts contain signs and symbols to convey the author's intended message. The cultural reflection within texts becomes particularly evident when studying documents from different historical eras, such as ancient times or the Victorian era, where sensibilities, values, assumptions, norms, and linguistic forms are uniquely specific to their respective contexts. This holds true for various artifacts from the 19th century, including old advertisements, dance sequences, clothing, and everyday items. If we acknowledge and interpret cultural artifacts from the past as reflective of their eras, it follows that we should apply the same approach to contemporary cultural objects, including brands. We might, then, describe cultural analysis as a methodology of "reading" culture as a collection of "texts" that conceal meanings that shape our current and past realities in profound ways. These meanings often go unnoticed due to the assumption that "this is just how things are," and it is our task to excavate them.

But why might this reframing be useful? Making the shift in viewing various elements of culture as "texts," and consequently asking what they are trying to communicate, forces us to engage with the culture in a more critical way. While the notion of considering everything as a "text" may initially appear abstract, it's remarkably practical. This way of viewing culture reminds us that every aspect of culture communicates *something*, just as a novel or a poem conveys a message or meaning. Whether it's an advertisement, a piece of art, or a social media post, cultural texts all convey both direct and more obscure messages about values, beliefs, desires, and cultural context that shaped them into being.

To harness advanced cultural insights, it's crucial that we sharpen our ability to notice, perceive, and interpret the cultural messages that surround us. While people undeniably provide invaluable insights to us through consumer research, customers can't be solely responsible for supplying the advanced insight into culture required for crafting culturally resonant marketing messages. That work is ours.

CONSIDER THIS: SOURCES FOR CULTURAL ANALYSIS

As you begin your cultural research, here are the kinds of cultural texts you might begin collecting for further interpretation and critical analysis:

- **Visual imagery:** Magazine covers, images, video content, screenshots, memes, visual art, and ads.
- **Cultural artifacts:** Items of popular culture, entertainment, and media, such as music videos, songs, artist performances, fashion items, mixed-media art, etc.
- **Social media content:** Posts, videos, comments, hashtags, influencers, social media scandals, debates, spectacles, and viral trends.
- **Cultural criticism and politics:** Opinion pieces, news articles, etc.
- **Academic and market research:** Peer-reviewed studies, published books, reports, and research articles.
- **Literary objects:** Novels, short stories, non-fiction, and fictional pieces.
- **Branded content:** Logos, taglines, products, brand stories, collaborations, campaigns, ad copy, and packaging.
- **Historical documents:** Letters, diaries, manuscripts, speeches, and official records from different time periods.
- **Consumer reviews and feedback:** Product reviews, customer testimonials, online forum discussions, and social media comments.
- **Language and communication:** Slang words, idiomatic expressions, language evolution, and communication styles in various contexts.

- **Subcultural expressions:** Music genres, fashion subcultures, subcultural symbols, and specialized subculture-related media.

- **Visual and performing arts:** Paintings, sculptures, theater productions, dance performances, and art exhibitions.

- **Media representations:** Movies, television shows, news articles, documentaries, and multimedia presentations.

- **Digital trends:** Social media trends, viral internet phenomena, online communities, and emerging digital platforms and tools.

This list is not exhaustive, but it is fairly representative of the kinds of texts that you would encounter when conducting cultural analysis. Depending on the specific brief, cultural objects you might want to explore could focus only on select categories. For example, a brief on inclusivity in beauty might lean more heavily into social media content, popular culture, health, and design and aesthetics. On the other hand, a brief focused on the future of sports might more eagerly take up cultural objects in the sphere of brand and product innovation, cultural criticism, and nascent trends related to leisure and lifestyle. The goal is to gain a *comprehensive* understanding of the cultural ecosystem in which your brand—and the broader consumer culture—operates. Next, we will examine how to collect and organize cultural objects, and then we will unpack how to begin to critically interpret them.

CHECKLIST

Here's a comprehensive list of topic areas to consider when evaluating a specific text, object, or artifact within a cultural context. You'll notice that these questions share similarities with those we've previously discussed when crafting high-level research questions; this is because the focus on representation and ideology in cultural analysis remains a constant. Broadly, we can organize the questions of cultural and textual analysis into the following categories:

- **Historical context:** Examine the historical backdrop of a cultural text. Understanding the time in which it was created allows for insights into how it might have been influenced by the sociopolitical events or shifts of that era.

- **Authorship and purpose:** Identifying the creators and their intentions behind the cultural text is pivotal. Consider their motivations, agendas, and the broader societal or cultural context in which they operate.

- **Distribution and accessibility:** Investigating how the cultural text has been disseminated and who has access to it sheds light on its reach and impact. This can also reveal power dynamics in terms of who controls its distribution.

- **Representation of identities:** Analyzing how different identities such as race, gender, class, etc., are represented within the text is a central aspect of cultural analysis. Identify patterns of representation and whether they perpetuate stereotypes or challenge them.

- **Power and marginalization:** Delve into power dynamics within the text. Who holds authority or agency, and who is marginalized or oppressed? This can uncover underlying power structures.

- **Affective and emotional dimensions:** Explore the emotional impact of cultural texts, including how they evoke feelings, empathy, or controversy. What does the text mean to evoke, and why?

- **Audience reception:** Recognize that different audiences may interpret the text in various ways. Consider how the intended meaning might diverge from how it is actually received—and why these discrepancies exist.

- **Appropriation and subcultures:** Explore how the cultural text has been appropriated or reconfigured by different subcultures or how it has been taken up in the mainstream, if different from its origins.

- **Cultural movements:** Consider how a cultural text might relate to or be implicated in broader cultural movements. Explore how the text aligns with or challenges the ideologies and values of cultural movements, whether they are related to civil rights, environmentalism, workplace culture, wellness, or other social and cultural shifts.

- **Future interpretations:** Consider how the meanings embedded in the cultural text might evolve over time. Analyze emerging trends and patterns that could shape its future interpretation and relevance.

These areas of exploration are not exhaustive but should provide a strong starting point. Specific questions you ask will depend on your research objectives and the particular topic or issue you are investigating.

Collecting and Organizing Cultural Data

Now that we have established the broader meaning of "text" in cultural analysis, let's clarify several data collection approaches. Ultimately, there is no single way to collect and organize cultural data; your preferred approach will largely depend on your learning style and preferred way of retaining information. Below, I will share with you some observations from my own process for collecting cultural objects and organizing research before we discuss how to analyze such data.

1. CONSULT A WIDE RANGE OF FORMAL AND INFORMAL SOURCES OF MEDIA

During my research process, I research, bookmark, save, and download objects of culture from as many sources as possible. The collection of texts I ultimately assemble are sourced from anywhere from social sites like Pinterest or Instagram to the headlines in the *New York Times* and the most recent studies from the *Journal of Cultural Studies*. Don't limit your research to a single discipline either. Cross-disciplinary approaches, drawing from fields such as anthropology, sociology, psychology, and history, can provide holistic cultural insights. Then, broaden your horizons by examining cultural artifacts from both local and global contexts. This provides a more comprehensive view of cultural dynamics, allowing you to identify both universal and context-specific patterns.

Don't forget to expand your analysis beyond mainstream culture. Explore subcultures and niche communities that may hold valuable cultural insights. These can often be the vanguards of emerging cultural trends. Stay attuned to real-time cultural events. Monitor social media trends, hashtags, and viral content—it might be helpful to bookmark items into a separate folder as you come across them. Then, dive into user-generated content. Platforms like Reddit, discussion forums, and user reviews can provide unfiltered insights into how individuals perceive and engage with relevant topics. If you have institutional access, leverage data analytics tools to sift through vast amounts of cultural data efficiently. Tools like sentiment analysis, natural language processing, word clouds, and data visualization can aid you in quicker pattern recognition.

2. EXPAND YOUR DEFINITION OF EXPERTISE

We have discussed extensively thus far the need to adopt a self-reflexive attitude. This means questioning who we see as an authority on any specific subject matter. Especially when it comes to cultural fluency, expand whose expertise you look toward and trust. Consult sources that cite and reference thought leadership not only of marketing leaders or trends analysts.

Artists, for instance, are able to capture and reflect the essence of culture through their creations. They offer unique perspectives on the world around them, often challenging conventional norms and inspiring fresh insights. Social workers and grassroots activists are on the front lines of societal change. Their experiences shed light on the lived realities of diverse communities and the ways in which culture intersects with issues of equity, social justice, and inclusivity. Public figures, whether celebrities, politicians, or community leaders, often serve as cultural touchpoints for what's gaining traction or admiration. Designers, in various fields from fashion to product design, interpret cultural aesthetics and values through their creations, too.

Expanding your sources of expertise means actively seeking out diverse perspectives other than your own.

3. AVOID RELYING ONLY ON TREND REPORTS

It is common to conduct desk research by reading existing articles or opinion pieces on cultural trends. These materials can often be repetitive and focus on sensationalized trends. Advanced cultural insights are produced by engaging in original thinking and analysis (more on this in the rest of this chapter!). We can only further deepen brand-relevant insights by observing cultural texts around us, in addition to consuming existing secondary research.

4. CONSIDER ORGANIZING YOUR DATA VISUALLY

I frequently utilize visual mapping tools like Miro, Mural, or Figma. This allows me to move different objects around more easily, organize thematically, and add notes and initial thought starters.

Part of your process will be to look for patterns and connections. Organize your cultural data thematically. Group similar objects or artifacts together by asking: What does this represent? What message or set of values does this convey? Are there recurring messages that persist in various contexts? For example, are there parallels in how wellness is increasingly being talked about in seemingly distinct categories, such as lifestyle, tech, and beauty? Signals grouped together soon start to form patterns.

Unlocking Innovation: Advanced Strategies in Cultural Analysis

But how do we identify what a text represents? Below we will review several methodologies that are helpful when you want to further level up your cultural analysis. Keep in mind, though, that these aren't hard-and-fast rules; they're flexible approaches that you can adapt and deploy creatively to meet the unique needs of your cultural projects.

We will start at a micro level by understanding what constitutes a sign and how meaning is communicated into the world. Then, we will examine how signs are used in culture to constitute "texts," which could be various forms of cultural expression, from books to memes and rituals. Finally, we will outline how signs captured across multiple texts form what we call "codes"—a set of governing "rules" that establish how meaning is taken up in culture. We will conclude with a framework for mapping cultural codes you uncover through your research.

How to Identify Signs

We're constantly inundated by a wide range of cultural texts in our daily lives, and these go far beyond mere written words or media we consume. Cultural texts constitute a wide spectrum of cultural expressions, from artifacts to symbols, each functioning as a repository of signs that hold and communicate deeper, symbolic meanings.

Knowing how to identify and decode signs is important, particularly for marketers, because it provides the keys to a hidden world of consumer behavior, motivation, and sentiment. Signs are not merely ornamental or incidental; they are the building blocks of cultural codes that influence how consumers perceive value, how they categorize products, and how they engage with brands. By analyzing signs within relevant cultural texts—be it social media trends, popular films, or even shifting political dialogues—marketers can unearth these hidden codes and better understand the forces shaping people's perceptions and expectations.

SIGN = SIGNIFIER/SIGNIFIED

The key lies in understanding the dual structure of the "sign." This concept in cultural studies originates from the pioneering work of Ferdinand de Saussure, a Swiss linguist who laid the cornerstone for the field of semiotics, dedicated to decoding the language of signs. According to Saussure, a sign consists of two parts: The "signifier" and the "signified." The signifier is the form that the sign takes—it could be a sound, an image, a word, or a ritual. The signified, on the other hand, is the meaning or idea that the signifier represents. In simplest terms, the signifier is the form; the signified is the mental concept associated with that form.

In our culture, signifiers carry mental concepts that structure our realities. A simple object can carry a multiplicity of meanings. Consider Figure 3.2: In a simple written word like "diamond," the letters D-I-A-M-O-N-D constitute the signifier, while the idea or mental concept associated with a diamond constitutes what we call the "signified." The diamond, in most Western cultures, represents more than just a geological formation. It symbolizes enduring commitment in a romantic relationship. It is also an emblem of high status and a signifier of luxury.

In more niche contexts, diamonds can also come to stand for the concept of mental toughness: Athletes or motivational speakers use diamonds as a metaphor for standing tall under pressure. These meanings are not inherent to the carbon structure of the diamond itself; they formed over time through language, marketing, cultural practices, and social narratives. From popular idioms like "diamonds in the rough" to marketing campaigns such as "diamonds are a girl's best friend," signs and symbols are constantly layered on with meaning over and over again. Language, media, and marketing are vehicles for this kind of signification.

Just like a diamond is both a material object and a symbol, every sign in culture has a mental concept attached to it. Think of popular symbols and how we have accepted and taken their meaning for granted. We do not question and, in most cases, we are unaware of how deeply the meaning of signs rests within our consciousness. These examples of signs are all around us. The image of a heart represents the idea or mental concept of love and romance. The scales represent justice, while the dove signifies peace. Humans naturally attach meanings and concepts to tangible symbols, making them more than just their physical form. It's how we construct and make sense of our lived realities.

Brands are signs, too, consisting of the signifier (the apple or the swoosh) and the signified—the associations that we attach to brand identity. This process of signification through representation and interpretation is not irrelevant to marketing. Far from it. It is why we are able to distinguish visual or even verbal brand signs: We can instantly link the swoosh with Nike, "I'm lovin' it" with McDonald's, or a bitten apple with Apple.

FIGURE 3.2 Visual Explanation of the Sign and Its Components: The Signifier
and the Signified

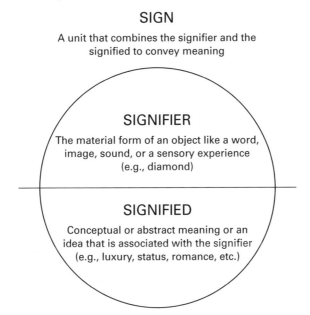

Created by Dr. Anastasia Kārkliņa Gabriel.

Take McDonald's, for instance: The company ingeniously leveraged how signs work in culture by advertising free internet in its restaurants using fries arranged on a red background to resemble a Wi-Fi signal. Likewise, Heinz-Kraft's "No one grows ketchup like Heinz" campaign used an image of a ketchup bottle sliced open like a ripe tomato, conveying the freshness of its ingredients. In essence, most successful brands are already deploying semiotics to craft messages that invoke unspoken meaning.

Moreover, when it comes to inclusive and socially responsible brand marketing, this model of the signifier and the signified is invaluable. By applying a semiotic lens, marketers can decode cultural texts to unearth the invisible codes that shape consumer perceptions, behaviors, and interactions. These codes are not arbitrary; they are born from recurrent patterns in signs across multiple texts, essentially forming the rules or algorithms of cultural meaning. This understanding can help to unlock insights into consumer behavior, societal trends, and competitive landscapes. By understanding what various signs signify, brands can tap into deeply held cultural meanings, align their offerings with them, and communicate more effectively with their target audiences. It's also a mechanism to safeguard against inadvertent cultural missteps. If you know how to derive meaning from signs, you can more easily spot potentially problematic or culturally insensitive elements before they become public mistakes.

This is useful both at the beginning of your process when you are conducting your research and formulating primary hypotheses and for proofing your work at the end of your strategic process. Marketing campaigns that have caused uproar and backlash lacked one thing: They failed to ask, what does this image, this story, or this campaign narrative signify in the eyes of consumers? This proficiency in semiotics essentially acts as a preemptive measure, allowing brands to fine-tune their messaging and visual cues to resonate with audiences while avoiding pitfalls.

In practice, you will not necessarily need to unpack every single sign that you collect as part of your data collection unless you are working on a granular analysis, as set forth by the brief. But understanding the signifier and the signified framework will allow you to approach any text that you deal with by asking: What does this signify? What does it represent? Developing this kind of analytical ability to perceive culture as a repository of signs, each signifying and symbolizing nuanced meanings—including the outputs of our own work—unlocks the true essence of cultural intelligence for brands that want to do better.

How to Identify Codes

Identifying patterns—spotting multiple signs that consistently appear in culture at the same time—leads you to recognizing "codes." Consider these codes as a collection of cultural "algorithms" shaping consumer behavior, emotions, and expectations. They consolidate various signs in culture to establish unspoken rules about "how things are."

When you notice that different cultural texts—like memes, news articles, or advertising images—are converging to establish a common understanding, you've now pinpointed a code. These codes are more than mere patterns; they help dictate the norms that guide how we think, feel, and act within a cultural matrix. In tracking these patterns and codes, we are capturing the cultural zeitgeist.

Codes establish a shared understanding of how things should be as they are circulated and normalized through cultural discourse, politics, news, marketing, and other forms of media. Think back to the example of a formal dinner: The unspoken code of professional conduct at a client event is itself a code that normalizes specific behaviors and expectations. The code of professionalism dictates what you should wear and how you should behave. On the other hand, in a marketing context, for example, a series of images from a luxury ad campaign that positions women in a specific light—say, as symbols of sensitivity or sexual desire—also constitutes a code. The brand doesn't just sell a luxury watch; it taps into an established code to capitalize on a specific narrative about what femininity is. In a broader cultural context, this normalizes a specific image of "how women are." Sometimes, the codes that brands lacking in cultural fluency tap into aren't conducive to inclusivity; often, they are outright harmful.

Now, consider how inclusive brands like Dove, Rare Beauty, or Fenty Beauty do the opposite. Conscious marketers deliberately tap into emergent codes that offer an alternative to dominant ones. In this case, these brands tap into cultural codes that promote skin and body positivity, diversity, and self-empowerment.

Can you see why our ability to decode signs and identify how they form codes is so essential for inclusive marketing? The process begins with recognizing significant signs and ascertaining their meanings through semiotic analysis. Next, we observe patterns in culture, where similar signs coalesce to form codes. We then articulate how these codes, when taken collectively, give rise to new cultural narratives—whether it's about body positivity, female empowerment, self-expression, or mental wellness. Crucially, we also examine how these emerging codes exist in tension with dominant ones. Equipped with this understanding, brands can strategize to align themselves with codes that complement their positioning (strategy) and activate against a new area of cultural opportunity (innovation).

By connecting the dots between signs and cultural texts, marketers can not only keep their finger on the pulse of culture but even anticipate future trajectories by identifying emergent codes. This underscores the transformative potential of cultural intelligence to catalyze inclusive innovation.

Strategic Cultural Foresight: The RDE Framework

Now that you have described, analyzed, and explained codes, we need to be able to understand where the opportunity for the brand actually lies. We do this by learning to distinguish what's in vogue, what's falling out of favor, and what's just bubbling on the surface. In cultural and semiotic analysis, we therefore categorize codes into residual, dominant, and emergent cultural forces. This gives your brand a full 360-degree view of the cultural playing field.

The concept of mapping cultural change through residual, dominant, and emergent cultural dynamics comes from the work of Raymond Williams, a Welsh cultural theorist, who introduced this framework in 1977 to better trace and understand shifts in societal values and practices. Williams understood that culture is not a static entity, but a vibrant, dynamic force continuously shaped by competing undercurrents.

In the realm of brand marketing and semiotics, this idea has found a powerful application. It offers marketers a unique lens to decipher the cultural nuances embedded in their brand communication and the wider market dynamics. By using this model, marketers can gain a deep understanding of a brand's current cultural alignment, identify potential areas of opportunity, and spot potential risks.

This isn't just about being in touch with culture; it's about developing strategic foresight. Recognizing the dominant culture allows your brand to resonate with the current pulse of society. Recognizing the residual assists in steering clear of cultural missteps, thus avoiding potential damage to your brand's reputation. Yet, the pivotal point of competitive advantage? Spotting the emergent. That's where the window of opportunity is to be found.

Essentially, by identifying and understanding the residual, dominant, and emergent elements in a brand's story, marketers can make data-driven decisions about brand strategy in response to cultural shifts. It's an insightful tool that ensures that strategies are not only relevant today but also primed for the future. To employ this framework, begin by organizing the codes you identified into three categories of the Residual/Dominant/Emergent (RDE) framework. Let's return to the example of beauty to identify examples for each.

Residual

Residual cultural elements are those that once held a dominant position but are now waning. In identifying residual texts, one can often spot them through the outdated concepts, values, or practices that are now met with competing narrative.

Consider, for instance, marketing campaigns from beauty brands that prominently feature images of thin, young, and predominantly white or light-skinned models. These expressions of culture are residual because they adhere to standards that are gradually being supplanted by more inclusive and diverse representations of beauty. In a parallel vein, the once-prevalent dieting culture that promoted thinness as the ideal has been increasingly overshadowed by narratives advocating wellness, mental health, and body positivity.

Another example of this is the shift in advertising narratives around masculinity. Older campaigns often glorified stoic, rugged individuals who epitomized traditional masculine ideals—think Marlboro Man or Old Spice's "The Man Your Man Could Smell Like." These depictions now fall into the residual category as newer narratives advocating emotional vulnerability, empathy, and a broader definition of strength gain cultural traction.

These elements may still wield influence, albeit diminished, as dominant culture evolves and new trends gain traction. If anything, tensions persist as some factions attempt to hold onto these waning norms. Recent instances of conservative pushback, like controversies over trans-inclusive swimwear at a major U.S. retailer or the rise of content creators advocating traditional notions of masculinity, underscore the ongoing battle over values that are receding. This is what Stuart Hall understood as culture—a site of ideological struggle.

Dominant

Dominant cultural elements, in contrast, are the drivers of our current cultural core. They encompass the widely endorsed ideas, values, and norms that wield discernible influence. Identifying dominant codes enables marketers to understand the central narratives and norms that resonate in culture the most at this time.

For instance, in the beauty industry, the current dominant ideals of beauty may emphasize diversity, body positivity, and individual expression. Marketing campaigns that feature a diverse range of models of different sizes, ethnicities, and ages align with these dominant beauty standards. By reflecting the prevailing norms, brands can connect with a wider audience and resonate with their desires and aspirations.

Yet, dominance isn't a synonym for permanence either. Dominant cultural forces are subject to change, and as they evolve, they challenge and reposition what's residual, diminishing its societal grip. As dominant ideas undergo transformation, they contest and reconfigure residual elements, incrementally diminishing their influence. By recognizing and adapting to the changing features of dominant cultural forces, businesses can skillfully maneuver through the cultural landscape attuned to prevailing values.

FIGURE 3.3 Cultural Forces at Play: Emergent/Dominant/Residual

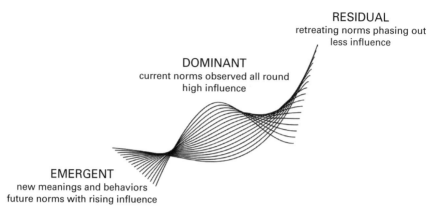

Original illustration by Dr. Anastasia Kārkliņa Gabriel.

Emergent

Emergent cultural elements represent the exciting and evolving trends, ideas, and practices that are beginning to sprout and shape the cultural landscape. They are the seeds of change, challenging established norms and offering fresh perspectives. These emergent codes signify the progressive evolution of culture, pushing boundaries and igniting new narratives that push back against what is. They possess the potential to redefine established conventions, disrupt the status quo, and inspire transformative shifts in societal values and behaviors.

The emergent realm is where new opportunities are found. Effective cultural strategy involves capturing these emerging trends before they become mainstream, thereby positioning your brand not just as a cultural participant but as a pioneer. By spotting these early trends, your brand can harness cultural shifts, not just follow them. This isn't just about reacting to culture; it's about shaping it.

As cultural innovators, brand-driven businesses that recognize and embrace these emergent cultural elements position themselves at the forefront, capturing the imagination of early adopters and carving a path toward the future. Mapping cultural signals onto this framework not only helps to illuminate the trajectory of cultural change but also enables us to anticipate future developments, providing valuable strategic insight for the brand's positioning and business strategy.

This proactive stance offers a competitive advantage in the fast-paced world of business. That's the power of cultural intelligence in action. It is where cultural innovation takes root—an opportunity to identify and leverage what's emerging on the cultural horizon.

Identifying the Right Cultural Narrative for Your Brand

By analyzing texts, identifying cultural codes, and strategically mapping your brand's territory within the RDE framework, you can identify opportunities to challenge, align with, or innovate within emergent cultural landscapes. When identifying a cultural narrative for your brand, look for a new counter-narrative or emergent cultural force that aligns with your brand's purpose and positioning. Of course, you can play it safe and engage with the dominant narratives in a way that makes the most sense for your target audience and strategic objectives. But identifying ideas, narratives, and trends within the context of the emergent cultural forces is still an invaluable exercise for ensuring that you can anticipate where the culture is headed within your category and what this means for your brand. Ultimately, the right narrative entails recognizing the counter-narrative or emergent cultural force that resonates with your brand's values, purpose, and target audience.

This exercise can also be invaluable for ensuring your marketing strategy is keeping up with the times. A few years ago, I worked for a client that was one of the pioneers in the clean beauty space. Over the years, however, the brand lost most of its relevance, as new beauty brands started to dominate the market. Strategically using the signifier/signified model to analyze the cultural landscape and map the beauty category onto the RDE framework helped this client to see where they fell behind in comparison, even in terms of visual language, packaging, and brand voice.

Follow this checklist to reflect on identifying emergent territories of opportunity that will complement your brand and strategic marketing objectives:

1 **Authenticity and brand fit:** Ensure the territory authentically aligns with your brand's values, purpose, and positioning. It should resonate with your brand identity and create a genuine connection with your audience.

2 **Social and cultural relevance:** Assess the territory's relevance to current societal conversations and issues. Consider how your brand can contribute positively, offer a unique perspective, and connect with the values and aspirations of your target audience.

3 **Consistency across touchpoints:** Test how the territory fits into your brand's messaging, visual identity, and marketing campaigns. It needs to complement a cohesive brand narrative that resonates with your audience across all touchpoints, from your website to social media channels and beyond.

4 **Long-term viability:** Evaluate the territory's potential for enduring relevance and adaptability in the face of future cultural shifts. Ensure it can evolve and remain compelling over time.

5 **Test and iterate:** Gather feedback from your target audience. Iterate and refine the narrative based on the reception, allowing you to fine-tune the cultural strategy and ensure it resonates effectively.

In Conversation with Ambika Pai

Ambika Gautam Pai is the Head of Brand at TIAA. She is a mom of two and the host of Corner Office Breakdowns, a podcast that aims to analyze workplaces through the lens of equity, emotional attunement, and an understanding of ourselves. She is currently writing her first book, which dives deeper into these ideas. She's a career-long strategist who was most recently Chief Strategy Officer at Mekanism, and has worked on initiatives in sport, technology, women's health, politics, and consumer goods.

AKG: Ambika, as we are recording this interview, you're just wrapping up your tenure as the CSO at Mekanism after 15 years in the advertising industry. Please tell the readers more about who you are and what moves you as a strategist.

AP: I've been in the advertising, or advertising-adjacent, industry for my entire career. I realized I now want to apply the strategic mindset and skillset I developed over the last 15 years to humanity—to the human condition and to make the world a better place. I've had a taste of this kind of impact in various ways. I worked on Joe Biden's design identity, and my team and I got lactating breasts on TV for the first time ever, which was a significant moment in both my career and personal life. I've managed to help flip conversations and culture on multiple projects. Usually, this involves finding out and centering the truth—working on things like vaccine hesitancy, reducing sexual assault on college campuses, and even understanding how to position a tequila brand. All of this work comes from the truth. In this industry, we have access to some of the deepest pockets and loudest microphones in the world, and so with great power comes great responsibility. We need to use these tools in a way that pushes the world forward. That is my personal definition of strategy and communications, and how I hope to identify myself going forward. I am focusing on deepening my own practice, understanding my conditioning, and working to unlearn and relearn things. Then I hope to apply that knowledge to the challenges that plague us as a society.

AKG: Some might argue that as marketers, we are here solely to serve the bottom line and sell the product through strategic persuasion. What's your vision of culture in marketing?

AP: I first understood that business impact and cultural impact could co-exist when I was at Wolf & Wilhelmine. I was one of the partners at this small brand strategy shop, and we didn't do creative work. We solely focused on strategy and then partnered with creative agencies or internal creative teams at our client organizations to bring things to life. By untethering strategy from a creative output, we were able to strategize with much greater integrity. We didn't have to worry about making it immediately palatable to consumers or those concerned with the financial bottom line. Instead, we could focus on the purity of the truth.

What shocks me is that old-school strategists claim that we're diluting the art of strategy by not focusing it on a traditional creative process. But the traditional creative concept isn't best at creating work that is inclusive. As strategists, it's our responsibility to speak to the real-life experience of our population, what motivates them, and what they struggle with day to day. It's a flawed assumption to say that a strategy that's truthful, impactful, inclusive, and conscious can't also be beneficial for your business. In fact, I believe we've yet to see the full potential of how successful businesses can be when they adopt this kind of thinking.

AKG: What you said resonates deeply with me. We're moving in the right direction but only scratching the surface of potential. What does it mean to do truly culture-defining work in this industry?

AP: It all begins with research. To me, true innovation starts with a profound understanding of consumer needs, the essence of humanity, and identifying gaps in culture where these needs aren't being met. Take, for instance, Billy. They tackled the issue of the pink tax, bringing a conversation that was typically behind closed doors into the open. They showed women that they were paying a premium for pastel-colored products when there was no real difference in the product itself. They were addressing the business implication of dismantling the capitalistic practice of charging women more for basic products, coupled with not just an understanding of women and the realities of their bodies, but actually putting that understanding into action. For so long, marketers portrayed women in a perfect, sterile manner—through the male gaze. However, women no longer subscribe to those roles and ways of being. It was time to acknowledge that women have body hair and portray what it's truly like to shave hair. Why did we depict razors just swiping over perfectly shaved legs?

In my view, it all starts with this kernel of truth, focusing on the human experience as it interacts with a category, a product, or culture. It's not just about identifying a market gap; it's about understanding the human experience within it. Now, regarding the industry's transformation and the inevitable shifts in the world of business, equalizing the importance of the bottom line and service can unlock tremendous potential. We're not diminishing the significance of the bottom line; rather, we're elevating service, betterment, equity, and inclusion to the same level. This is the human aspect that has been missing from business.

AKG: How does one begin to understand what you call here "the essence of humanity"?

AP: We begin by questioning our own truth. What is truth, after all? I recall the discussions about entering the post-truth era in the news, questioning the credibility of institutions. We've challenged the truth when it comes to institutions, but we've yet to question the truth within ourselves. This is where my work, particularly in my podcast Corner Office Breakdowns, comes into play. It involves breaking down the paradigms of leadership, challenging assumptions, and addressing conditioning to question which ways of working are genuinely our own, and what we've inherited by following the rules.

In my approach to strategy, I always strive to balance inherent knowledge—what feels right, human, and instinctual for the work—with inherited knowledge, which comes from engaging with the people we're building for and allowing them to teach us and share their insights. It's this interplay between inherent and inherited knowledge that guides all of my work because, without both, we're not truly speaking the truth.

AKG: I didn't plan to ask you this but this isn't discussed enough within this profession, so I find it important to bring up here. Could you share your thoughts on the day-to-day life of a strategist, particularly in terms of facing the discomfort—or maybe vulnerability is a better word—of this kind of introspection?

AP: This is my favorite topic in the whole world. My friend Valerie Nguyen and I gave a talk back in 2018 focusing on instinctual leadership. Instinctual leadership entails leading based on your own belief system, taking into account your background, your identity as a human, your life experiences, and the knowledge you've amassed over time. And for me, each time I assumed a leadership role, whether managing individuals or leading groups, I was acutely conscious of their unique internal experiences and personal stories that had brought them to that point. This is the essence of being an authentic leader—recognizing not only your instincts but also fostering an environment where others can hone and activate theirs. By repressing these instincts, we're essentially cutting ourselves off from our true selves.

The reality is that there's a substantial amount of self-work required, not just for emerging professionals entering the workforce but also for those at the highest echelons of corporate America. As leaders, you bear immense responsibility for the state of the world, the workforce, the products we create, and how this country generates income, among other things. However, this responsibility often stems from ego and conditioning rather than a genuine understanding of oneself and others.

4

Communication:
From Performative Marketing
to Inclusive Representation

WHAT TO EXPECT

What the previous chapter aims to show is that marketers who strive to be conscious and genuinely inclusive can no longer afford to see representation as only who is represented. When we begin to adopt a lens of cultural intelligence, we see representation as something more profound. Our research processes and analytical approaches have become more rigorous and more precise. It stops being merely a checklist of demographics to represent or a quota to fill, although this doesn't suggest that diverse casting and hiring isn't a priority. Instead, when we expand our perspective on culture, the definition of cultural representation becomes more expansive. We might even realize that to consider representation merely as the presence of a diverse set of faces in marketing collateral is to underestimate its transformational power.

   With this in mind, we will explore the following questions in this chapter:

- How does viewing marketing through the lens of cultural codes change the way we think about representation?

- What are the key principles for creating marketing strategies that are genuinely inclusive and culture-shaping?

- How do power relationships affect both the stories that are told and how they're received, and what can marketers do to address this?

- How can lessons from the study of culture make inclusive marketing more effectively attuned to the needs and perspectives of diverse audiences?

Embracing a more critical orientation toward culture, representation, and the function of ideology starts to influence not just marketing outputs but the entire brand ecosystem. When marketers adopt a culturally intelligent approach to marketing, the entire approach to briefing, research, and the process of building and executing a marketing strategy demands a new level of rigor and critical thinking. This new approach starts to form the core of our messaging, shapes the narratives we construct, confronts existing norms, and fosters a more critical engagement with brands' role in culture. This engagement becomes not just transactional or extractive but relational and much more intentional in how we engage with cultural knowledge.

Cultural representation, then, is about more than just diverse visuals in an ad campaign; it also involves recognizing, respecting, and actively engaging with the meaning (cultural messaging) that gets embedded throughout all marketing communications. This new understanding demands that conscious marketers who strive to be inclusive and socially responsible consider not just who is seen, but how they are seen, portrayed, and engaged with. In cultural studies, representation is not just concerned with "who" is shown but probes deeper into the "how"—how the narratives, ideologies, and messages are conveyed and disseminated by brands. Let's anchor us in this new paradigm for how representation as that which constructs social reality can be meaningfully taken up in inclusive marketing. As discussed in the previous chapter, representation is a process of communicating meaning. And so, to simplify, we can think of cultural marketing as a form of messaging—disseminating ideas and ideologies into the culture about who we are and what we value.

By offering more complex, nuanced stories and truthful representations of diverse audiences, marketers can actively challenge stereotypes and help cultivate a more inclusive brand worldview. Adopting this approach offers the advertising and marketing industries an opportunity to atone for and rectify past mistakes. Representation, in this sense, should be seen not only as a reflection of human diversity in media but as a vehicle for more inclusive societal messaging and cultural change by means of leveraging media and technology to promote belonging, not unconsciously perpetuate more harmful narratives.

Consider a brand that merely casts models diverse in race or gender expression and body size but fails to tell more inclusive stories or offer meaningful solutions to its diverse audiences. Such a campaign might technically be "representative" of some level of diversity, but it's also a missed opportunity to truly embrace the richness of representation from the perspective of culturally disruptive storytelling.

In contrast, when brands tell stories that resonate with people's full range of human experiences or use their media platforms to challenge prevailing societal norms and support more inclusive services and products, they tap into the true power of cultural representation in marketing for social good.

That potential is to uplift, amplify, and advance positive change through culturally nuanced and emotionally resonant cultural codes. That's why the learnings from the previous chapter are so critical to cultural intelligence. Once we can accurately decipher codes and land at advanced cultural insight, we can choose to leverage this knowledge in ways that are ethical, genuinely inclusive, and impactful. Because the end goal of inclusive marketing is not just to reflect but to redefine normative codes and move culture forward.

Building Culturally Disruptive Brands: Core Tenets of Cultural Fluency

At the level of ideology, culture-shaping marketing is disruptive. It's an approach to a brand's worldview that refuses to simply "fit in." By offering target audiences an ideological alternative that they desire—a new code for making sense of the world—brands drive both commercial differentiation and meaningful social impact with respect to the inclusion of historically excluded audiences.

Culturally disruptive representation is underlined by cultural fluency. As a reminder, cultural fluency refers to a brand's capability to engage in culture with resonance, integrity, and measurable impact by consciously using media to shape cultural conversation. Culture-shaping marketing that leverages inclusive and socially conscious representation for commercial success and social good rests on strategy that works to:

- subvert and overturn traditional stories that perpetuate inequality;

- shed light on enduring inequities while redistributing influence and resources;

- drive inclusive innovation to design for a more equitable future.

Embedding these key values-driven principles should start at the beginning of your process and stay central to everything you do, from ideation to research, strategy, and creative activations. These principles should shape your objective setting, market and consumer research, cultural analysis, methodology design, and the means through which you communicate your value proposition (language, visuals, imagery, partnerships, etc.).

What makes this so essential is that making it a habit to continuously ask yourself where your team is with respect to these principles is what will help your brand future-proof your strategy against the common mistakes discussed. And, of course, it will only maximize the impact in the long run.

Return to them as often as possible to ask: Am I following and centering these principles in my research, strategy, creative, and marketing outputs? Embracing these principles as the bedrock of your approach is key to cultivating a culture of accountability, both on a personal level and throughout your team. This ongoing practice of self-reflection will provide a safeguard against inconsistencies, gaps, missteps, or contradictions that could weaken your brand's messaging and dilute the impact. In the fast-paced world of cultural marketing, where trends and consumer expectations are evolving and shifting, such adaptability becomes even more crucial.

The principles outlined below are informed by insights from cultural and media studies, disciplines that have extensively explored the impact of media—including marketing and advertising—on culture and society.

Subversive Storytelling: Disrupting Exclusionary Norms

An approach to telling a brand story or marketing a product or services in a way that pushes against normative cultural codes and instead drives new, culturally innovative counter-narratives that reflect the complexity and nuances of the human experience.

Subversive storytelling serves as a conscientious approach to marketing that invites us to question and destabilize accepted social narratives, codes, and myths and encourages critical examination of these widely held beliefs. Drawing on theories of Antonio Gramsci, Stuart Hall, and other critical thinkers of culture and media, this tenet is about coming out with marketing that offers nuanced and rich counter-narratives that reflect the intricate fabric of human experience. The endgame here isn't merely to avoid causing additional harm through stereotypical tropes or normative codes but to consciously affect a substantive shift in cultural perception. Subversive marketing communications consciously integrate social responsibility into strategy.

Subversive doesn't mean loud or explicitly driven by purpose, by the way. Subversive representation simply means that you are conscious about refusing to tap into normative codes and are committed to discovering and leveraging codes that instead promote inclusivity and belonging.

Some brands will opt to be more explicit and outspoken; these are businesses driven by social purpose. Think Dove, Nike, and Patagonia. Their differentiation is driven by their intent to make headlines and inspire public debate. Other brands might more subtly integrate their commitment to move away from exclusionary representation into brand storytelling. These brands might not shout about social issues or make headlines, but they intentionally integrate inclusivity and belonging into the brand experience. Of course, the brand's approach to representation still must be anchored in a commercially viable strategy.

Any culturally fluent brand can adopt a subversive strategy to culture-shaping, subversive representation; the approach will reflect the brand personality, target audience, and long-term business objectives.

CASE STUDY
Gillette's First Shave, the Story of Samson (2019)

In 2019, Gillette released an ad that proved to be a culture-defining moment for culturally subversive marketing. The campaign, titled "First Shave," featured a young Black transgender man named Samson talking about his transition. Then, guided by his father, who affirms to him—"you're doing fine, you're doing fine"—we see Samson experiences the rite of passage that is his first shave. This is followed by the following copy on a black background: "Whenever, wherever, however, it happens, your first shave is special" (Durkin, 2019). With this campaign, Gillette not only broke stereotypes but normalized a new form of trans-inclusive representation.

The brand pushed against the dominant cultural codes at that time. Traditional razor ads often amplify hegemonic masculinity—rugged athletes and smooth shaves dominate the screen. These often feel less like advertisements for razors and more ads for a type of masculinity that is socially desirable. Gillette's decision to focus on a transgender man subverted expectations and opened the door for nuanced conversations about what constitutes masculinity today. The narrative intentionally distanced itself from heteronormative tropes, instead offering an intimate, emotional moment between a father and his trans son—thus, not just advertising a product but also normalizing inclusive representation of trans people in mainstream culture.

Consider this: The "First Shave" campaign didn't merely avoid perpetuating harmful stereotypes; it actively sought to diversify the narrative around masculinity and family to include a historically underrepresented group. The ad garnered both praise for its inclusivity and criticism from those uncomfortable with its disruption of traditional gender roles. Yet, the campaign's aim was not to comfort but to challenge and invite cultural belonging.

Gillette's "First Shave" serves as a prime example of how culturally fluent brands leverage subversive marketing strategies to not only engage with audiences in a deeper, more meaningful way but also to instigate real social impact. It showcased that brands can help normalize a more equitable vision for society—this is subversive marketing in action.

Power-Shifting: Leveraging Media and Capital for Social Good

A principle focused on deliberate reconfiguration or redistribution of influence, power, and resources within a given system or structure. For brands, this means harnessing media influence, resources, and financial power to drive positive social change. This involves utilizing media and technology not only to amplify historically marginalized groups but to drive meaningful, measurable social impact within disadvantaged cultural communities.

Navigating the cultural landscape with cultural fluency isn't only about asking: How do we make our brand appealing? The question is: Whose voices are we amplifying? Whose perspectives is our brand bringing into focus? This can look like hiring and compensating cultural advisors from historically marginalized audiences, partnering with grassroots organizations, and redirecting a slice of profits back into specific communities or social causes. But it's more than just a financial play—power-shifting directs not just the flow of money, but also time and expertise into the communities that brands engage with.

Power-shifting isn't just corporate social responsibility reimagined. It has to align your brand's core values with real-world social impact, going beyond mere optics to drive differentiation in a market where consumers aren't just buying a product, but backing brands that reflect their values. Power-shifting ensures that your brand doesn't just engage or borrow from the culture of marginalized communities; it seeks to interrupt cultural extraction that has historically characterized the advertising and marketing industries.

In marketing, we hear the term empowerment often. But power-shifting as a concept implies a more dynamic process with a dual focus. It aims not only to uplift but also to actively disrupt and reduce the disproportionate influence of historically dominant groups.

The idea of shifting power emphasizes the role of reallocating capital and resources for social good. It is what makes the brand's social impact measurable. It also underlines the inherent agency of historically excluded groups: Moving from "giving voice" to others to using resources to create platforms where historically marginalized communities can tell their own stories—in their own words. This is a shift from a paternalistic form of marketing, where businesses capitalize on being seen as saviors, to a more horizontal approach where brands act as platforms of shared influence.

Power-shifting enables brands to move beyond merely borrowing or extracting value from cultural communities. The alternative is clear: Contribute, compensate, and leverage existing resources without centering the brand. Create platforms and democratize media to enrich the cultural conversation, not just extract from it.

CASE STUDY
The Advil Pain Equity Project—Redressing Inequities in Healthcare

The conversation surrounding healthcare inequities is complex and multidimensional, and Advil took it upon itself to challenge systemic biases in pain diagnosis and treatment of Black patients. This mission has crystallized into the Advil Pain Equity Project, an initiative that tackles the egregious disparities in Black health in the United States (Payton, 2023; Advil, 2023).

Advil partnered with Morehouse School of Medicine and BLKHLTH, combining scholarly research and grassroots activism to illuminate the issue of pain inequity in Black communities. Choosing to go beyond marketing the pill bottle, Advil conducted an extensive survey with Morehouse to identify the gaps and challenges in the healthcare system related to pain equity. The brand then launched "Believe My Pain," a subversive, power-shifting storytelling campaign that included digital roundtables with healthcare professionals, advocates, and affected community members.

The project opened up a crucial conversation around racial bias in healthcare, and the "Believe My Pain" campaign amplified voices often overlooked, silenced, and otherwise relegated to the margins. By integrating medical expertise and intimate stories of pain, Advil succeeded in not only directing public attention to the issue but also driving the cultural conversation around the need to transform healthcare protocols around pain management and emphasize racial equity.

Consider this: This is a case of a brand effectively "power-shifting" by allocating both financial and intellectual capital to address systemic inequities in the industry where the brand is a major player. Advil didn't just cut a check; it facilitated cross-sector partnerships, utilized data-driven approaches, and engaged in story amplification to challenge the silence surrounding a painful issue for far too many.

Through these concerted efforts, Advil didn't merely borrow from the dialogue about healthcare disparities and positioned itself at the center; it provided a stage and paid media for this critical conversation to happen, proving that when a brand aligns its core values, positioning, and customer needs around broader cultural issues, the result is a deeply resonant and meaningful impact that transcends the commercial space.

Inclusive Innovation: Designing For a More Equitable Future

A forward-looking approach that employs foresight and futures thinking to go beyond understanding current or short-term trends and aims to shape long-term business objectives by ingraining a culture of innovation into the brand's DNA to explore transformative possibilities for the future.

Strategic foresight helps brands develop useful tools to prepare for what's to come. Developing foresight is about looking beyond the immediate horizon and strategizing for what lies ahead. But this is not just about trendspotting; it's about actively participating in the process of using cultural intelligence to imagine more inclusive futures.

By proactively considering how emerging technologies, social movements, or cultural shifts with rising influence might impact its target audience and the culture at large, a brand can position itself as a forward-thinking leader rather than a reactive follower. Drawing inspiration from futurism and speculative thinking, strategic foresight invites marketers to go beyond the status quo, not only more boldly but also to act on it.

In practical terms, this means integrating forward-thinking insights and having a broader vision for your strategy. Taking calculated, strategic risks as a cultural leader pays off, whether that's exploring emerging technologies, experimenting with new mediums, or leveraging emergent cultural codes. As we discussed in the previous chapter, innovation is an inseparable part of cultural intelligence.

It's crucial to point out here that historically marginalized communities have been visionaries in re-imagining and advocating for radically different futures that are inclusive of all people and the planet. Lived experiences and communal wisdom are legitimate sources of knowledge and innovative thinking. Given brands' immense influence in culture, marketers have the opportunity to responsibly use media and technology for good: To amplify these existing narratives and share access to media platforms.

CASE STUDY

Telfar's Dynamic Pricing Model—Building an Inclusive Future of Luxury

While most luxury fashion brands use high prices to establish exclusivity, Telfar chose to look ahead and envision a different future, one that is inclusive and equitable. The brand, famous for its tote bags featuring a bold "T," pioneered the dynamic pricing model. It was a groundbreaking initiative that employed strategic foresight to analyze the existing industry landscape and innovate against it by democratizing luxury by reducing cost barriers and increasing access.

Telfar collaborated with supply chain experts and data scientists to reimagine fashion pricing for the long term. This wasn't just a tweak; it was a radical rethinking enabled by their pricing tool designed to track real-time demand. Unlike conventional surge pricing, Telfar's pricing model decreases the price as items sell out. The "sold-out" price is then set as the product's new, permanent price (Chen, 2023).

The launch of this innovative model instigated a broader industry conversation about the very concept of luxury as inaccessible and exclusionary. In a press release, the brand boldly stated that "Telfar Live disrupts existing notions of supply and demand, scarcity and value perception—proposing a new mathematics for Black cultural innovation: Cool people ≠ rich people—therefore—cool clothes ≠ expensive clothes" (Pauly, 2023). By focusing on long-term cultural shifts toward inclusivity and financial equity, Telfar effectively used strategic foresight to position itself as an innovator not just in fashion but in the cultural ecosystem at large.

Telfar's strategy successfully integrated futures thinking and cultural foresight. By proactively considering how trends in consumer behavior and cultural inclusivity would evolve, Telfar identified a space of opportunity and innovation in the fashion industry. This is the power of aligning a brand's vision with future societal goals and cultural trends. Foresight is the cornerstone of cultural innovation.

Leveraging Reception Theory
to Fine-Tune Message Resonance

One of the main misconceptions about inclusive marketing is that it most applies to big players who already engage in purpose-driven marketing as part of their positioning. Let's practice questioning assumptions. For one, we already know of many marketing examples in recent years that resulted in public scandals, scrutiny, and backlash around cultural insensitivity or lack of inclusivity that had nothing to do with brand purpose or social impact. These campaigns received widespread criticism even though their aim was primarily to market the product rather than directly challenge, subvert, or shape the cultural conversation.

Every brand is involved in navigating cultural codes because ideology is inherent to all media communications. Get it wrong and you risk public backlash, as several notable failures make painfully clear. There was the infamous campaign of a reality TV star solving social unrest with a can of soda. Another example we mentioned before was that of a retailer that used a Black child to model a hoodie with a phrase referencing a monkey. A luxury fashion brand pulled a turtleneck design after it was pointed out that it resembled blackface. A deodorant ad received backlash for equating whiteness with purity. Some of these examples happened before 2020 but even more recent instances of egregious missteps abound, from a luxury brand that designed a hoodie with strings resembling a noose to an automaker that chose to cast a renowned Black Lives Matter activist in a commercial for a luxury vehicle. Cultural fluency is no longer optional. It's the future of marketing.

The mistakes brands make in regard to cultural sensitivity and inclusion happen all too frequently when they do not need to happen at all. In fact, they should not happen. A brand that embeds cultural intelligence as an in-depth and ongoing practice will have considered and prepared for possible responses to their strategy and subsequent outputs. But how can conscious marketers arm themselves against such pitfalls?

To answer this, I'll now introduce you to a vital framework drawn from the disciplines of cultural studies and media theory—reception theory. While it may sound like something relegated to scholarly journals, its implications for marketing are both real and urgent. As the name suggests, reception theory helps us understand not just what message is being sent out into the world but how it's being received and decoded by your audience.

Using Reception Theory to Avoid Preventable Mistakes

Remember the signifier and the signified model that we covered earlier in this book? Everything we put out into the world means something. Signs and symbols convey meaning that's often hidden and concealed as collective common sense. And everything that is put out into the world (by marketers, artists, politicians, and creators) is received, perceived, and interpreted. Because representation constructs reality around us, what we see represented to us in mass media is *normalized* to us.

Stuart Hall, one of the founders of the discipline of cultural studies, highlighted that representation is tied to systems of knowledge and power. Media messages are not simply "sent" as straightforward information but are encoded with meaning by content producers. During the encoding process, creators draw upon their own "frameworks of knowledge," ideological perspectives, and what Hall calls the "relations of production"—the institutional structures in which media content is produced. The media content, then, is not just a set of images or sounds but a "meaningful discourse," shaped by various social, cultural, and economic factors at play.

In the context of Stuart Hall's Encoding/Decoding model, "meaningful discourse" refers to the complex set of messages, signs, and symbols that are organized and structured in a particular way to convey specific meanings or ideologies. This concept emphasizes that these media texts are designed to communicate more than just basic information—this captures the essence that we discussed in the earlier chapter when we examined how meaning is transmitted through representation. The underlying idea is not just to look at media texts as isolated units but to understand them as parts of a larger social and cultural conversation—a discourse—that shapes and is shaped by multiple forces and stakeholders. For further explanation, see Figure 4.1.

Adopting this framework, we can understand marketers as media producers who imbue media content with their own ideological frameworks, knowledge, and values. It's no coincidence that we spent so many pages earlier in this book discussing the importance of questioning our own assumptions and biases as a practice central to cultural fluency. This places equal emphasis on the creator and the consumer, showing that meaning is not simply "sent" or "received" but is actively constructed on both ends.

FIGURE 4.1 A Visual Explanation of the Encoding/Decoding Model by Stuart Hall (1973/2000)

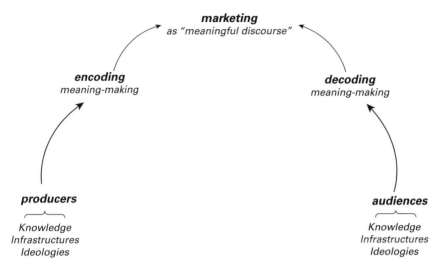

Modified and adapted by the author to fit the marketing context. Original illustration designed by Dr. Anastasia Kārkliņa Gabriel.

Audiences decode these messages based on their own cultural frameworks, knowledge, and experiences. Hall also asserted that audiences are not passive vessels that submit to the knowledge, information, and popular media they consume. Audiences actively participate in this transmission. In "Encoding, Decoding" (1973/2000), Hall proposed that the communication process is structured by inherent dominance, meaning that media producers—including advertisers and marketers—have the power to encode specific messaging into media outputs that get circulated at scale. Nevertheless, the audiences, he asserted, can decode these messages in different ways. In this sense, the audience is not a passive recipient of mass media but actively interprets and constructs meaning based on values, subjectivities, and lived experiences.

But why does this matter so much for inclusive marketing? For one, brands striving for cultural fluency can't afford to see marketing communications as a one-way transmission. When adopted in the context of conscious marketing, Hall's framework can enable us to produce more sensitive, culturally relevant, and socially responsible work. Understanding how an audience might receive intended messaging transcends the scope of traditional marketing, which often focuses solely on consumer need-states and problems to be solved. Understanding how to meet consumer needs is no longer sufficient; conscious marketers must also anticipate how messages will be decoded and interpreted across diverse audiences to pressure-test the work and ensure that the brand's subversive, culture-shaping messaging strategically anticipates any risk that innovation inevitably entails.

In previous chapters, we discussed the importance of learning to identify cultural codes, those intricate webs of signifiers and meanings that give shape to societal narratives. Once the brand has identified cultural territories to play in, the next step for conscious marketers is to operationalize this knowledge into actionable strategies that consider audience reception.

The power of understanding the interpretation of messaging in marketing can't be overstated. Of course, marketers have the responsibility to use such approaches conscientiously to make their outputs more inclusive and move away from performative gestures. Please use these academic frameworks with care and consideration.

Using Reception Theory to Deepen Audience Insights

At the heart of Stuart Hall's reception theory is the understanding that an audience isn't a homogeneous, passive entity that uniformly absorbs marketing messages. Instead, the audience comprises various individuals, each bringing their unique cultural contexts, experiences, and interpretations to the table when consuming media content. Hall's reception theory breaks away from the traditional communication model where the sender encodes a message, and the receiver decodes it exactly as the sender intended. The encoding and decoding process is not always in sync, leading to varied interpretations of the same message.

For marketers seeking to effectively practice cultural fluency, little is more crucial than understanding various audience segments and anticipating potential reactions to messaging. Advanced cultural insights that you would have collected through cultural research and analysis, as it was described in the previous chapter, will equip you with the knowledge you need to form a more nuanced, comprehensive understanding of the audiences on the receiving end of your messaging. This framework will be also particularly useful for pressure-testing any strategic messaging, brand narratives, or campaign ideas you might produce, with a focus on detecting bias, hidden misconceptions, or gaps in cultural knowledge.

Seeing audiences as diverse groups of people with multiple viewpoints helps us avoid oversimplifying, flattening nuances, and stereotyping. When I consulted for strategy studios, market research consultancies, and creative agencies, I often heard questions like, "What does the Black community think about this?" or similar asks about "the LGBTQ community" or "the Latinx community." My immediate response to such questions is to underscore how these single-story narratives risk reducing diverse, complex, and nuanced communities into monolithic entities. This act of simplification isn't merely problematic; it actually serves the ideological functions of racism, sexism, classism, and other forms of oppression, which aim to marginalize and subjugate by erasing the complexities of humanity within historically oppressed communities. By reducing an entire group of people to a single narrative, we inadvertently uphold the structures that disenfranchise them. In marketing, such generalizations can lead to misguided strategies that either miss the mark or perpetuate harmful stereotypes and biases.

Therefore, it's essential to adopt a more nuanced and thoughtful approach that considers the multifaceted nature of audiences and their varied interpretations. That's where reception theory is a useful, practical tool to help steer conscious marketers away from generalizations, prejudices, stereotypes, and one-dimensional stories. The premise is simple: On the receiving end of media, audiences interpret messages in ways that reflect their own lived experiences, societal norms, and personal beliefs.

Hall specifically proposed three positions from which audiences may decode a message. Hall did not specifically talk about marketers (rather, his focus was on media producers more broadly), but for our purposes, I will ground the explanations below in the context of marketing communications.

Dominant or preferred reading: The audience fully accepts the message as it was intended, without questioning its assumptions or ideological underpinnings.

So what? This can be seen as a win for marketers, but it's worth noting that this doesn't always occur. Plus, certain messaging consistent with the status quo and the dominant point of view can potentially conceal harm, bias, and stereotypes that culturally intelligent marketers ought to avoid. Think here about the time in marketing when sexist advertising was widely accepted and normalized.

Negotiated reading: In this case, the audience broadly accepts the intended message but modifies it to fit their own experiences, perspectives, or circumstances. They may agree with parts of the message and disagree with others, leading to a negotiated understanding of the intended message.

So what? For marketers, this suggests that even when a message is generally accepted, there could be elements that don't resonate or even alienate parts of the audience. Consider a hypothetical beauty brand campaign that features models of various body sizes and physical mobilities, showcasing them in high-end, designer clothing. The audience might appreciate the brand's attempt to be body-inclusive but will question the accessibility of high-end clothing to marginalized groups. By predicting and considering this response, brands can proactively address the nuanced perspectives that audiences bring to the table. It offers an opportunity to fine-tune the campaign before it's even launched, considering the elements of inclusivity, such as socioeconomic status and accessibility.

Oppositional reading: The audience understands the intended message but rejects it, interpreting it in an entirely different or opposing way. This usually occurs when there's a significant disconnect between the message and the audience's experiences or worldview.

So what? The infamous example of a soda brand featuring a celebrity mitigating social unrest by offering a can of soda serves as a textbook case of oppositional reading. The intended message may have been to encourage unity and peace, but audiences rejected it and interpreted it as trivializing serious social issues for commercial gain. This disconnect resulted in widespread backlash. Similarly, a deodorant that had intended to communicate the benefits of its invisible deodorant range by equating white clothes with purity failed when audiences rejected this message altogether, citing racial connotations. Had the brand decoded the sign by identifying the signifier or the mental concept associated with the signifier (the ad copy saying "white is purity"), the oppositional reading would be easier to predict.

This framework of understanding audience reception should encourage marketers to step outside their own perspectives and consider how their messages might be decoded differently by different audience segments, thereby informing the creation of more effective, inclusive, and culturally sensitive marketing campaigns. Incorporating reception theory serves as a reminder that brands aren't just talking to their audiences; inclusive marketing is equally about listening to those on the receiving end.

From Demographics to Values: A Culturally Fluent Approach to Consumer Insights

Reception theory departs from traditional consumer segmentation by advocating for a nuanced, audience-centric approach to understanding how people interpret marketing messages based on *cultural values*. Marketers have long known that different audience segments interpret brand narratives and messaging in different ways—why would advertisers fear showing diversity of sexuality or gender expression in ads, for instance? However, these differences have traditionally been seen through a very narrow lens of demographics. Relying solely on basic indicators like age, income, and location—commonly used for constructing and targeting personas—falls short in capturing the complexity of executing an effective and impactful cultural strategy.

Consider a popular meme that has been circulating on social media for quite some time. It depicts both Ozzy Osbourne and King Charles III. At a glance, the two could be segmented into similar demographic categories—both are British, white, and male of a certain age. Traditional marketing strategies might place them into the same audience persona based on these demographic markers. However, when we consider values, lifestyle, and cultural affiliations, the two could not be more disparate. Osbourne, a rock musician known for his rebellious spirit, contrasts sharply with King Charles III, a figurehead of tradition, heritage, and royalty. It's a stark reminder to brands that evolving toward a values-based approach ensures greater accuracy and precision when engaging diverse audiences.

CASE STUDY
Inclusive Advertising from Amazon Ads

As reported in AdWeek (2023), in 2023 Amazon Ads launched new audience targeting, including segments like eco-shoppers and "allies of diversity," to enable "advertisers to reach consumers who reflect [Amazon's] own leadership principles." The latter segment, for instance, aims to identify and target consumers who have shown signals of allyship—active commitments to fostering change through advocacy and sponsorship. By aggregating first-party shopping and streaming data, Amazon identifies audiences based on several attributes:

- purchase of books and educational materials on topics like women's studies, race relations, human rights, cultural policy, and immigration;
- fandom for artists who promote DEI;
- consumption of multilingual content with English subtitles.

While some questions remain about the way business models can more ethically engage data on behaviors and attitudes related to diversity and inclusion, this example is relevant insofar as it signals to us a new reality: Brands are increasingly aligning their marketing strategies—including audience segmentation and targeting—with social consciousness. And for good reason.

Cultural intelligence poses a commercial advantage. Brands that leverage culturally nuanced audience insights are better positioned to navigate an increasingly complex marketplace, making them more resilient, adaptable, and ultimately, more competitive.

Below is a list of key marketing activities where the principles of reception theory could be applied, from the initial stages of market research to the evaluation of campaign success. The goal here is to elevate your marketing practices, ensuring they are not only effective in reaching diverse audiences but also proactive in strategizing how to respond to various interpretations of your marketing strategy to maintain cultural relevance, protect brand equity, and practice authentic, responsible marketing that advances equity and inclusion:

1 **Market research:** Consider adopting and applying the principles of reception theory to inform the design of your surveys, focus groups, and interviews. Use the premise of this theory to identify how different audience segments might interpret and respond to questions, stimuli, and more. Then, use these learnings to sharpen and improve your research processes.

2 **Consumer insights:** Rethink your assumptions about your audiences to design a more nuanced approach to uncovering human and cultural insights. These should go beyond demographic data to include values, social beliefs, and cultural perspectives that influence what the audience thinks, wants, believes, and needs.

3 **Campaign planning/content creation:** This is the primary use for reception theory. During campaign development, account for possible audience interpretations. Preemptively identify possible misunderstandings and tailor your communications strategy accordingly.

4 **Crisis management:** Anticipate and prepare for potential public backlash to marketing messages. Decide on what you will stand for. Preemptively develop strategies for effective and nuanced responses when audiences interpret messages in unexpected or oppositional ways.

ACTIVITY: DEVELOPING CULTURALLY INTELLIGENT MESSAGING

A crucial part of Hall's theory is the idea of polysemy—that a single message can have multiple meanings. Marketers must consider this when crafting messages, as different audiences might interpret the same message differently. For the first step, take some time to select a recent or your favorite piece of media content. This could be a television advertisement, a billboard ad, a social media campaign, a blog post, or an email newsletter. Select a piece of media that explicitly has a cultural lens to it. If you can't find any examples, go to Google News, type in relevant keywords, such as "inclusive" and "brand," and then choose a recent news story or press release. Avoid selecting an opinion piece. Take some time to browse the content you selected on the brand's website, YouTube channel, or social media page where the campaign lives. Next, take some time to analyze this content and identify its potential for multiple interpretations:

1 **Reflect on your interpretation**
   Consider how you personally interpreted the message. What was your immediate response? What emotions did it evoke? Did it change your perception of the brand in any way? How did you interpret the message? Why do you think you interpreted it that way?

2 **Consider alternative interpretations**
   Now, try to put yourself in the shoes of different types of consumers. How might a person of different age, cultural background, ideological viewpoint, or lifestyle interpret the same message? Are there elements of the message that could be perceived differently depending on the viewer's context? What are some possible alternative interpretations of the message?

3 **Ideology and representation**

Reflect on the different ways you and others might interpret the message, considering the concept of polysemy, which means that the same message can have multiple meanings. How does the concept of polysemy apply to this media piece? Did recognizing the possibility of various interpretations change your perception of the message? How do ideology and normative ideas figure into it? Is it subverting or reproducing dominant codes?

4 **Play around with the messaging**

Based on your reflections, consider how the message might be adjusted to either broaden or narrow its possible interpretations, depending on the brand's objectives. The previous chapter discussed residual, dominant, and emergent cultural dynamics. In your interpretation of the message, what signs can you identify here? What codes can be categorized as either dominant, residual, or emergent? If you were to revise the message to lean into the emergent codes more, what changes would you make to the content, copy, or format? How would that, in turn, impact the reception?

5 **Predict, anticipate, prepare**

How might the messaging be adjusted to better control its reception? By the way, this does not mean watering it down or giving in to the demands of the loud, hateful minority. Instead, I mean, how would you make the storytelling more incisive? Given the multiple interpretations of the message, can you anticipate any adverse reactions or backlash? If so, from which audience segments and why? If a backlash occurs, how would you plan to respond in a way that acknowledges the diversity of audience interpretations while maintaining the integrity of the brand and what the brand stands for?

Representation in Marketing as Cultural Meaning-Making

The use of reception theory in marketing and advertising amplifies a crucial insight: Representation is not a one-dimensional, fixed transmission of images and stories but a complex interplay of cultural processes that produce meaning. It's a complex process that injects meaning into culture, which audiences then receive and interpret through the lens of culture. Brands that grasp this fluidity position themselves to be more culturally fluent and capable of navigating uncertainty that is endemic to cultural evolution.

The true work of inclusive marketing and advertising starts by treating representation not as mere surface-level diversity showcased in ads but as a conscious process of cultural meaning-making. Recognizing that inclusive marketing plays a role in constructing cultural meaning imposes an added layer of accountability. Interrogating how messages are delivered to audiences, what societal norms they reinforce, and which cultural ideologies they challenge or disrupt is what genuinely inclusive marketing and advertising is all about.

Before closing this chapter, let's touch on some key areas and guidelines to consider in relation to cultural fluency and inclusivity when devising how brands communicate meaning.

Communication Styles

This should be a no-brainer but still has to be said. Do not attempt to mimic language and slang that originates with your target audience. For instance, too many brands appropriate AAVE (African American Vernacular English) to signal relevance or attempt to resonate with Black audiences or even Gen Z. Instead, ensure that people who belong to and represent a specific linguistic community are not only present in the room but actively involved in the creative process. The complexities of culture are best untangled by those who live them—people deeply embedded in specific subcultures, regional identities, or linguistic groups.

Compensate and seek diverse input and perspectives to ensure an accurate portrayal of language, slang, and communication styles. Embrace the expertise and insights of those who intimately understand the nuances and cultural intricacies of specific linguistic forms. Better yet, hire partners who can act as cultural interpreters and guide the process from start to finish. It's not just about having diverse voices in the room, but about extending agency and decision-making power to people from cultural communities the brand is engaged with.

Visual Language

Incorporate visual symbols and imagery into your storytelling that hold cultural significance and resonate with your target audiences. Ensure these elements authentically represent the traditions, values, and aesthetics of the cultural communities you aim to portray. Use these visual cues to convey deeper meanings and trigger emotional responses that align with the cultural context. Be vigilant to avoid stereotypes and clichés in favor of diverse and nuanced visual representations that mirror the complexity of human experience. Engage with artists, designers, activists, or cultural advisors who can offer insights into the symbolism and visual language pertinent to the culture. Put to use the learnings about meaning-making and signification to evaluate the underlying messaging of the symbols you use.

Cultural Artifacts

In your storytelling, incorporate both cultural artifacts and everyday objects that hold symbolic or experiential significance within particular communities. These elements can serve as touchstones, grounding your narrative in authentic, lived experiences. Pay close attention to the details—whether it's clothing, accessories, or specific objects—that are integral to cultural expression. By including familiar objects, you can evoke a sense of familiarity and authenticity that resonates on a deeper level. Defer for guidance to consultants, experts, and insiders with cultural expertise and lived experiences in these cultural contexts. This is an opportunity to represent lived experiences, cultural nuances, and everyday experiences that are otherwise underrepresented or entirely missing from popular culture and media representations. Cultural artifacts, symbols, and rituals often hold deep-seated meaning that reflects broader values and beliefs. This work has to be done with intentional care and attention.

Take Sephora's "Black Beauty is Beauty" campaign as a benchmark example. The campaign is so impactful not merely because it showcases the legacy of Black beauty, from the local hair salon to Harlem's drag ball, but because it does so through a lens that is accurate and authentically representative, down to the smallest visual cues and signifiers. This level of cultural fidelity doesn't just happen—it results from strategic planning, informed collaboration, and a profound respect for the culture that the brand engages.

Context Matters

Pay close attention to the cultural, social, and historical contexts when crafting your narrative. Address themes or issues that hold real significance within the target culture, thereby deepening the audience's engagement with the material.

Advocate for a co-creative approach by involving those who are well-versed in the relevant cultural contexts. Their contributions during the development and refinement stages can add layers of accuracy to the narrative, which is imperative in inclusive storytelling.

Know Your Lane: Everyone Already Has a Voice

All too frequently, I hear colleagues in the marketing industry talk about a cultural community and say that they are eager for the brand to "give them a voice." While the intention behind this statement may be well-meaning, it is important to approach such aspirations with caution and self-reflection. The notion of "giving a voice" assumes a power dynamic in which one group can grant or bestow representation upon others. Yet, true empowerment lies in creating space for a diversity of voices to be heard, amplified, and respected—on their own terms.

Instead of assuming the role of gatekeepers, marketers should strive to be facilitators and amplifiers of existing voices, causes, and initiatives that have been silenced and actively unheard in contemporary society. That's where power-shifting comes into the picture. This entails creating platforms, campaigns, and initiatives that provide opportunities for individuals from historically marginalized communities to share their stories, perspectives, and experiences directly. It requires actively listening, valuing the contributions of historically excluded groups, and ensuring marginalized people have agency and control over how stories are portrayed within the broader marketing strategy and campaign messaging.

By shifting our mindset from "giving a voice" to "amplifying existing voices," we foster a more inclusive and equitable approach to cultural strategy. We recognize the inherent value and worth of every individual's story and acknowledge that our role is to uplift and share the platform rather than speak on behalf of others. Ultimately, the goal is to build trust, credibility, and loyalty by demonstrating a genuine commitment to inclusivity, social responsibility, and positive social change.

The role of the brand isn't to confer a voice upon others but to remove barriers in media that obstruct voices from being heard more widely—and loudly.

BEST-IN-CLASS

For further inspiration in culturally fluent advertising, consider exploring these exemplary brand campaigns, all of which are available for viewing on YouTube:

- Chevrolet, "Mrs. Hayes" (2023)
- Sephora, "Black Beauty is Beauty" (2021)
- Airbnb, "We Accept" (2017)
- Dove, "As Early as Five" (2022)
- Alzheimer's Research UK, "Change the Ending" (2023)
- Apple, "The Greatest" (2023)
- IKEA, "What If?" (2018)
- Nike, "Dream Crazier" (2020)
- Starbucks, "Every name's a story" (2019)
- Degree, "#BreakingLimits" (2021)
- LEGO, "Let's get the world ready for girls" (2022)
- Etsy, "Gift Like You Mean It" (2021)
- Heineken, "Worlds Apart" (2017)
- Dove, "Reverse Selfie" (2021)
- Olay, "#STEMTheGap" (2022)

In Conversation with Coco Videla

Coco Videla is a cultural strategist and an advocate for building a fairer, more inclusive society. She collaborates with purpose-driven brands and organizations to reimagine, rewrite, and transform fiercely held narratives that make up culture. After spending nearly two decades working in advertising for multimillion-dollar brands, Coco knows what truly makes a brand a cultural leader: Powerful stories. Because stories change people. And people make change.

In 2013, Coco founded The Village, a collective of progressive thinkers and storytellers committed to bringing conversations that matter to the forefront through cultural research, creative strategy, and content creation.

Coco has brought her cultural expertise and foresight to some of the most iconic names in the world such as Nikon, Virgin, Waldorf Astoria, Cotton Council, Danone, Nestlé Waters, Tide, Olay, Revlon, Away Travel, and Ulta Beauty, among others. She has held senior-level roles at The Assemblage (VP, Marketing), AR New York (Head of Global Strategy), Y&R/WPP (VP, Global Strategy), and Saatchi & Saatchi (Regional Strategy Director). Her work has been recognized across the industry, including winning awards from Cannes, Clios, and Effies.

AKG: Coco, you write, "In my work, I hope to contribute to a more equitable and inclusive society by reimagining and rewriting the narratives that make up culture. For two decades, I have helped purpose-driven brands and organizations become cultural leaders through powerful stories. Because stories change people. And people make change." What makes you so passionate about inclusivity in marketing? How did you get started in this line of work?

CV: I came into this industry from the intersection of journalism and acting. I studied journalism, and then I realized I was too opinionated to do straight-up journalism! What I loved most in acting was understanding all of the background of a character and the context in a story. For me, this was the foundation. Because every time you talk about someone's individual experience, it becomes a story, right? That's how I came into advertising.

Though I've held roles in advertising agencies that required me to lead strategy for a brand—and that's obviously very much about marketing—I feel like I am now more somebody who works alongside marketers. I'm much more interested in culture and the consumer. Intentionally, I now try to stay away from knowing too much about the brand, so I don't get trapped in that bubble. This way, I can always talk to people who are in that bubble about things that are happening outside of it.

In 2000, I came into Saatchi & Saatchi to help translate some journals from a research study. Consumers were given journals to fill out, and I was tasked with translating them from Spanish into English. Story after story fascinated me. I had just moved to the U.S. six years earlier. It was quite an experience to see all of these different Spanish-speaking countries lumped into one—like we're just "the Hispanics," the "Los Hispanitos." Part of me was proud to be Hispanic, but I also didn't always appreciate how others saw us.

Reading all these stories, I was inspired. Not long after, working closely with big P&G brands like Tide, Head & Shoulders, and Pampers, I approached the planner who hired me with an idea. In advertising, Latin women were mostly seen in three roles: The overwhelmed mother who is all about the kids, the woman who cannot speak English and isn't portrayed as intelligent because she always relies on the kids to translate, and then the sexy "hot mama" Latina. I wanted to change this narrative.

And so, I thought, "Let's set aside these stereotypes for a moment. I'm going to share 12 stories with you." I collaborated with a friend who happens to be a playwright. We conducted extensive research, undertaking a series of ethnographies across the U.S., and engaging in conversations with ordinary women. Our focus wasn't on any specific brand; it was purely about their lived experiences.

Upon our return, my playwright friend and I crafted monologues that represented the diverse women we had interacted with. It was essentially our way of saying, "Here's what we truly desire. Here's how you can genuinely understand and represent us." We produced and performed the play in Puerto Rico, where the P&G hub was located at that time. The impact was profound. I had never seen so many clients so emotionally moved—some to the point of tears.

We intended the play to be humorous, but by the end, we wanted it to resonate deeply, and it did. We had the play here in New York and we invited clients like General Mills. And so, that became one way for me to say, "Let's set aside the PowerPoint for a moment and infuse some humanity into this."

At that time, I didn't frame it in terms of "culture." It wasn't front of mind for me, but in essence, that's what it was, right? Because it was about my culture and a desire for my culture to be understood in a more nuanced way. The projects that resonated the most were those where people left thinking, "I want to do work that genuinely impacts and makes individuals feel represented." Not just another commercial about an overwhelmed mother.

AKG: How has the experience of discovering those stories and producing that play influenced the trajectory of your career and your current approach to running your own studio and collaborating with agencies and brand clients?

CV: I personally could never tackle a brief without first connecting with the intended audience. That was always my guiding light. As planners or strategists, we're usually driven by ensuring that the audience's voice is heard and that they have a seat at the table. I've always seen my role as amplifying the voices of those who aren't represented. Of course, I've faced challenges because I can't represent every audience. I used to think I could.

One significant learning curve for me has been recognizing the importance of collaboration. For instance, when I was a regional strategist for brands in EMEA, I obviously couldn't speak for everyone in those regions. To address this, I would partner with local strategists from our different offices. Whether in Senegal, Nigeria, Saudi Arabia, or Russia, I'd team up with a local expert, which allowed us to craft more authentic stories. I've often felt that's what typically happens in our industry. This outsider's approach, where someone observes and then leaves, doesn't sit right with me anymore.

AKG: How does this realization affect how you work now?

CV: I want the story to originate from those sharing their experiences. In our research at Culture Studio, there's a method called participatory action research that Dr. Nisha Gupta introduced to me. We look for cultural advisors who provide an expanded and more diverse lens. So, for our recent project at Culture Studio, we're incorporating not just initial expert insights but continuously involving them throughout. They guide our questioning methods and the themes we explore. We also experimented with digital ethnographies. I'm just not someone who settles for one method. I'm in a constant state of experimentation.

AKG: I know you have engaged cultural analysts (that happened to be me!), psychologists, researchers, and so on. I was privileged to work with you while still in graduate school, finishing my doctorate. Could you expand on the merit of this interdisciplinary approach?

CV: The danger is that we can get cocooned in a bubble, especially if we've been in an agency or brand setting for a long time. The language becomes homogenized, and before you know it, everyone's echoing the same ideas.

This realization struck me during the 2020 elections, where I volunteered in areas unrelated to advertising. It introduced me to this whole other set of communities, their language, the way they were talking about issues. The way they were talking about their experiences was just so different and illuminating and inspiring... and also depressing because how could we be so disconnected?

These worlds exist and have such different agendas. Now, when I undertake a major project, I work with freelancers to bring fresh perspectives. All of these elements have reshaped the way I construct my team and our research methodologies.

I want to work with people who are going to teach me, challenge my way of thinking. I want people that I can debate with and have good disagreements with. In this industry, we need to have the confidence to have those disagreements with the clients and among each other.

AKG: For the last three years, you've been running a cultural research program for one of the largest beauty retailers in the U.S. What results are you observing with your clients through your efforts? They evidently return to your studio, year after year.

CV: I began collaborating with this client back in 2019 when we were initially delving into the evolving understanding of gender. In our initial research, we didn't even distinguish between gender and sexuality. That's the starting point we had, and that's where the entire team's understanding was anchored. Now, fast-forward to just three or four years later, observing their enthusiasm and confidence in choosing someone like the trans influencer Dylan Mulvaney to engage in their recent initiative was commendable.

Beyond that, supporting Mulvaney despite the backlash marked a significant shift for the brand. Though it may seem like incremental progress, this is a monumental change over the last four years. It was brave! In this work, you have to be super patient. There was a lot of compassionate learning. It was almost like therapy with the clients. I felt like we created that space for them to ask questions that maybe they felt uncomfortable asking in other places.

That's why I like this idea of *compassionate learning*. For clients who feel scared to ask questions in other spaces, I felt like we had created that unique space for them. Lately, that's been my passion: How can we get people more comfortable with being uncomfortable?

AKG: I resonate with this! I recently wrote a piece about that. These wins that are achieved once we work through discomfort can have a ripple effect in the industry. It's so important to model that for others.

CV: I almost want to say that to achieve this, one must remain pure and untethered to anything that might censor you. It's essential to have a partner, whether an agency or a brand representative, who knows the brand in and out. This partnership can then offer the market and decision-makers concrete, actionable steps, not just display some impressive trends or issues they should be aware of. The true magic unfolds when you can say, "Here's how these cultural trends can profoundly affect your specific business."

And if the Barbie movie, for instance, taught us anything it's that we need to let research and creative partners do their thing. Let them do what they do best. And then, we can combine the work that is infused with cultural insights with some genius marketers who can successfully take it to market.

5

Consciousness: Building Ethical Marketing Practices Beyond Buzzwords

WHAT TO EXPECT

We have just considered the importance of communication and transmission of messaging in marketing. Brands are in the business of producing and communicating meaning to the public through marketing as a form of media discourse. If there is anything to take away from the previous chapter, it's that language, be it verbal or visual, matters for how strategic messaging is received in culture. As marketers, we turn narratives, insights, and strategic messages into storytelling that moves people into thought and action. What we tend to overlook, however, is the specific language we use to talk about the work that we want to do in inclusive marketing. In this chapter, we will explore the following questions:

- Why is inclusive language important in marketing strategy?

- Why are we drawn to buzzwords in inclusive marketing, and what purpose do they fulfill?

- How do buzzwords harm efforts to foster genuine inclusivity?

- What does intersectionality truly mean? What are its origins?

- What does it mean to be an "intersectional" marketer?

- What are the most common pitfalls, and how can they be avoided?

Language matters, not only for the messages we communicate to our audiences but also for how we name, understand, think, and communicate with each other about ideals, principles, and practices that make up our day-to-day practice. At the time of writing there are currently too few resources available to marketers that establish a set of foundational principles, definitions, and frameworks—a shared language for successfully executing cultural fluency in the marketing context. Without a shared language, how do we know we are moving in the same direction and with similar objectives?

Masquerading as a shared language, buzzwords quickly take hold in our culture. As brands scrambled to navigate issues of representation in 2020, buzzwords quickly became a part of the marketing lexicon. Too quickly, brands claimed the labels of "intersectional" and "inclusive" without knowing what that truly meant. Before we knew it, business professionals interested in becoming more conscious and socially responsible claimed to be "intersectional." How much harm or good has this rushed adoption of interdisciplinary terms done—particularly without proper cultural literacy training in the industry? Only time will tell.

On one hand, catchphrases can be helpful when they consolidate complex ideas into digestible, actionable terms in equity work. At least, that's the hope—that we would act and execute on what we learn. Conversely, our somewhat uncritical adoption of trendy buzzwords, like inclusion, intersectionality, or allyship, can also sacrifice nuance and precision. It reduces complex cultural issues to hollow phrases that signal that we "get it" without much else.

In this sense, we might think of buzzwords as signs that have come to absorb new layers of meaning through assimilation into the mainstream. This is particularly problematic given the urgent need for substantive dialogue in an era marked by performative gestures and stagnant progress in advancing inclusion. That's the danger: Buzzwords can offer brands a semblance of relevance with minimal effort. Brands use signifiers lifted outside of their original context to signify progressiveness without action or investment in real work. The cost is steep: Concepts become hollowed out, stripped of their intrinsic value and depth.

And then, there's another insidious layer to this: Appropriation. In co-opting nuanced ideas born from the struggle and resistance of marginalized people to systems of oppression, corporate industries engage in a form of intellectual theft. Appropriating knowledge without respect for its origins commodifies and capitalizes on the very concepts that were crafted to challenge for-profit systems and practices of extraction in business. This isn't just irresponsible marketing; it's a form of ideological colonization.

In the end, this does more than simply compromise our integrity as producers of media that has real impact on people and culture. The appropriation of anti-oppressive concepts and frameworks serves to dilute, whitewash, and effectively neutralize movements striving for genuine social change and radical transformation of social structures. It impedes our collective efforts for inclusivity and equity, not just within the industry but across the broader cultural landscape. This is more than an innocent lapse in judgment—it's an ethical issue that immediately demands correction.

The Misuse of Intersectionality in Modern Marketing

From "diversity" to "inclusivity," no other term has been arguably misappropriated, misused, and co-opted in the business world than the concept of intersectionality, coined by renowned Black feminist legal scholar Dr. Kimberlé Crenshaw in 1989. Whenever I have worked alongside clients and marketing colleagues as a consultant, it was common to hear the term "intersectional" used to describe an array of things: Brands, marketers, research participants, or approaches to strategy. But when I recently casually polled marketers in my circles and asked them to define the term "intersectionality," without even asking them to explain the conceptual framework in detail, most marketers fell short in offering a simple definition.

You might have noticed this yourself: In marketing settings—whether in team discussions or in dialogue with clients—the term "intersectional" is often used as a stand-in marker for "diverse," which is another problematic term on its own. It is not uncommon to hear that the research would benefit from "intersectional" or "diverse" participants or that the strategic narrative should focus more on "intersectional issues." I was not surprised to learn that the most common answer among marketers I talked to was that "intersectionality" simply meant including people who have multiple identities or diverse backgrounds.

Right? Wrong. Though this emphasis on ensuring diversity in representation isn't entirely off the mark, it's a gross oversimplification of a deeply nuanced concept. More so, it's a missed opportunity for untapped potential: Understanding intersectionality can benefit and elevate strategy and communications from shallow, performative marketing to meaningful brand impact.

In pointing this out here, my aim is not to demand some kind of academic purity from the business world but to emphasize important aspects that marketers can't ignore: "Inclusive" marketing that lacks respect for marginalized knowledge and relies on appropriation is, in fact, not inclusive at all. Anything less than respect, accuracy, and appreciation is appropriative and exploitative of knowledge produced, lived, and experienced in historically oppressed and excluded communities.

Misused, such terms can undermine the very principle of our practice and perpetuate the systems of inequality and marginalization they were designed to highlight, challenge, and dismantle in the first place. Buzzwords sound nice, but they serve neither our teams, customers, nor clients. At the very least, they make for a lousy strategy that is bound to have obvious holes.

With this in mind, in this chapter we'll clarify what intersectionality is and what it isn't. This isn't to say that intersectionality—an analytical framework for analyzing interconnected systems of discrimination and not just recognizing our differences!—must form the core of your marketing strategy. Even if your work isn't directly purpose-driven, neglecting an intersectional approach compromises your ability to execute marketing in an inclusive way.

An intersectional approach, then, isn't just a tool for more effective marketing; it's a responsibility, a demand for ethical conduct in how we engage with and represent the complexities of the human experience in the commercial sphere.

Intersectionality, Power, and the Perils of Simplification

In 2020, McKinsey published a report with evidence to suggest that companies in the top quartile for ethnic and cultural diversity had a 36 percent higher likelihood of having above-average profitability (Krishnan et al., 2020). It rather quickly became clear that not only was acknowledging diversity the right thing to do from a societal perspective, but it also made good business sense. The terminology that was popularized between public figures, activists, and equity advocates naturally entered the business world. Intersectionality was one of these terms.

Between May 24, 2020, and May 31, 2020, the week when George Floyd was murdered in Minneapolis, MN, searches for the term "intersectionality" increased by 137 percent (Google Trends, 2020). Recognizing this shift, the marketing world quickly adopted the language of diversity, equity, and inclusivity to resonate with an increasingly socially conscious audience. Yet, what followed was a cautionary tale for conscious marketers: A bandwagon effect that prioritized buzz over substance.

In an interview with *Vox*, Dr. Kimberlé Crenshaw, the scholar who originally coined the term, jokingly remarked that "seeing other people talking about intersectionality" was like an "out-of-body experience." That's hardly surprising: The term spread far and wide, gaining rapid popularity in the mainstream owing to more activist content flooding social media platforms. "Sometimes I've read things that say, 'Intersectionality, blah, blah, blah,'" Crenshaw noted, "and then I'd wonder, 'Oh, I wonder whose intersectionality that is,' and then I'd see me cited, and I was like, 'I've never written that. I've never said that. That is just not how I think about intersectionality'" (Coaston, 2019). In a clickbait culture that reduces radical ideas into bitesized memes, accuracy has become even more important for preserving the integrity of cultural knowledge moving from academic and activist circles into the mainstream.

This inconsistency in interpretation matters more than we have dared to admit. Appropriation and extraction of cultural knowledge is a real problem in corporate space, marketing and advertising included. If intersectionality is to be used and employed in marketing practices that aim and claim to be inclusive and socially responsible, this knowledge must be honored and understood not as an easy-fix buzzword but as a complex framework for unpacking the role of our identities and how they are implicated in systems of power and oppression.

The ethical use of concepts from marginalized scholars, activists, and organic intellectuals hinges on a dual commitment: First, to rigorously understand the theory in all its complexity, ideally by engaging directly with the work of the original scholars or their intellectual descendants; and second, to apply the knowledge in ways that are consistent with its original imperatives of elevating the most marginalized people and dismantling inequities. Truly "intersectional" marketing does both. This is how a theory becomes more than an analytical tool: It serves as a grounding framework for strategic, principled action.

Back to the Basics: What is Intersectionality?

The term intersectionality was first coined by Kimberlé Crenshaw, a prominent civil rights advocate and leading scholar of critical race theory, in a

1989 paper titled "Demarginalizing the Intersection of Race and Sex: A Black Feminist Critique of Antidiscrimination Doctrine, Feminist Theory, and Antiracist Politics." Contrary to how the term has been taken up in corporate spaces, Crenshaw didn't refer to intersectionality through the lens of "diversity"; in her paper, she explicitly called intersectionality the answer to existing "*anti-discrimination* framework" that failed to consider people with multiple experiences of marginalization (Crenshaw, 1989). This wording matters.

Crenshaw's motivation was to articulate the unique experiences of individuals subject to multiple, overlapping forms of oppression. In her work, she observed that the experiences of Black women could not be fully understood by considering the dimensions of either race or gender alone. Instead, their experiences were shaped by the intersecting systems of racism and sexism, creating unique forms of discrimination not recognized by existing legal frameworks or social discourse. Intersectionality, therefore, served as a lens to uncover these overlapping oppression systems and illuminate how they compound and intensify one another. It revealed the limitations of single-axis frameworks that looked at social identities in isolation and ignored the complex, intertwined reality of people's lives.

The legal case that Kimberlé Crenshaw referred to in her seminal 1989 paper was DeGraffenreid v. General Motors. The case was filed in the United States District Court for the Eastern District of Missouri in 1976. The plaintiffs were five Black women, including Emma DeGraffenreid, who brought a class action lawsuit against General Motors (GM), alleging that the company's seniority system perpetuated the effects of past discrimination. They argued that GM had discriminated against Black women specifically by not hiring them until 1964 and then laying them off disproportionately in the recession of the early 1970s.

However, the court refused to allow the plaintiffs to combine racial and sex discrimination into a single category of discrimination. It insisted that the women had to prove that GM discriminated against all women or all Black people. In this context, the court did not acknowledge that the experiences of Black women could be distinct from those of white women or Black men and dismissed the case. The court stated:

> The plaintiffs are clearly entitled to a remedy if they have been discriminated against. Yet they should not be allowed to combine statutory remedies to create a new "super-remedy" which would give them relief beyond what the drafters of the relevant statutes intended. Thus, this lawsuit must be examined to see

if it states a cause of action for race discrimination, sex discrimination, or alternatively either, but not a combination of both (Crenshaw, 1989).

The court thus refused to consider the combined, overlapping effects of race and gender discrimination, asserting that the women could not prove they were discriminated against either as Black individuals (since the factory employed Black men) or as women (since it also hired white women). This perspective overlooked the unique intersection of racism and sexism faced by Black women. In this way, Crenshaw argued that the existing anti-discrimination framework in legal theory erased and further marginalized Black women, making it impossible for them to seek the redress they were owed. By focusing on this case, Crenshaw illuminated the limitations of traditional civil rights law and feminist theories at the time. For this reason, she coined the term "intersectionality" to capture this complex phenomenon and to advocate for the recognition of overlapping forms of discrimination in applied law, legal theories, and the broader society.

Over the years, the concept of intersectionality has been expanded beyond its initial scope. It has been adopted in the broader social discourse, activism, and corporate lexicon. Intersectionality, and other terms like equity and justice, have come to signify less the dissent against the dominant frameworks and commitment to anti-oppression and more a marketable commodity that lends businesses a veneer of social consciousness.

It lets us off the hook. It suspends the responsibility to grapple with deep-seated systemic issues of discrimination that the term meant to expose and bring into the light of public awareness. The purpose of appropriation is to depoliticize and dilute, but it's hard to pick up on that when the term is used in a positive context that we can all support: Increasing diversity in representation; one of the important goals of the anti-oppressive agenda, no doubt. Yet, the framework was never meant to stop there, to only consider the presence of multiple identities at the table.

In her later work, Crenshaw clarified that intersectionality is not about "adding up" different forms of discrimination, nor is it a way of ranking or comparing experiences of oppression. In Crenshaw's own words, "Intersectionality is a framework for understanding the ways that multiple forms of inequality or disadvantage sometimes compound themselves, creating obstacles that are often not understood within conventional ways of thinking." It necessarily involves examining the social, political, and economic structures that create and perpetuate inequality and then working to dismantle these forms of discrimination. As Vox essayist Jane Coaston

(2019) further elucidates, "Intersectionality operates as both the observance and analysis of power imbalances, and the tool by which those power imbalances could be eliminated altogether."

Putting Intersectionality into Practice: Implications for Marketers

What does this all mean for marketers striving to market in a way that is genuinely inclusive and responsible? For critics, it might seem daunting to unpack histories of Black feminist thought in the context of business decisions and concerns such as brand equity, return on investment, and other things that matter to brands like customer lifetime value, conversion rates, or sentiment. Why does any of this matter then?

Put simply, if you want to leave a mark and capture the attention of consumers, then doing the bare minimum in this cultural climate isn't going to get you there. Adopting intersectionality as a critical lens is a pivotal step toward unearthing more meaningful, precise, and culturally incisive cultural and consumer insights that can fuel brand storytelling that moves people. Brand storytelling that is not only emotionally moving but moves people into action. That captures mindshare in a way that transforms awareness into loyalty, converting passive onlookers into participants in your brand's story. It's a way to transcend superficiality and venture into a realm of authenticity. And what is more powerful in the marketing world than authenticity—than being real and telling real stories about real people grounded in real lives and deeply felt lived experiences?

Consumers today crave genuine, heartfelt stories that reflect their realities and validate their experiences. This makes for stories that aren't just palatable but are relatable, memorable, and capable of eliciting emotional connections. To optimize brand storytelling for genuine social impact and help solve actually relevant problems in the lives of their audiences, conscious brands must understand not only how identities intersect but why they result in lived experiences of oppression and create these problems in their lives in the first place.

At the end of the day, what you give is what you get. If brands focus on more than merely ticking off boxes and invest in research and strategy that is seriously attentive to cultural and social issues, then they can move closer to marketing that is not just culturally intelligent but also fundamentally human, and not in a fluffy kind of way. This is about substance, rigor, and integrity. Real recognizes real.

CASE STUDY
REI's Trailmade Collection

The outdoor retail brand REI takes its guidance directly from an inclusion advisory panel of Black, indigenous, people of color, LGBTQ+, body positive, and adaptive communities. The brand works with outdoors groups like Unlikely Hikers, Latino Outdoors, 52 Hike Challenge, The Venture Out Project, and Fresh Tracks at the Aspen Institute. Through this partnership process with historically excluded groups, the brand learned that it was challenging to find technical gear for all body types. Since then, REI has focused on discovering innovative opportunities for the product and the brand around sizing, gender inclusivity, and affordability.

REI's Trailmade collection now provides gender-free gear such as backpacks, sleeping bags, and hiking apparel. But the brand didn't stop there. The collection is not only inclusive of genderqueer customers but also attentive to inclusive sizing options across the line.

But they didn't stop there either. Marginalized people are most economically disadvantaged by interlocking forces of racism and classism, so REI has also made an effort to make products like a gender-free sleeping bag affordable to more people, pricing it under $100. In this way, the brand combined fit, function, and financial fit, inviting more people to be part of their brand's story and into the outdoor lifestyle community. More information is available in the press release at www.rei.com.

A few weeks after launching the collection, REI's Cooperative Action Fund invested $4 million in non-profits working to create a more equitable outdoors. This investment included the addition of 18 new partners to the brand's growing network of non-profit partners. New grantees included organizations like Hike Clerb, that equip Black, indigenous, women of color with tools they need to heal in nature, and Latinas en Bici, which exists to support the "well-being of Latinas through weekly bike rides and multi-cultural events" (REI, 2023).

Why is this meaningful for intersectionality? REI considered how to address multiple forms of exclusion to meaningfully expand the brand's inclusivity. The brand simultaneously understood how lack of size inclusivity, lack of gender-inclusive gear, and lack of accessible options are connected to customers' experience in the outdoor retail category and addressed these issues. The brand didn't simply include models from various identities in its marketing materials to signal how "diverse" and "inclusive" it was. REI listened to cultural community partners and integrated insights about multiple ways in which genderqueer people, low-income people, Black and indigenous people, and people of color are disadvantaged in the outdoor category. The brand didn't need to go out and find a cultural issue to speak about. The most meaningful work happens in our own backyard. REI focused on applying an intersectional analytical lens to their own vertical, seeking to better understand and make a tangible impact on the customer's journey.

Brands can start by asking: Am I considering customers that are most disadvantaged? What historically excluded audiences might have unique experiences in my category based on intersecting forms of discrimination and exclusion that exist? How can we shift our strategy to de-center dominant groups? How can we instead center insights about the experiences of those most excluded and disadvantaged across multiple axes of oppression? Conscious marketers who work to integrate intersectionality as a frame for critical thinking don't need to create some lofty, revolutionary change. You can start small but meaningful. Then, build it up.

Start Here: Eradicate Buzzwords from Your Practice

As brand marketers and strategists, we value simplicity. It is often said that the mark of an effective marketer is explaining complex ideas in accessible, relatable terms. Yet, in our quest for simplicity, we must be careful not to oversimplify to the point where we unintentionally strip the nuance and complexity out of the concepts we are trying to convey. Brands yield more power than we realize: The words shape perceptions, and marketing messaging can either educate or mislead. Omissions and gaps marginalize and exclude simply by perpetuating the status quo. And in an industry where responsible representation and conscious messaging matters so heavily, the call for accuracy and sensitivity is paramount. We need to understand the essence of cultural concepts if we are to communicate, apply, and embed them accurately and with the creative simplicity that we so value in this profession.

When we choose to eradicate buzzwords from our practice, we commit to doing the hard work—delving deeper, understanding better, and communicating with precision and respect for human experiences. This is not a restrictive but a liberating move. It allows marketers to engage with audiences more profoundly, recognizing their multifaceted experiences regarding their own identities and how this intersects with their customer journey.

If we choose the easy route and resort to easy fixes, buzzwords, and shortcuts, here is what brands have to be prepared to be held accountable for—often in the court of unforgiving public opinion:

Commodification: When intersectionality is reduced to a buzzword in branding, it dilutes its transformative power as a tool for social critique. This commodification fails to honor the struggles and realities it was designed to address, diminishing both the integrity of the brands and their accountability to marginalized communities. The framework becomes a product in itself, a commodity that is used to serve the bottom line.

Tokenism: Tokenism is the practice of making a symbolic effort to appear inclusive, diverse, or progressive by including members from marginalized groups, often in a superficial or minimal manner. Brands may claim to be "intersectional" by merely including diverse faces in campaigns or initiatives. This superficial engagement can amount to tokenism, as it ignores the underlying structures of inequality that intersectionality aims to dissect and challenge.

Appropriation: When brands deploy intersectionality primarily for financial or reputational gain, they risk exploiting a framework built on the lived struggles of marginalized groups. Such co-optation not only invites consumer skepticism but also recreates unequal power dynamics. Corporations win, while cultural communities from which such frameworks emerge are left behind. Not acceptable.

Selective attention: In an effort to drive relevance, brands tend to latch onto cultural moments, like Black History Month or Pride Month. This often leads to selective attention: Brands ignore less "marketable" aspects like disability rights or economic justice or fail to show up during the other 11 months of the year. When brands jump on the bandwagon or cherry-pick issues that are considered "safe" or commercially beneficial, the principles of intersectionality are betrayed. Putting intersectionality into practice implies commitment to wrestling with what's been overlooked, excluded, sidelined, and silenced.

Common Pitfalls and How to Avoid Them

Based on the above, here are five more detailed common mistakes and how you can resolve them by correcting the use of intersectionality in your strategies.

Oversimplification of Demographics and Identity Markers

It might be tempting to include demographic groups or seasonal moments associated with historically underrepresented groups in market research and call it "intersectional." For example, you could target so-called "multicultural" audiences without considering how race and ethnicity, gender identity, gender expression, and socioeconomic status might figure into your audience's experiences, beliefs, values, and unique needs. Recognize the multifaceted identities within your target groups. Rather than treating these demographics as homogeneous groups, aim to understand the complexities within them.

Overlooking the Role of Intersectionality in Consumer Data

For instance, you might see lower engagement rates from a marginalized racial or ethnic demographic, and attribute it to factors like lack of disposable income without considering how intersectional experiences and other factors might influence consumer behavior. A culturally fluent marketer will immediately recognize the racial undertone and probe further. What about the product, the brand, its history, or marketing communications that underperform with a specific slice of the audience? To ask thoughtful, probing questions, marketers need to operate out of cultural knowledge about the broader function of race, ethnicity, and age in culture. It is not the consumer's role to critically unpack their experiences, only to share and narrate them.

One-Size-Fits-All Strategy

Creating a strategy aimed at "women" without considering how experiences might differ at intersections of race, class, and other factors is a failing option. Your strategy has to consider not only identity markers but their impact and societal implications for the experiences of your target audiences. This is not to say that there is no common denominator that gets at a profoundly human experience shared by people with different identities. It is, however, to say that by overlooking differences between people within your target audiences, you are missing out on deep, powerful insight—design strategies to understand a diversity of experiences within your target audience. For instance, if you are looking to engage moms, be sure to consider a range of experiences of motherhood that are shaped by other factors, like age, disability, or class. It leads to more resonant and rich storytelling. To be inclusive your creative might need to incorporate stories, ideas, symbols, and artifacts outside of traditional considerations that generally focus on dominant groups (white consumers, men, heterosexual/straight people, etc.).

Tokenistic Representation

The creative stage is where misunderstanding of intersectionality can be most glaringly obvious. Stories that don't quite fit those who are cast. Inauthentic narratives that feel forced run the risk of turning into and perpetuating stereotypical portrayals. Casting singular models from marginalized groups just to check the box. The list goes on.

The solution is to start early. Start by doing your homework. Invest time and effort in understanding the lived experiences of the identities you aim to portray. Ask often and regularly—who is in the room? This might involve conducting interviews, surveys, and focus groups or consulting with advocates from said communities and experts who can share advanced knowledge, lived and otherwise. It might also mean intentionally creating hiring opportunities for those who are culturally fluent within a specific community or a cultural group that directly contribute to the creative process—as writers, directors, and consultants.

PRO TIP: USE INTERSECTIONALITY AS A CRITICAL LENS

Here's one way to think about the role of intersectionality in marketing more concretely. Don't conclude that applying intersectionality as a critical lens in marketing should always evoke issues of power, marginalization, or discrimination within your brand storytelling or any campaign strategy. Instead, consider how you can apply this lens to ask questions, probe further, and ensure that your process is not perpetuating harmful dynamics that are the result of interlocking systems of power, marginalization, or discrimination.

The application of intersectionality is less prescriptive and more preventative. Use it to anticipate potential gaps in knowledge, areas of oversight, and practices that could inadvertently lead to direct or indirect harm. Apply what you learn here to hold yourself, your team, and the brand accountable. Intersectionality does not begin with asking, "How many people have we included to signal 'diversity'?" Rather, intersectionality begins with making it a habit to ask, "In what ways are systems of power showing up here in ways that people are cast, interviewed, researched, treated, partnered with, or represented—and how are we interrupting them?" Intersectionality is not a specific output. It's a mode of critical thinking. Use it regularly.

Checklist: How to Know You Are on the Right Track

Here are a few indicators that you're using the framework of intersectionality correctly and ethically in your marketing strategies:

- **Insight generation:** Your marketing efforts take into account the diverse range of social identities that exist in society. Instead of solely focusing on general human truths, it should also expand this inquiry and consider the lived experiences of people from different backgrounds. This doesn't mean that the messaging needs to address social inequalities directly, but it should demonstrate an intention to avoid one-dimensional, incomplete stories. This aligns with Crenshaw's emphasis on intersectionality, which helps to expose and understand interlocking systems of power and how they affect people who hold multiple marginalized identities. It is important to ask yourself whether you are truly representing the multifaceted identities of the individuals and communities you engage with or if you are oversimplifying their stories and contributing to their historical exclusion from marketing.

- **Strategic messaging:** When it comes to brand storytelling, it is not enough for brands aiming to be inclusive to just steer away from egregious stereotypes. Brands have the power to challenge one-dimensional narratives through strategy and creative direction that integrates actively subversive storytelling elements that push against dominant cultural codes and offer more expansive stories. In line with Crenshaw's intersectionality theory, brands can expose how forces of oppression marginalize and exclude not necessarily by only running campaigns driven by social issues but by proactively embedding inclusive, counter-stereotypical stories throughout brand messaging.

- **Campaign impact:** If the brand aims to be genuinely culturally innovative, consider the ripple effects of its actions on broader social issues and causes for greater inclusivity. Rather than just speaking to diverse audiences, is the brand amplifying existing social initiatives and redistributing influence within the organization? As with the REI case study, partnerships with cultural advisory groups can be a stepping stone for the brand to not only engage with cultural groups but also bring them into the strategic marketing process. Is the brand helping to solve real issues for customers and address existing gaps in inclusivity within the category or within relevant adjacent spaces in culture?

We must recognize that concepts like intersectionality weren't created to make marketing more effective; they were designed to address real, lived experiences of discrimination and injustice. This doesn't mean brands can't use these ideas thoughtfully. However, it does mean that applying such concepts in the marketing sphere should be linked to a genuine commitment to making a systemic impact. At its heart, achieving cultural fluency is about respecting and honoring the roots and intent of these important ideas, many of which emerged from deep struggles for equality and justice. I hope the knowledge shared in this chapter will help you do just that.

In Conversation with Tameka Linnell

Tameka Linnell is the SVP of Cultural Fluency and Integrated Strategy at Dentsu Creative. Previously, she was the SVP of Strategy and Marketing at Zimmerman Advertising and the President and Chief Strategy Officer at the Human Collective. For decades, Tameka has been in the business of understanding consumer behavior and growing brands based on insights and evidence-based marketing practices—always putting the consumer first. She has had the unique privilege to learn from and work with the best in the industry: Best-in-class global brand leaders (Burt's Bees, American Express, McDonald's, Mars Wrigley, Nike, adidas, Coca-Cola), healthcare innovators (HCA, University of Miami Health System), and nimble digital startups. In her approach, Tameka applies marketing laws of growth to brands and businesses, ensuring that evidence, not opinion, drives strategies, recommendations, and creativity.

AKG: Tameka, could you please tell the readers a little about who you are? What areas of strategy and marketing do you specialize in? How do you find meaning in your work?

TL: At the highest level, I lead the cultural fluency practice at Dentsu. I'm the SVP of Integrated Strategy there. As you know, the conversation around cultural fluency started in 2020, right around the time most inclusive marketing programs were kicking off at agencies and companies. This was around the George Floyd case. In 2021, Dentsu called me because they wanted to start a practice focused on embedding inclusion into the creative process. I thought that was commendable at the time because not many agencies were doing that. I had this opportunity to set it up and set the stage for what that would look like at a big general market agency.

AKG: What has that been like?

TL: There's interest in cultural fluency when a client asks for it, or there's a specific need. But making this work really requires a cultural transformation at the agency. And that's where I felt like I hit a brick wall over time. Despite all the initiatives and workshops, only a few people—maybe 50 to 100 out of thousands—show sustained interest. We tend to engage only when it benefits their specific account or a client asks for it. I have enough experience to figure out how to have an impact still, but I alone can't transform the culture of a global organization. It takes all of us.

AKG: That's a striking contrast to what we saw just a few years ago, during the height of social upheaval, when there was so much attention to cultural fluency. How would you articulate the importance of inclusivity and cultural fluency in brand marketing and business for readers who feel like there's a case for it but don't know how to put it into words themselves yet?

TL: I'm a Black woman, a mom, and someone working in advertising—with all of the hats I wear, I'm so highly aware of the, again, the power that we wield as marketers in these visual forms that we put out in the world. I'm in an industry that has such profound power. We don't recognize—or we're not conscious of—the power that we hold. We're in meetings all day, discussing statistics and data, talking about how many images people see daily or their time on TikTok and other platforms. All those images, many of which are paid for, are chosen by us. We are paying people to represent our brand. We are using our own mental models and the way that we see the world to choose people, to select them, to advocate on behalf of our brands. So all of that shapes the way that people see themselves and it shapes the way that we see others.

Not to sound trite but I do believe that we all have a responsibility to create change, right? At the very least, we must be conscious of what we're doing every day. Whether you want to change it or not, that's on you. But there is no question that we shape how people see themselves and how they view others. We should all be conscious of this, at least. That's my personal point of view.

AKG: What does this look like in your work with clients?

TL: Let me start by saying that I don't think it's my job to change how someone else sees the world. That's work individuals have to do on their own. What I do believe is that there are ways to show that if we make these changes—if we're more inclusive in our actions, in our briefs, in our casting, on TikTok, in the influencers we select—it will have a positive impact on your brand or business. It's unfortunate that we're still in a position where we have to prove this. It seems like a no-brainer that people have been underrepresented in this country—and around the world. You only have to look around: The Supreme Court has eliminated affirmative action, and women's rights are being rolled back. So, working alongside industry leaders and my clients, what I believe I can do is begin to show both quantitatively and qualitatively the benefits of these changes. I'm still trying to crack that code because it's so multifactorial; there are so many variables. But I do believe there are ways to prove this will positively impact your brand and business. If we approach this emotionally, we'll likely be shut down.

AKG: Innovation is inherently risky. The risk might be higher than staying comfortable and complacent but so is the reward. Still, even the most well-intentioned leaders can be fearful of the unknown in the process of change—changing mindsets, approaches, and so on... How do you approach this?

TL: Progress may be slow, but as I always say, it's still progress. Progress often feels like two steps forward and one step back. I frequently hear about leadership or senior executives still experiencing some resistance to inclusivity in marketing, and there's a palpable fear of trying new things. But there are steps that brands can take that are both comfortable and meaningful.

AKG: What will finally move the needle forward?

TL: What we need is a true generational change of guard, so to say. Until that profound shift takes place from a leadership perspective, we're still going to be navigating these waters.

AKG: For those who are ready to increase the brand's cultural fluency, what steps do you encourage your clients to take?

TL: Let's get clear that cultural fluency has broadened since I started in advertising and marketing nearly 25 years ago. Back then, it was all about being multicultural. There were multicultural agencies, Black agencies, LGBTQ agencies, Asian agencies. Everything was segregated, mainly along lines of race and ethnicity. When we started focusing on cultural fluency, the first thing I said was that we need to expand beyond just race and ethnicity. In today's world, that's still critical, but we also have to look toward the future. That's where intersectionality comes in. Cultural fluency now considers age, gender, gender identity, sexual orientation, religion, size inclusion, socioeconomics—all the various aspects of identity.

Think about the recent census. There was a massive increase in people identifying in multiple categories. It wasn't that the population exploded; people just now had the freedom to identify the way they wanted to. We can't ignore signals like that. The core of cultural fluency is being expansive and inclusive, not limited to race and ethnicity. Understanding that identity is complex is vital.

Now, how do we action this cultural fluency? There are three main ways: Intersectionality, counter-stereotyping, and nuance. Intersectionality is about recognizing the multiple identities we all carry. Counter-stereotyping involves actively working to shift existing stereotypes. This requires awareness of our own biases and also a commitment to making small, meaningful changes. I read a study saying that it's easy to adopt a stereotype but difficult to change our perceptions even with repeated exposure. I see that as a challenge for repeated exposure.

Finally, there's nuance. I'm not a fan of the word "authenticity"; it's too open to interpretation. I prefer "accuracy." Whether we're selecting influencers, designing a set, or writing a social post, it's all about capturing the nuances—dialect, language, hair texture, skin tone—that make identities unique. This leads to a more authentic representation, however you want to define "authenticity." In my view, "accuracy" is a much more actionable term.

AKG: Accuracy is such a useful term here. What are some of the practices and protocols you cultivate on your team to maintain such rigor and effectiveness?

TL: Starting with a grounding conversation about cultural fluency is crucial. We need to have a common language and shared understanding of what we're aiming for. It's not just about attending a "cultural fluency workshop"; it's about really understanding what that term means for all involved. So, laying down that foundation with plenty of content is the first step. We dive deep into the tenets of cultural fluency, look at real-world examples, discuss cultural moments, and figure out when to engage and when not to. Where a brand is in its journey dictates the next steps. For some, it's about evaluating their current standing. It's essential to reflect on their historical role, perhaps in perpetuating stereotypes. Brands sometimes resist this retrospective look, focusing solely on the future. But understanding where you've been is integral to knowing where you're going.

Our research methodology blends various approaches, including representation assessments through the lens of cultural fluency and intersectionality. We leverage AI for scale, particularly when analyzing thousands of images. But AI has its limitations. It can't pick up on nuances, especially in areas like sexual orientation. For example, if our AI proxy for orientation is intimacy, it may misinterpret a mother-daughter relationship as a romantic one. We're aware of the limitations, and we supplement AI with human analysis.

We've got multiple tools at our disposal. In addition to AI, we conduct workshops and have our Creative Council at Dentsu. This group helps us vet strategies and creative works against the targeted cultural groups, ensuring our output is both relevant and resonant. We also use a proprietary tool called Mindsight, which taps into System 1 thinking. Brands often worry about alienating their core consumer base while diversifying their marketing. With Mindsight, we've found that diverse representation usually elicits a positive emotional response even from those who don't directly identify with the imagery. This insight is critical for CEOs who are concerned not just about their consumer base but also their shareholders. It shows that inclusivity isn't just a moral imperative; it's good for business too. Our approach is multifaceted, always evolving, and committed to being as accurate and resonant as possible.

6

Community:
Brand Accountability and
Co-Creation as the New Model
of Brand Engagement

WHAT TO EXPECT

In this chapter, we'll dissect the concept of "community" to understand its role in contemporary brand marketing, zeroing in on social impact, brand accountability, and co-creation as a model of community engagement. By the conclusion, we'll collectively be equipped to tackle these questions:

- Why adopt a critical lens when considering how consumers perceive brands within a capitalist framework?
- How can brands meet the expectations of socially conscious consumers?
- What is brand accountability, and how can we best operationalize it?
- Why is co-creation the best approach for responsible and inclusive marketing?

As a marketer, you've no doubt encountered another buzzword dominating the headlines: "Community." The notion of "building community" with customers has been at the forefront of the industry conversation since the pandemic fundamentally reshaped how people understood what it means to belong and be in community with others.

Community-led growth strategies have since become a focal point for brands keen on tapping into more organic forms of engagement. By engaging consumers in spaces where they bond and socialize, brands are able to find connections with customers who are willing to pay for the experiences and value-aligned offerings. Engaging communities is also an opportunity for brands to activate in specialized niches relevant to the brand or the product.

In "Belonging to the Brand: How Community is Reshaping the Marketing Landscape," *Forbes* contributor Shep Hyken (2023) defines communities in the marketing context as those "customers willing to evangelize their brands" in the form of positive reviews and referrals. Drawing on Mark Schaefer's book *Belong to the Brand* (2023), Hyken outlines three commercial advantages of community to brands: Brand differentiation, market relevance, and brand loyalty.

Communities are seen as the future of brand loyalty in an age of consumer skepticism and overwhelming choices. Luke Hodson (2023) of Nerds Collective, for instance, argued that "Community engagement should no longer be an afterthought, but central to brand strategy." Indeed, numerous wellness and beauty brands have started to engage and include loyal customers in product development, offering fans ways to benefit from exclusive offerings.

Thought leadership in industry publications, however, is almost exclusively focused on how brands can benefit from engaging in community, whether it's insights and feedback or repeat sales. What is conspicuously absent is a conversation about the responsibilities that brands might have to communities when engaging them. Apart from the singular voices of cultural strategists and inclusivity consultants, such a conversation is strikingly absent from the business discourse at large.

This is hardly surprising, though. The capitalist mode of production has historically depended on accumulation and extraction (Harvey, 1982/2005; Wallerstein, 1974). Despite innovation and technological progress that has improved consumers' quality of life, capitalist structures have normalized business models within which brands are incentivized to extract value from culture to drive maximum profits. Historically, cultural communities have been, therefore, treated as an open-source reservoir of symbols, rituals, artifacts, and practices that brands can use for inspiration.

This has set the stage for brand-driven businesses that have drawn freely from subcultures and marginalized communities without acknowledging or compensating cultures of origin. Consider how luxury brands, fast-food chains, or athletic brands have in the past appropriated elements from indigenous cultures, global cuisines, or streetwear. Cherished cultural symbols were converted into marketable products or campaign themes.

In 2014, for instance, Raquel Laneri and Connie Wang (2014) reported on an "assimilation-themed campaign" run by a well-known luxury brand; the campaign featured "vintage photographs of Native Americans dressed in tweedy jackets, chambray shirts, and European-style ties." This was a jarring instance of cultural extraction, which blatantly disrespected indigenous history; the brand did issue an apology. Fast-forward almost 10 years and recent journalism has also reported on the continued historical appropriation of Black streetwear and hip-hop culture by the most loved brands in the world (Holt, 2023). The examples abound, although, in the last few years, more brands have intentionally turned to "cultural appreciation" instead (Schroeder, 2021). This is movement in the right direction.

At the fundamental level, however, the paradigm has remained the same. Most brands still extract value from cultural communities but fail to provide any value in return. Truth is, we simply don't have existing models for doing otherwise. But as the concept of community gains prominence in marketing strategies, we stand at an inflection point: This is an opportunity to shift from an extractive to a more synergetic engagement with culture.

The choice is clear. Brands can continue engaging cultural communities, subcultures, and historically excluded groups as sources of creative inspiration or data points for profit maximization. But conscious marketers can also choose to adopt a more reciprocal way to relate to cultural partners, advisors, organizations, and identity-based groups. To do this, however, we first must fundamentally deconstruct what's been accepted as a given way of doing business and draw on critical imagination to create new models of cultural cooperation. It's high time to flip the script.

Consumer, Customer, User, or a Person? Navigating a Culture of Consumerism

The impulse in the industry to change our language, perspectives, and outlook on culture and people is already there. Over the years, marketers have advocated against using terms like "consumers" when describing people who purchase and use the goods and products brands market. This is often seen as the first step toward building a more authentic and genuine community with customers. Industry veteran Elliot Begoun, for instance, proposed that marketers swap the term "consumer" for "collaborator."

"Join me in dropping the term "consumer," wrote Begoun (2021), "and instead embrace the building of community."

This makes sense: The term "consumer" can be seen as reducing individuals to mere acts of consumption under capitalism. A more nuanced terminology, some argue, might help us to view people that brands serve through a lens that doesn't reduce them to strictly their economic function in a capitalist system.

This idea certainly starts with good intentions. It's more challenging to think holistically about building community bonds when your customers are placed in a strictly commercial context. When a range of KPIs, from purchase frequency to customer lifetime value, measures the value of customers to the business, it's hard to remember the human aspect. Conscious marketers who genuinely care about resonating with customers and solving their real, everyday problems naturally feel moved to see their audiences as people, just like them. Of course, a purely transactional perspective can quickly diminish this human aspect of the customer-brand relationship. This is an inclination that reveals a kind of discomfort with marketing's rigid commercial focus. Not surprising. The most frequent complaint I encounter when talking to marketers about culture is that they want their work to do more good in the world.

But here lies the problem. Simply changing our language sidesteps a more pressing reality: The pervasiveness of extraction as a mode of engagement in marketing doesn't go away if we simply change the words used. It's a step in the right direction, no doubt. But, being deeply entrenched in capitalist modes of relations, it's a systemic issue we can't simply wish away by renaming it. Adopting euphemisms or dropping specific terminology from our vocabulary starts an important conversation but doesn't necessarily solve the problem at stake.

In fact, brands cannot earnestly build community, leverage cultural fluency, and make a positive social impact on individuals without grappling with how brands are implicated in consumerism. If we are too eager to change our language without interrogating the structures that brands uphold, we run the risk of putting up a façade of progress while leaving the underlying issues unaddressed. We have to dig deeper. As Innocean's global head of innovation and partnerships, Mordecai (2020), writes in an op-ed in *The Drum*, "Brands must break free from established tropes that define how they do business. Or to put it another way, they need to start thinking anticapitalist to be more pro-consumer."

Mordecai makes a compelling point: To be more pro-consumer, marketers need to start thinking in more critical, anti-capitalist ways. Some, too, argue in favor of what they call "conscious capitalism." It is left up for debate whether consciousness is fully compatible with an economic system erected upon the exploitation, exclusion, and oppression of marginalized people; where profit generation is a mode of unequal extraction of labor, resources, and value. While we may disagree on this, we can agree on one thing: It's the only system we currently have. And so what we can do is work together to make it more equitable for all.

As much as we might wish it to be different, economic precarity and insurmountable levels of inequality shape the everyday reality of consumers. If conscious marketers invest time in understanding the broader cultural ecosystem within which brands operate—an ecosystem that shapes people's lived realities—then they will gain a deeper insight into people's perspectives on brand image, social impact, and expectations for accountability. Brands that want to do better might even realize why consumers call out business for unfair practices as fervently as they do.

Increasingly, people recognize the extent to which brands are directly implicated in ruthless profit-making within a society where anti-capitalist sentiment has steadily grown among consumers. In 2019, Pew Research Center found that two-thirds (65 percent) of Americans had a positive view of "capitalism" (Atske, 2019). By 2022, Pew observed a decline of 8 percentage points, with 57 percent viewing capitalism favorably (Nadeem, 2022). From slogans like "Eat the Rich!" to "I do not dream of labor" to "lazy girl jobs" and ideas about "soft life" and "radical rest," the younger generation is struggling to cope with the realities of late-stage capitalism (Barth, 2023).

CONSIDER THIS

Millennials, and even more so Gen Z, whose attitudes will shape the future of marketing, are increasingly turning their backs on capitalism.

In 2019, those aged 18 to 34 were split pretty evenly between those who viewed capitalism positively and negatively: 49 percent vs. 46 percent, respectively (Wronski, 2021). Two years before that, that gap was much larger: 58 percent against only 38 percent. Even the favorable view among young Republicans has fallen from 81 percent in 2019 to 66 percent in 2021. Further, attitudes toward capitalism grew more negative among racial and ethnic groups and were particularly pronounced among Black Americans (Edwards, 2023).

Then there's another report from the Center for the Study of Capitalism that revealed that Gen Z "holds overall lower positive views about free markets, especially the profit system" (Elson and King, 2023). According to the study, only 45 percent of Gen Z vs. 51 percent of Millennials agree that the current profit system teaches positive values like hard work and success.

Still, Edelman paints an even bleaker picture. Young consumers, in particular, increasingly see those holding power in society as divisive and antithetical to harmony in society. Edelman's Trust Barometer study estimated that 62 percent of consumers globally see "the rich and powerful" as a "dividing force that pulls people apart" (Edelman, 2023). This metric was comparable to "hostile foreign governments," which was seen as a divisive force by 61 percent of consumers, almost on par with corporations and the elites.

In our efforts to humanize customers, attention is often lost to this macro context that shapes the views and perspectives of ordinary people in the broader culture. Brands need to be aware of these shifts in culture to deliver on marketing that is able to more eloquently speak to the present moment. Simply changing our language won't suffice; we must also begin to shift perspective and practices when it comes to engaging consumers—and speaking to customers, or just "people," if you will. Marketers might want to see individuals as more than "consumers," but they certainly are consumers in the context of modern-day economic structure; there's no escaping that.

We can't forget that, nor should we run away from it. It's a central piece of cultural insight that brands should take seriously to know how to speak to people and show up in communities or within niche spaces. Because advertising, as Mordecai notes, "is an expression of consumer capitalism."

Socially conscious consumers know this and are already three steps ahead, prepared to hold brands accountable for their actions or rather lack thereof. Brands better catch up to this new reality, and soon. Unless you are looking to implicitly show that your brand understands its economic power and is willing to wield it responsibly, you are already falling behind on the opportunity to stand out in the cultural marketplace of forward-thinking competitors. If you want to market inclusively, accountability is the name of the game.

What Is Brand Accountability?

Accountability, in its most basic form, can be defined as the obligation to account for one's actions, decisions, and subsequent outcomes. Accountability requires one to be honest about one's responsibilities and understand the potential impacts of one's actions on others. This isn't merely a function of legal obligation within a system; it's a moral commitment to honesty, transparency, and integrity, fostering trust and mutual respect.

In activist and trauma- and oppression-informed communities, where the now-popular term stems from, accountability is seen as a cornerstone of community building. That's why it's imperative to the conversation that the industry is having about the future of community building in marketing. When we translate the concept of accountability into the context of brands, accountability takes on an equally, if not more, profound significance.

What we colloquially term "calling out" is, from the consumer's perspective, a call for greater accountability. To be authentic and emotionally resonant in brand communications, marketers need to understand where their inclusivity-focused audiences are coming from.

For socially conscious consumers, brands are not faceless corporations that sell products and have no bearing on society and culture. The aforementioned study from the Center for the Study of Capitalism actually found that 44 percent of adults aged 18 to 34 agree that the CEOs of big businesses should be more involved in solving social problems. Increasingly, newer generations are more sensitive to the fact that brand-driven businesses are corporate entities with identities, values, and considerable societal influence not only within business but also in society. Here is the paradigm shift that brands need to make: For businesses that are looking to future-proof their success, accountability can no longer just be about meeting sales targets, achieving marketing KPIs, or only being accountable to stakeholders. Brands are now also accountable to the people; not merely as consumers as units of economic transactions but as participants whose input and feedback extends beyond the point of sale.

CONSIDER THIS

Accountability is one of the ethical forces in the cultural intelligence model of culture + strategy + innovation. Brand accountability starts with recognizing the role and impact that your brand or client has within society and outlining its responsibility toward consumers, workers, and necessarily also the environment. This will require a commitment to continual self-reflection, learning, and improvement. In being held accountable by the public, brand marketers are asked to exercise the courage to accept tough feedback and the humility to admit when mistakes have been made. Moving from fear of being wrong into embracing what it means to be a change agent, action is how brands can unlock and leverage more authentic and genuine interactions with audiences. Later in this chapter, we will unpack how fear sabotages brands and why marketing professionals will win when they fearlessly leverage the power of authenticity, humility, and brand accountability. This process starts with first understanding how socially conscious consumers think.

I Want My Brand to Be Accountable. Now What?

Understand Where People Are Coming From

Inclusivity in marketing without actual social impact in communities that marketers want to engage in remains little more than tokenism, and tokenism is, by definition, not only detrimental but fundamentally exploitative. This is the first lesson of community building and brand accountability. Marketing strategies that use historically excluded communities to *appear* progressive without ever directing material resources or institutional power to make a positive social impact are akin to optical illusions. But sooner or later, the illusion begins to fade. Eventually, audiences catch on.

The reality of tokenistic gestures and performative actions soon becomes evident. Modern-day consumers are hypersensitive and aware of the fact that brands are capital-driven corporate entities that seek to benefit when customers purchase and consume products and services. That's why consumers engage in boycotts: They know their power as drivers of revenue and market share for brand. Marketers need to understand this to produce culturally savvy marketing that isn't detached or insensitive. By this, I mean that if you want to understand today's customers and fulfill their culture-driven expectations, you'll need to understand how socially conscious consumers think.

Sure, you might opt to drop the term "consumer" from your vocabulary, but my suggestion is actually to embrace and interrogate it more deeply. Here's a harsh truth: Ordinary people are under no illusion that they are "in the community" with brands, even the brand they adore. More than that, consumers today know that they hold the economic power to either support and amplify your brand—or, if not boycott it, then at least seriously consider a competitor.

This isn't a call for every marketing campaign to suddenly become a rallying cry for social justice. That's not the point here, and this kind of strategy of community engagement would probably backfire anyway! What consciously minded marketers must grasp is that, as consumer attitudes increasingly shift toward inclusivity and heightened accountability, future marketing efforts will be assessed against these evolving expectations.

Learning from the Activist Discourse

Besides all the data, I know this with a great degree of certainty because I spent over a decade of my career as an academic, being a part of socially conscious, grassroots activist communities. This experience significantly informed my consulting practice in marketing. What I know to be true is this: Ordinary working people don't think like marketers. If you want to build genuinely inclusive and responsible lines of communication with customers, take the time to understand how conscious customers think about consumption, brands, and capitalist relations in today's society.

As a young activist—a decade before brand accountability was even picked up by marketers in the mainstream—I myself actively criticized brands for hypocrisy, even occasionally calling on others to boycott brands. I am biased, of course, but socially conscious consumers aren't entirely unreasonable. They get indignant and loud on social media when brands make inclusivity- and equity-related mistakes not because consumers are vindictive, maliciously petty, or bought into so-called "cancel culture" (more on the myth of cancel culture later in this chapter!) as some critics believe. It's because people see brands as corporate entities looking to benefit from consumers like them by incentivizing them to purchase and consume goods. Indignation from socially conscious consumers—which, as research shows, is an ever-growing segment of the population—stems from people's hyper-awareness that they are *consumers*—and not just people—to brands.

This explains widespread consumer skepticism. As more brands attempt to align with social issues or cultural causes, public trust remains elusive. In fact, the gap of consumer trust is only widening. Consider that in 2019, a Sprout Social survey of over 1,500 U.S. consumers found that more than half (53 percent) believed that brands only take a stand on social issues for public relations or marketing purposes (Sprout Social, 2019). Fast forward to 2023; this number is now significantly higher. Adweek's senior reporter

Paul Hiebert (2023) reported in July 2023 that a new survey found that 76 percent of adults in the United States now believe that "brands take a stand on social issues to help generate more sales." Changing the terminology without addressing the roots of how brands show up in culture is like putting a new coat of paint on a crumbling house. It might make us look and feel better but it doesn't change the problem on our hands.

Don't assume that simply by ceasing to refer to your customers as "consumers" and opting for the more empathetic term "people," you'll change how your marketing audiences perceive brands in the context of corporate greed and subsequent distrust. Rather than denying or side-stepping the realities of our market-driven world, lean into them. Face it head-on and see it from people's perspective. At the end of the day, this is what it means to build community: Learn to deeply understand the people your brands serve. It begins with self-awareness. Then, you can begin to build strategies that resonate rather than agitate and aggravate.

Show Up or Perish: A Better Way to Build Communities

While most marketers might fear backlash or public outrage, the consequence of being a brand that lacks accountability and social engagement is actually much more pervasive and detrimental. Just look at the data shared above. What's at stake is a loss of opportunity to innovate and differentiate your brand. Most of all, it's a lost opportunity to build consumer trust, brand loyalty, and ultimately, growth in market share in the long term. Think for a moment about most iconic brands: No brand that "lives rent-free" in people's minds achieved this status by playing it safe. Innovation is inherently about risk tolerance—and the willingness to try.

Leading with Humility

Innovation requires out-of-the-box thinking. There is inherent value in thinking about customers beyond business metrics—as multifaceted individuals who bring their experiences, values, and perspectives to every interaction with your brand. This means recognizing that behind every purchase is a person making choices, not just about what to buy, but also about which brands align with their values, reflect their identity, and contribute positively to their lives and, increasingly, the broader society.

Understanding customers more multi-dimensionally enables us as marketers to enrich brand positioning with respect to contemporary culture by aligning the brand with consumer values. This reorientation does not negate the importance of commercial metrics. Rather, it enriches these metrics with a depth of understanding that allows brands to build their customer base and enhance their market performance sustainably. After all, when customers feel valued and understood, they are more likely to engage, advocate, and remain loyal to the brand, ultimately driving long-term profitability and growth.

But what does this mean in practice? Always start from a position of humility.

- **Zoom out.** Learn to see the bigger picture and see your customers beyond the problems you can solve with your product. Your brand isn't their entire world; it's a pretty small part of it.

- **Seek feedback.** Building community starts with equalizing the playing field and listening to voices that have been historically overlooked, excluded, or silenced. What perspectives have been often neglected? Start there.

- **Be ready to be held responsible.** Understand that striving to be culturally relevant means being ready to shoulder responsibility for your brand's actions (or inactions) in the cultural arena. Take this responsibility seriously and be prepared to learn, even when it might be uncomfortable.

Zoom Out

As marketers, it's easy for us to get so involved in the details of creating and managing brands that we lose sight of the bigger picture. While emotionally resonant brands can certainly capture consumer attention and loyalty in powerful ways, marketers need to remember to connect with people on a wider level. This means understanding the broader societal and cultural factors in people's lives.

Avoid becoming isolated within a marketing bubble. When you broaden your perspective to truly comprehend consumers' lives in their totality—not just in terms of buying habits but also societal pressures and cultural contexts that people navigate—the heightened scrutiny under which brands find themselves becomes more understandable.

Start here: Public call-outs of brands for problematic behavior aren't frivolous or without substance. Instead, they arise from real-world offenses and harms that brands inflict, impacting or triggering something about the lived experiences of consumers in meaningful ways.

Remember that consumers' lives extend beyond the marketplace. Of course, it may seem tempting to brush off consumer complaints or label them as mere instances of "cancel culture" or purposeless outrage. In some instances that might be the case. However, don't make the mistake of choosing to ignore or deflect real issues—that will only further undermine the brand.

Avoiding hard conversations or trying to sidestep criticism won't make it disappear. Instead, it might exacerbate the issues and leave lasting damage to brand reputation and consumer trust. Confronting and addressing these concerns head-on is not just the right thing to do; it's a strategic imperative for longevity and relevance.

Seek Feedback

To build community with your audiences, it's crucial to foster a culture of listening within the organization, particularly when it comes to amplifying voices of those traditionally underrepresented, marginalized, or ignored in the marketing process. In a world where historical inequities are increasingly challenged, brands can't afford to recreate old patterns of exclusionary practices. Each voice in your audience represents a distinct perspective. When taken together, these collective insights can serve as invaluable guides in shaping the narrative, improving offerings, and innovating in ways you wouldn't think of otherwise.

Start here: Identify and acknowledge the voices that have been neglected, be it audiences from certain socioeconomic backgrounds, gender identities, racial and ethnic groups, or people with disabilities, among others. When it comes to your cultural marketing strategy, double down on including these historically silenced or overlooked perspectives.

Remember that soliciting feedback isn't just about addressing customer complaints or queries; listen and make necessary changes based on how people feel about the brand. Seek feedback diligently, listen empathetically, and act consciously. Don't forget that perspectives from marginalized communities should be adequately remunerated and amplified by sharing your brand's platform, resources, or a percentage of the revenue.

Be Prepared to Be Held Responsible

As brands aim to connect on a deeper level with their customers, they must understand that stepping into the cultural landscape means accepting accountability for their actions—and inactions. This is true for all of us who engage in the public sphere. Actions have consequences and we will be held accountable when we cause harm. Why should it be different for brands? Brands must be prepared to answer for their decisions, actions, and impact, regardless of how uncomfortable or challenging it may seem to integrate social consciousness with business considerations.

Start here: Acknowledge that each decision you make as a brand has potential implications—both intended and unintended—that ripple through society. When consumers feel that your brand has overstepped boundaries, misappropriated culture, perpetuated harmful stereotypes, or neglected its commitment to sustainability, they will demand accountability.

In such instances, it's crucial not to dismiss or paint real concerns and issues as just another instance of a "cancel culture" mob. Instead, view them as calls for greater responsibility and accuracy in marketing.

Defensiveness or evasion will not vanish these issues; it may only amplify them, causing more harm to your brand's reputation. Being held responsible is an opportunity to learn, grow, and better align your brand with your community's values. It's a chance to showcase your brand's commitment to acting in ways that are ethical and socially responsible.

When you bravely face criticism and apologize sincerely for mistakes and take concrete actions to correct them, this demonstrates a level of brand maturity and authenticity that can't be achieved through marketing campaigns alone. Get ready to be held responsible and learn from your missteps. Anything less is risk aversion that mistakenly leaves transformative opportunities on the table.

CASE STUDY
Apple, "Mother Nature" (2023)

In 2023, Apple took a risk when reporting on its progress toward the brand's sustainability goals. Previously, Apple's VP of Environment, Policy, and Social Initiatives, Lisa Jackson, would discuss the company's eco-friendly initiatives, often from unique locations like Apple Park's roof. This year, her segment followed a "Mother Nature" comedy sketch. Starring Octavia Spencer, the short film aimed to showcase Apple's strides toward achieving carbon neutrality for all its products by 2030. It also announced that the new Apple Watch will be the first item to meet this goal.

The script features Spencer as "Mother Nature" arriving to the team meeting to grill the tech giant on its progress toward becoming more environmentally sustainable. At the end, Tim Cook appears in a face-to-face encounter with Mother Nature. He promises that by 2030, all Apple products will have net-zero climate impact. Mother Nature asks, "All of them?" "All of them," Cook affirms. "They better," she responds, raising her eyebrows. The camera zooms back in on Cook. Looking straight in her eyes, Cook says assertively, "They will."

While some lauded the ad as brave, others accused Apple of "greenwashing." As we learned in the chapter on communication, audiences will always have different interpretations of messages they receive. But as *Inc.com* tech columnist Jason Aten (2023) notes, the ad was effective, even though some didn't find it funny or even conscious enough. "The point here isn't just that Apple is devoting itself to making real progress on the issue," Aten wrote, but that the brand is "highlighting its progress in comparison to its competition."

Apple directly took on the challenge of accountability. The ad communicated humility, commitment, and the brand's willingness to be challenged. More than that, Apple communicated tangible steps it was making to reduce its negative impact on the climate. Instead of dodging responsibility, it spoke directly to the community of not only stakeholders but also people. The brand set a benchmark in corporate accountability through transparency and proactive action.

Beyond the Fear of Being Wrong

Authenticity demands courage to be wrong. In this era of consumer expectations, marketers must be bold enough to stand up for ideas and beliefs that complement their brand positioning and mission, even amidst potential controversy. When a brand's engagement in social causes aligns with its ethos, it enhances consumer respect and admiration, fostering a stronger emotional bond. Transparency is key to this. This doesn't only imply admitting mistakes, but it also means granting consumers an insight into the brand's processes—its supply chain, hiring practices, sustainability efforts, influencer partnerships, and creative campaigns. As with anything, transparency nurtures trust, the cornerstone of brand loyalty. But none of this is possible if marketers make business decisions out of fear of backlash, criticism, or "being canceled." Adopting the term "cancel culture" across trend reports and industry conversations has been one of the most detrimental missteps in the marketing profession in recent years.

The rhetoric around "cancel culture" breeds a climate of apprehension, leading to inaction or bland, superficial engagement with audiences that is bereft of genuine commitment, authenticity, and ability to step into cultural leadership. It creates a binary world where brands are either "in" or "out," where consumers are either "for" or "against," and where we are divided into "them" and "us." This language breeds fear, and fear is the enemy of authenticity. Authenticity requires courage to show up in ways that align with what your brand believes in and stands for, to take risks, and to be open to criticism. This is what innovation is all about—you can't do something extraordinary and distinctive without having the courage to try to do something new and unexplored.

But fear of "cancel culture" discourages this kind of boldness, inhibiting brands from having real, challenging conversations that might push you and your team out of your comfort zones in ways that will only benefit your business in the long term. This rhetoric of fear and apprehension is not only misleading but also oversimplifies the complexity of the cultural ecosystem and robs brand marketers of an invaluable opportunity to leverage cultural and social issues to make a positive societal impact in addition to pursuing forward-thinking business opportunities and in doing so, advancing brand differentiation in the market.

Cancel Culture = a Loud Minority

Critics of socially conscious and responsible marketing argue that marketing strategy has been hijacked. Brand purpose and social impact are seen as detrimental to the bottom line, as that which puts the entire brand at risk. Certainly, there have been a few examples in recent months that showed the effect that consumer boycotts can have on sales. Yet, few examples exist of brands being "canceled" to the point of business failure or non-existence. The notion of "cancel culture" often exaggerates the actual impact of public backlash. The term simplifies complex social accountability mechanisms, amplified in the digital era.

Certainly, we can easily think of moments of controversy and missteps that have earned brands a place in the headlines or even damaged sales. Yet, from Pepsi and Dove to H&M, these and other brands that had previously made inclusivity-related mistakes and were publicly held accountable have continued to thrive and grow regardless of past mistakes. The concept of "cancel culture" as such tends to overstate the impact of such supposed "cancellations."

Another warning: The "cancel culture" narrative tends to portray consumer criticism as impulsive and unreasonable, undermining legitimate grievances, especially from historically marginalized groups. It is often the case that the balance of power remains unchanged, and the "canceled" people, organizations, or brands continue to hold significant influence.

It's also crucial for conscious marketers to distinguish between unwarranted attacks on social media and genuine calls for justice and inclusivity. The very idea that there exists a monolithic, organized "cancel culture" can be misleading, particularly when it comes to understanding the complexities of cultural dynamics in the digital age.

In recent years, "cancel culture" has been used to represent an allegedly widespread social trend where individuals (often celebrities, public figures, artists, or popular brands) are "canceled" or socially ostracized following behavior deemed offensive or unacceptable by a particular group of consumers. But this notion simplifies and even misconstrues the multifaceted mechanisms of social accountability and critique that have been amplified in the digital age.

Above all, we make it seem that the social accountability we see today is in any way a new phenomenon. Think for a moment about the beginning of this book: The calls for accountability and social responsibility of advertisers can be traced back to the sixties. What has primarily changed is the platform and scale at which this can occur. The advent of social media has democratized the process, giving voices to individuals who were previously unheard and allowing a wider range of perspectives to be shared and discussed. Silencing marginalized communities could only benefit those who have something to gain from sustaining the status quo.

The discourse on "cancel culture" frames these accountability mechanisms and dissenting viewpoints as impulsive and unjust, implying an absence of legitimate concerns. But this assumption actively undermines legitimate grievances that people express, particularly those from communities that have been historically oppressed, overlooked, and underrepresented.

None of this is to excuse toxic language and unwarranted attacks that do, indeed, characterize contemporary social media culture. Yet, it is essential that we draw a line and ensure that the voices of those offering constructive, even if harsh or critical, feedback are heard.

The digital age has allowed a broader range of voices to participate in cultural conversations, leading to increased demands for integrity and responsibility. Brands can rise to meet these expectations, not merely as a reactionary step to avoid being "canceled," but as a proactive strategy to build trust, credibility, and authenticity with their key audiences. This is a conscious, responsible way to do marketing.

Key Lessons for Brand Accountability

Sure, being "called out" by consumers is less than ideal, but it is not an automatic death sentence for a brand. On the other hand, avoiding engaging in real cultural innovation eventually might be. If you're up for the challenge, here are a few suggestions to keep in mind.

You Can't Fake It—Being Real Starts from Within

You will fail at coming across as an authentically inclusive, culturally resonant, and socially responsible brand until and unless your team gets clear on what your brand stands for in regard to contemporary issues in culture and society. Authenticity cannot be reduced to a marketing tactic, although it certainly can and should be central to your strategy. Authenticity is a way of doing business as a brand that encompasses commercial impact but is not limited to it. You have to get clear on what is core to your brand's DNA and how that core positioning aligns with contemporary culture and movements for equity and inclusivity. Going through a series of discussions and exercises with your team to identify your zone of impact and innovation opportunities will help you prepare and strategize what your brand is ready or not ready to do.

Courage to Address Difficult Topics

Brands that are willing to confront challenging issues, accept their missteps, and actively work toward solutions are brands that stand out among the rest. They build stronger bonds with their consumers and begin to command respect within their industry. An example of this would be brands like Fenti and Patagonia. In this sense, a "brave" brand is more than a mere producer of goods or services; it becomes a living entity that can affect change, inspire loyalty, and set a benchmark for social impact and brand responsibility. This approach moves beyond superficial marketing tactics and into a realm where a brand stands for something greater than itself—it evolves into a cultural participant with a voice that resonates deeply within its community.

Transparency Is Non-Negotiable

In an age where information is just a click away, transparency goes beyond revealing the functional aspects of your brand, like pricing or supply chains. It extends to your values, your culture, and how you respond when you make a mistake. It's about being open with your intentions and actions and holding yourself accountable for the impacts your brand creates. Start here: Let your customers see behind the scenes. Volunteer information concerning working conditions, sustainable materials, and your efforts to advance equity both within your own organization and across communities relevant to your brand. Make transparency a cornerstone of your brand's ethos—it's not just expected; it is essential.

Pull Up or Shut Up: Why Social Impact Matters

In cultural marketing, brand authenticity rings hollow without generating a substantial material impact on the communities your brand seeks to engage, amplify, or support. The mere act of rolling out a campaign is not enough; there must be evidence of genuine commitment to making a material difference. This doesn't always necessitate financial contributions or high-profile donations. However, there must be an unequivocal demonstration that your brand is devoted to actual change rather than superficial gestures.

Why does this tangible impact hold such importance? It ties back to a critical point addressed earlier in this chapter. Today's consumers are not just socially conscious but also commercially astute. They perceive brands as profit-driven entities operating within the capitalist machinery of consumer culture. Aware of the economic advantage brands gain by appearing culturally relevant, today's consumers won't hesitate to question the brand's intentions.

This is not only about protecting the brand reputation, although that is certainly an important aspect. Consider how we discussed the importance of considering the dynamics of power and oppression in the earlier chapter. The same line of thinking applies here. Responsible marketing calls for marketers to recognize societal imbalances, including power imbalances between brand-driven businesses with economic power and historically excluded communities with a comparative lack of resources. It demands an understanding that, as business entities, brands hold significant resources and influence. This positions brand-driven businesses uniquely within society, particularly in relation to marginalized communities that have long been underserved. As corporate entities, brands are inherently positioned in a place of power due to their extensive resources. Brands operate in societies where economic and social inequalities often translate into power imbalances. These imbalances can perpetuate, and sometimes even exacerbate, the marginalization experienced by certain communities. And so, if brands genuinely wish to engage with these communities in a responsible and authentic way, they need to recognize this inherent power dynamic. Rather than acting from a position of control, brands should approach their engagement efforts as a form of partnership, one where their resources can be leveraged to support and amplify the community's efforts.

Co-creation as the New Model of Brand Engagement

So, how can your brand foster a real difference? Consider Figure 6.1. The key to community engagement is not in reinventing the wheel but in supporting and amplifying the existing endeavors of those on the ground. Collaborate with community leaders, support their efforts, and use your brand's platform to shine a light on their work. This approach is crucial because marginalized communities have been historically underserved and under-resourced. By shifting the focus from your brand onto communities your brand wants to engage and existing initiatives within these communities, you'll have an opportunity to foster much-needed support and build an authentic reputation. Ultimately, this grounded authenticity, demonstrated through real, tangible impact, is what distinguishes inclusive brands from performative ones.

FIGURE 6.1 The Essence of Community Engagement

Original framework created by Dr. Anastasia Kārkliņa Gabriel.

Values and principles: Align on a set of values and guidelines that seek to challenge dominant ways of engaging with audiences and amplify marginalized perspectives from the communities the brand engages. In short, what do you stand for?

Commitment to growth: Develop sustainable strategies to seek and integrate community perspectives and feedback and create processes for how current strategies will be revised and improved over time. What feedback loop do you have in place?

Reciprocal partnerships: Establish frameworks for shared decision making and resource allocation between the brand and community partners, ensuring that initiatives serve community needs while also aligning with brand goals. How are you using community feedback to determine and prioritize where you show up?

Material impact: Supplement marketing communications, storytelling, and inclusive representation with impact-driven community initiatives that direct resources to existing community-based and community-initiated solutions. Beyond talking the talk, how are you walking the walk?

Brand responsibility: Implement a clear short-term and long-term strategy for how the brand will respond in the event of negative publicity. Identify how you will honor your partnerships and communicate with stakeholders, advisors, and involved community groups. Most importantly, how will you proactively prevent the brand from being unintentionally harmful?

CASE STUDY
The King Center Timeline

Microsoft's collaboration with The King Center, founded by Mrs. Coretta Scott King, represents an instructive case of a tech giant using its digital power for sociocultural preservation. Using an Azure-based Digital Asset Management solution, Microsoft (2023) partners with the center to "preserve and facilitate digital access to the world's largest repository of primary source material related to the life and work of Martin Luther King."

What stands out about this initiative, particularly evident in the 2023 Martin Luther King Day release of their "Dear Coretta" campaign, is Microsoft's low-key approach. "Dear Coretta" was part of a larger effort to digitalize the archive of photographs, recordings, and other artifacts documenting Mrs. Coretta Scott King's life's work. The tech brand didn't take credit nor center itself.

This was not a marketing play thinly disguised as social responsibility; in fact, Microsoft's logo was, notably, subtle in the campaign video, consciously taking a back seat to the central figures and themes of The King Center, its founder, and modern civil rights leaders.

This nuanced, "soft touch" strategy aligns well with the rising consumer expectation for brands to not just "do good," but do so without loudly proclaiming their own benevolence. Microsoft's collaboration with The King Center transcended mere tokenism. It was an example of meaningful social impact, offering a model for how tech companies can use their existing products or resources and genuinely contribute to fill an important need. The focus remained on the beneficiaries, stakeholders, and the cause at hand, rather than shifting the spotlight to the brand's charitable or socially responsible actions.

A New Paradigm for Innovation and Growth

Co-creation marks a paradigm shift in marketing. It pulls down the traditional corporate hierarchy and seeks to redistribute power and resources in a flawed economic system. The traditional business model typically functions top-down, with decisions being made at the top and trickling down. However, when truly engaging with cultural communities and moving away from engaging consumers to seeing them as people, we need to question and re-evaluate not only how brands refer to them but how brands treat them.

By nature, hierarchies establish divisions, with those in higher tiers possessing more power and control. This dynamic perpetuates imbalances and, in the context of brand activism, can lead to paternalistic or exploitative practices rather than community partnerships that are respectful, empowering, and supportive.

When community members from marginalized and historically excluded groups are absent in the decision-making spaces, the result is often a limited, unidimensional understanding of brands' so-called "communities." It also means that solutions and strategies are likely to be developed through a lens that does not fully capture the lived experiences of those these initiatives aim to support.

On top of that, assuming the role of a "savior" that brings solutions to community issues can easily slip into a form of cultural imperialism, where brands impose their own views, values, and solutions onto the communities on the receiving end of brand activism. Not surprisingly, this approach often fails to recognize the unique cultural contexts, lived experiences, and existing solutions within these communities, leading to interventions that may be inappropriate, ineffective, or even harmful.

On the other hand, the model of co-creation positions communities that brands want to engage not as passive beneficiaries but as active collaborators and decision-makers. Challenging hierarchies means shifting from dictating to dialoguing and from commanding to collaborating.

Initiating an open dialogue while embracing a more equitable partnership paradigm reorients the narrative from being "brand-led" to being "community-guided." Co-creation as a mode of engagement reorients how marketers can approach brand activism and social impact efforts: From vertical extraction to more horizontal collaboration. This necessitates that we acknowledge the innate wisdom embedded in the communities that brands aim to connect with. It demands that we rethink how brands participate in the redistribution of power and resources, how brands can foster a dedicated environment for community dialogue, and how brands can stay committed to commercial growth that takes community, adaptability, and inclusivity into consideration.

CHECKLIST: QUESTIONS ANY INCLUSIVE BRANDS SHOULD ASK

1 **Values and principles**

   o Does the campaign respect and value the knowledge, expertise, and capabilities within the community, rather than imposing external "solutions"?

   o Is the brand aware of and has it considered the power dynamics within the community and in relation to itself during the planning process?

   o Has the brand conducted comprehensive research on the specific challenges and existing solutions within the targeted community?

2 **Commitment to growth**

   o Has the brand set measurable goals to assess the campaign's tangible social impact and community benefits?

   o Is the brand prepared to learn from and act upon the feedback and criticisms from the community, both during and after the campaign?

   o Has the brand considered the potential implications of the campaign on the wider societal and cultural context within which the community exists?

3 **Reciprocal partnerships**

   o Has the brand engaged with influential community leaders and organizations for collaborative efforts in the campaign?

   o How is the brand planning to involve the community members in the design and execution of the campaign?

   o Has the brand taken steps to ensure it considers and amplifies the voices of marginalized or overlooked individuals within this community?

4 **Material impact**

   o What efforts has the brand made to give back materially to the community beyond the scope of the campaign?

   o Has the brand developed a plan for maintaining a relationship with the community after the campaign to ensure lasting, positive impacts?

o Does the brand have a contingency plan in place to rectify potential mistakes or unintended consequences within the campaign, particularly those that could negatively affect the community?

5 **Brand responsibility**

o Is the brand prepared to take responsibility and be held accountable for any negative impacts or controversies arising from the campaign?

o How will the brand hold itself accountable throughout the process? Will the team implement multiple review and feedback sessions with expert consultants and paid community members?

o Is the brand committed to transparency about the campaign goals, processes, successes, and challenges with all stakeholders, including the community, consumers, and the public at large? How will this transparency be upheld and put into practice?

In Conversation with Vanessa Toro

Vanessa Toro writes about culture, advertising, and society. She is a strategy director, responsible for providing strategic and creative direction for clients and partner agencies alike. Relentlessly focused on helping brands harness culture for over 15 years, Vanessa believes advertising should propel culture forward rather than merely functioning as its mirror. Dedicated to disturbing the status quo, Vanessa has served as a portfolio school instructor, an advisor to political campaigns, and an assistant to visiting street artists. She hates jargon.

AKG: Vanessa, you help brands harness culture and move people. What is your own vision for culture in the world of brands? In what unique ways do clients benefit from working with you, and what do you try to achieve in your work?

VT: My ambition is for brands to embody a symbiotic relationship with people and culture, not a parasitic one. Brands hold significant influence in the shaping of values, beliefs, and norms. Brands should be engaged contributors to culture and context, not passive organisms waiting to "tap into a cultural conversation." This is the promise and possibility that keeps me in the game. Even in the face of pervasive and scathing takedowns about advertising, strategy, and marketing, I still haven't given up on this busted industry.

Clients and partners benefit from my ability to move beyond spools of inconsequential data and spiritless psychographics everyone has access to, to peer into deeply held beliefs, unspoken codes of conduct, and nuanced expressions of communities. It is exquisitely important to me that as brands answer the call for cultural relevance and "representation" of historically silenced cultures and communities that it not be an extractive, exploitive transaction. That symbols and rituals and practices aren't taken out of context and trivialized for wider consumption.

There are so many narratives coursing through the fabric of the nation that need uprooting, reframing, and challenging. Why should a brand that is selling a product care about any of this? Because they exist in all of this.

AKG: More brands are invested in tapping into emergent culture, but as we know, this work is often filled with performative gestures and buzzwords. One of them is "community." How should brand marketers think about this idea of "building community"? What is the role of accountability and social impact in this conversation? Are these still relevant?

VT: My experience with art-based collaborations is closely tied to my vision of symbiotic relationships. Do we know what matters to the community we wish to engage? What they value? Does the brand have the right—or an opportunity—to uplift this dialogue? Are we willing to back it with an ongoing commitment instead of just dipping into the pool of cool?

When brands reference or harness a local culture or community, there is an ethical imperative for economic reciprocity and investment. It is never the case that there aren't already people on the ground doing the work that an organization or brand wants to activate against.

What efforts and systems are already in place, and how can you supercharge the efforts of locals? No one knows the needs and wants of a neighborhood or community better than the folks in it. We may be experts in telling stories and creating symbols, but people are experts in their truth and reality.

More broadly, when brand marketers speak about building community, I candidly struggle to see it mean much outside of products, services, and conduits for self-expression: Fashion, beauty, gaming, technology. I am not saying it's impossible for other categories, but it just doesn't make a whole lot of investment sense to expect strangers to connect meaningfully—and on an ongoing basis—in discussion about your breakfast cereal. The only community that naturally forms and truly persists is the complaint forum.

AKG: You have previously spoken about how agencies often overlook local talent and instead work with folks in default places, like NY or LA. Why should folks in the industry pause and think about that?

VT: This is a rather large pet peeve of mine because it reinforces the existing paradigm of exclusion and gatekeeping in an industry that loudly proclaims the opposite.

My frustration has many facets, from the erroneous belief—or expectation—that America's creative class reside in the two biggest and most expensive cities, to the post-George Floyd pronouncements that we will train and mold raw talent to create opportunities for new entrants into the field, but also ask for one to three years' experience. How anyone looks at the musical, fashion, political, and cultural landscape and doesn't cite the influence of Atlanta is beyond me. Black culture is the city's largest export and global currency.

Production companies and brands often fly into town—to the world's largest and busiest airport—to film rappers at their barber shops, the organizers ensuring reproductive justice and mutual aid in a growing dystopia, the civil rights icons who live among us, and the swell of creative that exists as just a regular feature of this city. And then they head back to their segregated-but-really-close-together little neighborhoods on the two coasts to edit the film, slap a bop over it, and act like purveyors of culture.

I've seen Atlanta shops import middle and senior talent from a handful of locations, providing relocation packages and industry press for those white folks, when our Atlanta creatives of color have had to leave to find opportunities at any level. It doesn't make any sense.

Curious, passionate, wild-hearted people exist everywhere. They're already making something out of nothing. They're not hard to find. Our inability to cultivate the talent growing beneath our feet says a lot about our staggering lack of imagination and the collective, deep embrace of the status quo, no matter how much we claim to detest it. There is a perception that advertising and marketing is a "progressive" endeavor but rarely has that proven to be true.

AKG: Much of this book touches on the idea of cultural innovation. How do you think about innovation? What does it mean to innovate responsibly?

VT: Co-creation is something often mentioned in marketing, the notion of listening to consumers' ideas and problems to develop new products or update existing ones. Some brands have built a feedback loop and ecosystem to unearth innovation opportunities.

In my mind, there's a comparable form of innovation through a cultural lens that goes beyond the expected functional and emotional benefits—which often are an undifferentiated value proposition coupled with a layer of vague emotional words.

How people use the products and their application can vary from community to community. People who've lived on the margins are wildly innovative—because necessity is the mother of invention. They've developed workarounds for existing products that never took their height, left-handedness, or gender into design consideration. Our elders should all hold patents!

7

Now What? Developing Cultural Intelligence Capabilities

WHAT TO EXPECT

You are now familiar with the four foundational pillars of cultural intelligence: Culture, communication, consciousness, and community. However, the question that arises is, what's next? Getting started on this task can often prove to be quite challenging. The process of change can be messy, and there are often no clear guideposts to follow. Too few companies currently have dedicated cultural intelligence teams, although the number is certainly growing. When these teams do exist, they can often intersect with social insights, consumer research, sales support, and market analytics.

Inclusive marketing as such is also commonly absent in existing practices. Continued education in cultural literacy is severely lacking. It can be assumed that marketing teams that analyze market trends or conduct consumer segmentation will, by default, be able to execute an inclusive marketing strategy. But that's not often the case. In this chapter, you will have an opportunity to reflect on the following questions:

- How can you begin the process of assessing your brand's current position?

- How can you align your brand with pertinent cultural codes?

- How do you formulate an approach that genuinely makes an impact?

- What core values should you leverage for an impactful cultural strategy?

Now that we have covered foundational elements of cultural intelligence, it is time to unpack how exactly marketers can leverage it in practice. I hope this book has successfully convinced you at least about one thing: That practicing cultural intelligence and becoming a culturally fluent marketer requires diligent attention to what is easily missed and overlooked.

Cultural intelligence is both an art and a science. In this work, marketers must learn to balance skills in cultural analysis with developing a certain kind of intuition and a critical eye. Beyond knowing how to analyze cultural movements and social shifts, we need to be able to lean back, assess, and make decisions in a way that sometimes will require us to place bets and put faith into ideas that have not been tried and tested.

As you are getting started, remember that it is entirely normal to feel like you don't know where to begin exactly. In what follows, I hope to offer you a few guiding posts and useful questions to consider. Of course, every brand has unique needs and a distinct positioning. But every effort to put cultural intelligence into practice starts with similar steps that you can adopt and apply to your brand or your client's, adjusting where you need to based on whether your brand is a legacy brand or a new startup.

It's worth remembering that mistakes will be made. That is okay. No brand, regardless of its size, track record, or legacy, will perfectly navigate every cultural opportunity. The willingness to be imperfect while learning, adapting, and earnestly engaging with culture and people will always resonate more deeply than mere tokenistic gestures or feigned perfection. Nothing is worse than playing it safe and doing nothing.

Start With the Present

The first and most critical step is to understand where the brand currently stands. Before a brand can effectively venture into the practice of cultural intelligence and innovative cultural marketing, you should first take time to introspect and evaluate the brand's current position. It can be all too tempting to rush and jump on the most recent cultural wave in an effort to seem in tune with the cultural zeitgeist. It is also much easier for brands to lean into big and obvious splashes in popular culture.

Consider here, for instance, the popularity of Barbiecore in anticipation of the movie's release, when so many brands jumped in on the opportunity to have their marketing "Barbie-fied." From Pinterest, Roku, and Bumble to Airbnb and Boohoo, brands saw an opportunity for cultural marketing to leverage and capitalize on the popular interest in Barbie as a doll and a historic icon (Dockterman, 2023). Some did so more intelligently than others, and it showed. This was both an exciting opportunity for marketing genius and a moment for forward-thinking brands to ask: Outside of the obvious moments of cultural spectacle, what is the brand's long-term vision and approach to driving the cultural conversation?

Latching onto trending moments might give a temporary boost in visibility. It might even increase sales. But this is not quite enough. It's the sustained, thoughtful engagement with culture that builds long-term brand loyalty and repairs past missteps.

Brand authenticity can't be crafted overnight or through a single campaign; it must be nurtured over time by showing up consistently and aligning brand values with actions. How is your brand showing up in the quiet moments, the everyday engagements, and the spaces where genuine cultural conversations are happening? What is the brand doing when nobody is paying attention? Those actions, with little recognition but full of intent for long-term impact, become the foundation for a brand that is truly aligned with its values. To get there, start by reflecting on where your brand is and where it has come from. Social responsibility starts with brands being willing to be accountable for the past, take action in the present, and plan for a more inclusive and equitable future.

Conduct a Brand Audit

Start by conducting an audit of your current approach to cultural strategy. Identify whether you are starting from zero or if you have already made strides in this domain. Delve into past campaigns, initiatives, and partnerships. What was the impact and did you see an ROI in terms of engagement, brand perception, and sales? Did your cultural marketing efforts resonate with the intended audience? Were your efforts culturally sensitive, socially responsible, and authentically inclusive? Be honest. Did you hear negative feedback or is there any way in which you might have missed the mark? Without question, the bottom line will always be part of your measurement toolkit. But embracing a more holistic approach that intertwines cultural relevance with business objectives will be a strategic imperative for long-term growth.

Grounding today's moves exclusively and only based on short-term commercial gains can rob the brand of the broader perspective needed for true innovation and a long-term vision. Pioneers of culturally disruptive marketing knew this long before cultural fluency became a mainstream conversation in the marketing and advertising industries. These brands didn't just jump onto fleeting trends; they tapped into deeper societal shifts, challenging prevailing narratives and sparking new dialogues. The long-term dividends are now paying off. Their campaigns weren't just about selling products but about reshaping perceptions and pushing boundaries. Is your brand living to its fullest potential?

Always Start from Within

In your brand audit, you would want to take a serious look at your internal team and their capabilities. Is there adequate representation and diversity on the teams? Do they possess the tools, training, and resources for effectively navigating the complexities of developing cultural strategy? Are there areas in which your team might benefit from the expertise of external consultants? To what extent might you need to lean on the cultural knowledge of people from the communities among your target audience?

Understanding where you currently stand isn't just about identifying gaps; it's about acknowledging the strengths you can build upon and the weaknesses you need to address. If your team is not aligned and empowered to execute your brand's innovative ambitions, invest in continued education.

Consider facilitating not only training with marketing consultants but also activists, community leaders, and artists. This gives you a solid foundation from which to craft a meaningful, impactful cultural strategy by expanding not only your team's marketing-specific skillset but also perspective, outlook, and cultural knowledge. You can think of the process I describe above in terms of the following specific steps that you can adopt to fit your brand's circumstances and particular needs.

EVALUATE BRAND PERCEPTION

Utilize surveys, focus groups, and social media analytics to discern how your brand is currently perceived by your target audience and the general public. Are there any misconceptions or negative perceptions that need to be addressed? Social listening tools are invaluable assets that you should take advantage of frequently. Marketers have a justifiable fear of facing backlash on social media, which can seem harsh and unforgiving. Rather than avoiding it, use real-time insights into consumer sentiment to your advantage. Leverage social listening to get real about where the brand is falling short and leverage it as a pathway toward growth.

IDENTIFY GAPS IN KNOWLEDGE OR PRACTICE

Get real with your marketing, insights, and strategy teams and understand your major areas of growth. Do you need more expert voices in the decision-making process? Is there a gap in your team's skillset that has been overlooked for too long? Cultivating a culture of honesty is the cornerstone of sustainable progress. They say knowledge is power—and, when wielded strategically, it actually is. Book a training program and repeat it every quarter until your teams are sufficiently empowered to fly on their own. Identify, too, any gaps in your current practices: Did the brand host an event to highlight a new inclusive campaign if it was not accessible to people using wheelchairs? Or perhaps, in a move toward gender inclusivity, your brand introduced a new size-inclusive line of products for women but did not make the language and messaging inclusive of non-binary individuals. Get honest about room for improvement.

GET HONEST ABOUT INTERNAL DYNAMICS

The culture within your company and on your team is directly implicated in the quality of your culture-driven outputs. It is challenging, if not impossible, to produce culturally fluent, socially responsible, and inclusive marketing outputs if the internal dynamics do not reflect values that make this work possible. Take time to conduct internal surveys and evaluations to understand how to maximize your team's superpowers. If you want to deliver conscious outputs and drive greater inclusivity outside of the organization, ensure that your own house is in order first.

Get Honest About the Brand's Past

Culturally fluent and inclusive brands that ultimately win don't shy away from their history. The advertising and marketing landscape is strewn with examples of brands that faced immense backlash because they failed to introspect and address problematic aspects of their history. Achieving cultural fluency requires diligent introspection not only into the present but also the past.

This process of deepening your brand's consciousness should not be limited only to marketing campaigns. A historical audit of your brand should aim to interrogate inclusivity, accessibility, and sustainability in every facet of your brand—from product development and UX design to cultural partnerships and event activations. By being transparent and acknowledging past track record, including any missteps, brands demonstrate growth, maturity, and, most of all, authenticity.

Sweeping any aspects of a brand's problematic past under the rug is not only disingenuous but also a strategic misstep. It doesn't pay off to avoid past harm as you are bound to repeat it. Once you are ready to conduct a historical brand audit and critically reflect on your past, consider the steps below.

BEGIN BY DIVING DEEP INTO YOUR BRAND'S ARCHIVES

Advertising Campaigns   In hindsight, were there any campaigns that seem insensitive or missing the nuance of a particular lived experience? What is the main learning for your brand today? Alternatively, are there ways in which your brand could have pushed the boundaries toward more innovation and cultural relevancy?

Product Lines   Has your brand ever produced or promoted products that may be considered exclusionary by today's standards? If so, has there been an acknowledgment, apology, or strategy to ensure such missteps aren't repeated in future campaigns and product launches? Alternatively, are there opportunities that, in hindsight, could help your brand champion inclusivity or drive conversations that resonate with the diverse needs and values of today's consumers?

Collaborations and Partnerships   Have there been instances in your brand's history where collaborations or partnerships were forged with entities or individuals whose values or actions might now seem questionable or controversial? In the same vein, it's crucial to contemplate missed opportunities: Were there collaborations that could have amplified marginalized voices or positively shifted societal conversations?

Sustainability   In a world increasingly alarmed by climate change and environmental degradation, your brand's approach to sustainability can't afford to be an afterthought. Have your sustainability claims been verifiable, or do they venture into the territory of "greenwashing"? What commitments has the brand made to sustainability in the past? To what extent have these been honored, if at all? Be honest.

CONSIDER THIS: ADDITIONAL AREAS TO INVESTIGATE

CSR initiatives: Corporate Social Responsibility activities, initiatives, and programs reflect a brand's values. Have there been past initiatives? Have past initiatives been genuinely impactful or were they more performative? How do these align with today's expectations of social responsibility?

Digital accessibility: This includes a brand's website, social media, mobile apps, and any other digital tools or platforms that customers interact with. How does the user experience and interface design of these platforms measure up against the current standards of inclusivity and accessibility? What improvements can be made?

Merchandising and retail strategies: For brands with a physical retail presence, how are products displayed? Are there enduring practices that could be seen as marginalizing certain groups or promoting stereotypes? For instance, in 2021, Sephora announced its plan to combat racial profiling and bias to improve the in-store experiences of Black customers (Bhattarai, 2021). How can your brand make the experience more inclusive for your customers? Are the brand's retail spaces accessible to people with disabilities or mobility concerns?

Reflect on the Evolution of Brand Associations

Consider the cultural context in which your brand has operated. Are there opportunities to refresh how your brand's positioning and messaging is expressed to drive greater cultural relevancy? Consider these areas below.

SOCIETAL CONTEXT

Establish the brand's starting point in culture. What are your brand's origins? During what eras did your brand flourish? On the other hand, when did your brand face challenges and uncertainties about its long-term future? Were there significant societal or cultural movements happening simultaneously? Did your brand contribute to, ignore, or challenge them? What has been your brand's historic role in either disrupting or contributing to the status quo? How has the category or the industry been implicated in societal exclusions?

For example, at an industry level, beauty brands have historically played a role in perpetuating narrow beauty standards that excluded diverse representations of beauty. Some have used light-skinned models in brand marketing, upholding colorism and racial prejudice.

CONSUMER ASSOCIATIONS

Evaluate the brand's engagement with historically excluded audiences. What meaning did consumers derive from your brand at different points in time? What about those groups that were historically excluded or overlooked within the category or by your brand? Were they neglected or celebrated? This requires more than just sales data or running numbers; understand the cultural context within which the brand engaged historically marginalized groups.

Consider carefully your brand's trajectory alongside the course of history and culture—how have the emotions, perceptions, and attitudes tied to your brand evolved along with cultural shifts in wider society? Drawing these parallels will help you identify crucial moments of alignment or misalignment between the past and the present.

A brand example of this would be the evolution of Barbie, a popular doll produced by Mattel. Initially, Barbie was meant to celebrate women. Throughout its history, however, it has faced criticism for perpetuating narrow beauty standards and gender stereotypes. Mattel recognized the need for change and responded to cultural evolution. Over time, the brand introduced dolls with various body types, ethnicities, and careers, aiming to be more inclusive and reflective of society's diversity. With a recent rebranding and the release of the Barbie movie, Barbie has been revived as a symbol of modern-day feminism.

CONTEMPORARY RELEVANCE

Consider how the brand's past shapes the lens through which the brand is viewed today, particularly in moments of public criticism. This is particularly relevant to the brands that have a history that might be associated with cultural appropriation. Are there opportunities to leverage your brand's unique historical context to gain a competitive advantage, or is there a need to distance the brand from certain historical aspects that no longer align with its values or the market landscape? What past harms, if any, have not been resolved by the brand in the present?

Consumer goods like Aunt Jemima and Uncle Ben's have undergone significant changes in their visual and verbal identities to address their historical use of racist stereotypes. While these changes came all too late, these brands were pressured to reject racist imagery and adapt to evolving societal norms. Of course, such imagery has always been unequivocally unacceptable, which is why brands need to engage in this kind of reflection proactively.

CONSIDER THIS: DON'T IGNORE THE PAST!

The cultural history of your brand can function not only as a retrospective analytical tool but also as a future-forward compass. Depending on the maturity and lifecycle of your brand, "history" could be as recent as 5–10 years ago. If your brand championed progressive narratives around female empowerment during the feminist discourse of the early 2010s, it sets a historical precedent for you to continue leaning into similar values today, albeit in updated and nuanced ways to match the evolving conversation on gender equality. Take Dove as an example: The brand has managed to evolve its efforts over time while staying true to its core mission, skillfully adapting to cultural shifts without losing sight of its foundational purpose.

However, if your brand faltered during a significant cultural movement—such as the protests against racial justice a few years ago—understanding the nature of that misstep can offer a roadmap for navigating similar challenges in the future. Rapid cultural evolution means that a brand's relevance can either be jeopardized or positively transformed in a relatively brief period. This underscores the ongoing need to evaluate, adjust, and pivot in response to the ever-changing cultural landscape of today's world.

Document and Create Reporting Processes

Consistently documenting and reporting on your brand's cultural insights, strategies, and cultural engagement outcomes creates a valuable historical record that can guide future decisions. By establishing a thorough and searchable database, you will enable your team to build upon prior knowledge. In dynamic and fast-paced organizations, where institutional memory can be short, such documentation serves as a brand's compass, ensuring its course remains steady and informed by its history. Consider these priority areas as you set out to establish a comprehensive documentation process to ensure that your efforts have a meaningful and sustainable impact:

Dedicate team resources: Assemble a dedicated team responsible for this historical audit and the introspection process. Consider establishing an ongoing process or task force responsible for ensuring proactive steps are continually taken to address past harms as necessary and to ensure follow-through on these initiatives.

Establish regular evaluation protocols: Gather all the findings, reflections, and insights into a comprehensive report. This document will serve as a point of reference and a resource for future planning, marketing, and PR strategies. By having a well-structured evaluation process in place, you'll be better equipped to track your brand's progress in addressing any outstanding issues and proactively engage in the necessary actions to respond to emergent shifts in culture.

Leverage data and analytics: Incorporate analytical tools to track the impact of your brand's initiatives over time. This can include social listening, sentiment analysis, and customer feedback to measure both tangible and intangible outcomes of your efforts over time. Data-driven insights will offer valuable feedback on how your adaptation strategies are resonating with the audiences. This data will help to inform future decisions and refine the approach to ensure maximum impact.

Other actions your brand might take include regularly convening community feedback through feedback circles, conducting focus groups, and engaging in stakeholder discussions. Collect feedback while documenting hesitations, excitements, and concerns expressed by participants. It's crucial to apply the same principles discussed in previous chapters: Ensure that the identities of those surveyed are diverse, honor ethical protections, and provide adequate compensation. Being comprehensive in the approach will allow the brand to gather valuable insights and perspectives to inform its cultural strategy more effectively, with less risk of getting it wrong.

CASE STUDY
Be Ready to Play the Long Game

Brands aiming for real transformation should take note: Meaningful change requires time and thoughtful implementation. Pinterest has taken a phased approach to increasing inclusivity in its search features, and its journey toward being a more inclusive platform serves as an instructive case study.

In 2018, the brand launched a skin tone filter to help users tailor beauty-related searches according to a variety of skin tones. In 2021, the platform added a hair pattern search, allowing users to specify searches based on six different hair types. Their latest addition, a body type technology, enhances the representation of diverse body types in women's fashion-related searches by fivefold. Initially focusing on wedding and women's fashion content, Pinterest plans to extend this technology in the future to other categories like men's fashion.

Change can't wait, and yet at the same time, time is of the essence. Time allows for testing and iteration, essential for any feature but even more so for those that touch on sensitive and highly personal aspects of identity. The point is, don't rush if it means you're otherwise going to make mistakes you'll regret.

Pinterest's example demonstrates how a brand can stay committed to inclusivity and care for its user base in a way that is integrated into its product development. Over time, Pinterest has evolved from a platform that primarily catered to a narrow idea of beauty and lifestyle to one that actively embraces the diverse experiences and needs of its users.

This kind of proactive initiative showcases a brand's ability to listen, learn, adapt, and deliver on the commitment to inclusivity, not in singular moments of "trends" but over the long haul. This reflects an understanding that more brand-driven businesses should emulate in tech and beyond: Inclusivity is not a one-size-fits-all endeavor. Different user groups have unique needs and preferences, and making a long-term commitment to change ensures that these nuances are addressed thoroughly and effectively over time.

Mapping Brand Purpose to Cultural Movements

Successful brands understand that they operate within a larger cultural framework, and those that recognize and adapt to evolving cultural shifts gain a competitive edge. This is not about chasing every trending topic but identifying the big-swing movements that align with your brand's core values and business objectives. By strategically positioning your brand within these relevant cultural conversations, you not only enhance its visibility and relevance but also forge deeper connections with your target audience.

ACTIVITY: ALIGNING CULTURAL OPPORTUNITIES WITH BRAND IDENTITY

To begin this exploration, start by considering broader questions about your brand's positioning in the marketplace. Reflect with intention on the inherent characteristics that make your brand unique, and the foundational values upon which it was built. These foundational reflections will act as the cornerstone for the ensuing steps. This exercise should be based on learnings from cultural research and analysis you have conducted based on the content in previous chapters.

Ensure you have a large sheet of paper or a whiteboard, along with a collection of colored pens or markers. Alternatively, use digital tools for convenience and documentation.

Place your brand's name prominently in the center of your chosen canvas. As thoughts flow, begin branching out to list your brand associations. Then, brainstorm cultural topics that might resonate or contrast with your brand's ethos. These could be abstract concepts that reflect broader cultural themes, such as community, belonging, or renewed desires for authenticity in culture or more specific social causes. You could also consider topics or issues of inclusivity where your brand or the category has fallen short in the past. How could you offer redress for past harms that continue to live on in the present?

Depending on where you are in your process, you could move to brainstorm at a more granular level. Do you see any connections to offerings and services that your brand already provides? What about narratives or psycho-social needs that the brand fulfills?

Take as an example a Starbucks ad that connected the issues of trans inclusivity to the everyday experience of coming to Starbucks and giving the barista a name for your order. The ad tells the story of a young trans teenager whose dad, teachers, and those he encounters continuously use the name that the teen no longer goes by. When the teen arrives at Starbucks, he has an opportunity to give the barista his actual name: "James," he says. There is an implicit emotional connection between a real painful issue for genderqueer, non-binary, and trans people and a point in the customer's journey at Starbucks.

Consider focusing on the benefits of the product or services that the brand offers. The case study of Pinterest mentioned above is a stellar example of how a brand can use its product to make a difference. Another best-in-class example is that of Rihanna's Fenty. Fenty disrupted the beauty industry by launching 50 foundation shades, later expanded to an even more diverse range, to offer an accurate match for a wide range of skin tones. This functional benefit—diverse shade options—filled a gap in the market, catering to consumers often overlooked by other brands. In doing so, Fenty not only met a practical need but also positioned itself as a leader in inclusivity. It exposed the inherent white supremacy that has dominated in the beauty market. The brand raised awareness of colorism and lack of inclusivity of people with darker skin tones, who for decades could not find a product that worked for them.

As you proceed with the exercise, be sure to list any emerging cultural codes that come to mind. This is where the Residual-Dominant-Emergent (RDE) framework, which we introduced earlier in the book, becomes useful. The depth of your exploration will depend on both your existing cultural knowledge and the extent of your brand's history. As you identify each cultural movement, delve into its nuances. Take into account both the emotional aspects and the tangible social issues affecting consumers. Reflect on specific colors, imagery, and slogans associated with the code as well as universally recognized symbols and icons that represent it. Also, consider the key figures or thought leaders driving these movements. Document these insights either through written notes or by adding relevant photographs, artwork, memes, or pictures. As you piece these elements together, you may discover obvious connections between these movements and your brand's core values, messaging, and visual identity.

Most critically, brainstorm actionable steps to translate these insights into potential strategies and activations. Organize these ideas into categories: The "wild card" options that are high-risk but potentially high-reward; the "safe bets" that align closely with your brand's existing ethos and have a higher likelihood of positive reception; and the "long-term investments" which may require more time and resources but offer an enduring impact.

Once completed, convene with your marketing, strategy, and cross-functional teams to discuss the insights unearthed, potential opportunities that emerge, and the challenges that might lie ahead. Use the reflection questions shared in this book to inspire a proactive discussion about your ambitions as you begin to build your inclusive marketing strategy.

This activity should just be the beginning, though. Cultural dynamics are in a constant state of evolution, necessitating ongoing monitoring and adaptation of strategies to remain not only relevant but also aligned with audiences and what they value. Use this as a way to get you started but don't stop here.

Seek Authentic Alignment

Authentic alignment in the context of a brand's relationship with cultural movements implies that the brand's engagement is organically tied to its core principles, values, and identity. It's not about cherry-picking what is popular or trending in the cultural spaces but more about finding cultural resonances that genuinely reflect and resonate with the brand's positioning.

Consider as an example the outdoor clothing company Patagonia. Patagonia's commitment to sustainability is reflected not just in their marketing but in their business practices, from sourcing materials to their stance on corporate responsibility and workplace conditions. This is an evident example of authentic alignment between a brand and the cultural ecosystem it aligns with.

Conversely, a forced fit occurs when a brand attaches itself to a cultural trend or movement without any organic or meaningful connection to its brand identity or values. The infamous campaign of a popular soft drink brand during the emergence of the Black Lives Matter movement is, perhaps, one of the most obvious examples. Campaigns that are obviously forced fit can be seen as opportunistic or inauthentic by consumers who are becoming increasingly savvy in scrutinizing brand authenticity. Forced fit can be easily identified by an inconsistency between the brand's identity, its past actions, and its messaging.

This is why evaluating the brand's past is so crucial—often, it might be more strategic to make a few smaller steps in the right direction than make a big splash out of nowhere. You can expect that jumping on the bandwagon is only going to invite increased scrutiny of the brand's past and has a high likelihood of being perceived as performative and exploitative.

The point here is, start with what you know—your brand. With a brand-first approach, you will avoid getting lost in the noise of everything that you could be doing. At least, at first. Over time, your team will develop an intuition for the kinds of campaigns, partnerships, and opportunities that are right for your brand but also push it in the right direction—toward genuine cultural innovation.

To identify and differentiate authentic alignment, brand leaders need to proactively and continuously reflect on the following questions:

Alignment with brand values: Does the cultural current under consideration align harmoniously with the core values that the brand upholds? Is it in line with the brand's personality and values?

Mission and vision connection: How does the brand's engagement with this cultural issue connect to the broader mission or vision of the brand? Does it contribute meaningfully to the larger purpose the brand aims to achieve?

Consistency with brand identity: Will the brand's involvement with this cultural issue resonate authentically with the audience's perception of who the brand is? Does it reinforce the image and identity that the audience already associates with the brand?

Audience relevance: Does the brand's engagement with this cultural issue address the needs, wants, desires, or challenges that the audience faces? Is it helping to solve emotional needs or practical problems for the audience?

Competitive landscape: What are the brand's competitors doing in relation to this cultural issue? Are there opportunities for the brand to differentiate itself and make a unique contribution? Where is the white space of opportunity for the brand?

Cultural sensitivity: Has the brand conducted thorough cultural research to ensure that its engagement is culturally sensitive and respectful? Is the brand ensuring it doesn't partake in cultural appropriation and is demonstrating cultural fluency in its approach?

CASE STUDY

Billie: The Rise of a Culturally Disruptive Brand

Consider a direct-to-consumer brand like Billie, which offers shave and body-care products. Founded in 2017, the brand positioned itself as a cultural disruptor of the "pink tax," which refers to the "gender-based price disparities" between products designed for "men" as opposed to "women" (Feingold, 2022; Shu, 2018). Billie ran culture-shaping campaigns to normalize showing female body hair in ads and media, among them the 2019 campaign that invited customers to participate in "Movember" by growing their facial hair instead of shaving it (Driver, 2019). Instead of focusing on their immediate business goal—selling more shaving products—Billie tapped into a deeper emotional register that resonated with female-identifying users. In its Instagram post on October 29, 2019, the brand boldly wrote:

> Newsflash: Women have mustaches too. So this month, we're outing our top secret lip hair for a good cause. Lend your perfectly good 'stache to our @movember team. We're matching 100% of contributions, up to $50,000.

In the campaign video published on Instagram alongside the above caption, a group of women announce that "women have mustaches, too" and are joining Movember. As the video announces without hesitation, "a stache is a stache." The campaign not only resonated but also communicated a sense of empowerment and collective defiance. And not only that—Billie matched 100 percent of contributions to support Movember, which is a global charity focused on raising awareness of *men's* health, such as prostate cancer, testicular cancer, and suicide among men.

The brand had to take risks, knowing it would face criticism. As part of its "Red, White, and You Do You" ad earlier that same year, Billie boldly posted pictures of models with over-grown hair in their bikini and armpit areas (Solé, 2019). This wasn't about being controversial for controversy's sake. Billie recognized a commercial opportunity in making a disruptive impact, identified a cultural narrative that was meaningful for their mission and the brand's target audience, and began to show up—with intention and consistency.

In the few years since then, Billie has emerged as a best-in-class example of a culturally fluent brand that not only understands the cultural conversation relevant to the brand but also shapes it. In 2023, Billie launched a board game, "Taking a jab at double standards affecting women with its cheekily designed, aptly named board game, 'No Worries If Not'" (Lobad, 2023). Retailing for $24.99, the game is a satirical take on obstacles that women have to go through within a sexist society, including the "Self-Doubt Spiral" and "Judgment Junction." In the statement, the brand explained that the "game is about 'The Game" women hate playing: Being forced to engage in people-pleasing, over-thinking, multitasking, over-apologizing," and other "real-life setbacks."

When I reached out to Georgina Gooley, the co-founder of Billie, she told me that "No Worries If Not" is intended to "point out the absurd and contradictory cycles of judgment women face in everyday life and hopefully helps women feel a bit more empowered to tune out external measures of their worth." But what does a razor have to do with challenging everyday misogyny? Everything, it turns out.

"Billie was created to be the antidote to an industry that has fueled many of the insecurities and harmful norms we feel compelled to subscribe to as women," Gooley explained. The brand's co-founders intimately understood the harmful narratives that negatively affected women's well-being and sense of self. "There's no shortage of messaging telling women how they should look, think, and behave," Gooley said, and Billie's purpose has always been to "champion womankind by taking aim at some of these pressures." "Instead of telling women what to do differently or change about themselves, we want to celebrate women showing up as they want to, for themselves," she clarified. Billie did what no other brand in its category was bold and visionary enough to do back then. They played the long game, and they succeeded.

How did they do it? Billie first set a new precedent among the competitors by focusing on a long-ignored issue within the category: Body hair. "We focused initially on normalizing body hair, putting women's body hair front and center in our work," Gooley noted. This was truly groundbreaking at the time. In its marketing, Billie has presented shaving as a choice, not an expectation—a radical departure from the norm. But the brand didn't stop there. "Over time, we expanded our product line-up and point of view," explained Gooley. This expansion was possible because Billie had invested in building a reputation with its audiences through a demonstrated commitment to fulfilling its purpose. "I think building credibility as a brand that authentically and unwaveringly lives up to its mission has allowed us to speak to the broader lived experience of womankind and the pressures we so often face," she told me. The results speak for themselves. Georgina Gooley co-founded Billie in 2017, and the brand celebrated its fifth anniversary in November 2022. Dubbed "The internet's favorite razor" brand, Billie was acquired by Edgewell Personal Care Company for $310 million in 2021 (Breen, 2023).

The brand's legacy? Culturally defining! Making body hair, something so inherently human that was shamed and stigmatized for decades, a new norm in media and, therefore, also in contemporary culture. Since Billie's launch, what was once unthinkable happened: Legacy brands began to show body hair. In an interview with *Entrepreneur*, Gooley added that this was "probably the biggest win for us— because even a small underdog brand can make a big impact and change a category that's a century old" (Breen, 2023). Billie's journey serves as a powerful reminder that bold, inclusive, and culturally conscious marketing can reshape industries and societal norms in ways that shift and improve the lived realities of real people.

With its strategic and visionary approach, Billie has now set the gold standard for how a brand can engage meaningfully with its audience while simultaneously challenging established cultural norms. The brand's authentic, impactful evolution in the marketplace is a testament to what having a vision and sticking to your values can achieve. This success laid the groundwork for the brand to expand into new cultural issues that go beyond body hair.

I ask you to consider this brand example for two reasons. For one, this case study highlights how a brand's authentic alignment with culture can naturally evolve. It can start with the product (in this case, a shaving razor) and, with credibility and earned cultural relevance and user trust, evolve into something more expansive and impactful. Billie began the conversation about body hair but has now earned its rightful place as a brand leader within cultural conversations about women's experiences more broadly.

This also showcases the potential for culture-shaping marketing to propel daring brands to the forefront of cultural innovation. Since Billie launched in 2017, other brands have followed their lead. Subsequently, legacy brands and brands like EOS (Evolution of Smooth) started showing women's body hair in their ads. The brand even tackled toxic gender norms around masculinity with its first men's shaving line in its "Unmanhandle Your Face" campaign (Nelson, 2023). Billie's impact has indeed been far-reaching—both in culture and commerce.

The lesson for marketers here is not to rush into things that will only backfire. Invest in cultural intelligence now. Take time to get to know the lived realities, challenges, and concerns that affect audiences relevant to your brand. Unpack cultural realities that shape people's lives far beyond the aisle where your product sits. Develop your brand's point of view on these lived realities in a way that is aligned with the brand's purpose. Then, do something meaningful about them.

Take inspiration from a brand like Billie. Over the years, Billie's interventions in culture ranged from something as simple as speaking to everyday rituals like shaving to commenting on more complex experiences of gender oppression that women face throughout their lives. Perhaps the most important lesson to take from Billie's leadership is this: Know what your brand will—or will not—stand for. Then, stick to it and let this knowing infuse how your brand moves in culture with clarity and a genuine commitment to incite social change.

How to Activate Cultural Territories

Use the Audit of the Brand's Past and Present to Define Areas of Meaningful Impact

Risk mitigation is crucial. But overcaution can lead to complacency and missed opportunities. Use your historical audit to pivot your strategy. Identify those areas where your brand has remained dormant, complacent, or actively harmful in the past and look for ways to lean into addressing these areas. Rather than writing these off as areas to avoid, consider them as territories ripe for redress and meaningful action.

If your brand once excluded, misrepresented, or stereotyped a particular historically marginalized group in its advertising, now might be the time to engage with that community genuinely. Remember that it's not only about rectifying past wrongs; it's about creating a sustainable and inclusive future. In identifying the zones where the brand was previously complacent or even damaging, it opens up new possibility for meaningful impact and redress. Within this new possibility, your brand can stand as a supporter, not an adversary.

Decide Where to Play in Culture and the Impact You Want to Make

Drawing on the content of previous chapters and the brainstorming activities above, work to align your brand with cultural topics or issues that complement its purpose and positioning. Identify areas where your brand's core values and expertise resonate naturally with cultural movements and consumer needs.

Be sure to look beyond the transient viral moments and short-lived trends. As my colleague Matt Klein (2023) notes, trends have lost their meaning as "we've come to confuse what is 'trending' with what is a trend." Look beyond the transient viral moments and short-lived fads on social media. Instead, look to align with broader cultural currents that possess real depth and staying power to actually influence people's behavior in the long run. Fleeting trends might offer a quick boost in visibility but deep-rooted emergent cultural movements are what will offer sustained commercial advantage and meaningful impact in society and culture.

Choosing how you want to play in culture requires more than just claiming a cultural territory; it asks brands to make conscientious investment in the area of culture that they engage with. Establish early on what you're willing to commit to. If you take a stand on an issue, be prepared to back it up with action. This could mean committing funds to a cause, partnering and sponsoring a cultural advisory, involving your consumer base in a larger cultural campaign, or producing a product or a service that solves an existing need among consumers or in the broader culture.

It's equally important to delineate what you won't stand for. Establish red lines that your brand will not cross, informed by your historical audit, brand values, and consumer feedback. Creating an ethical framework within which it operates is critical to building an inclusive strategy. If your audit revealed a past partnership with an organization or a person that contradicts your brand's core values, create and honor the ethical boundaries you will no longer cross. Similarly, if you anticipate some criticism for your engagement with issues pertaining to historically excluded groups, choose to stand by your beliefs as a brand.

This is not a "check the box and move on" scenario. Continue evolving and refining how your brand engages in culturally relevant spaces related to inclusivity. Employ the toolkit of cultural intelligence, drawing on cultural analysis, semiotics, and the decoding of emergent cultural codes. These specialized tools need to be integrated alongside your standard methodologies, from social listening to market analysis. While cultural intelligence is not a mere add-on, it needs to effectively augment existing marketing frameworks.

All too frequently, inclusion, equity, and diversity are treated as peripheral processes in marketing. If the brief doesn't call for it, they are often sidelined or altogether ignored as irrelevant. To build an inclusive marketing strategy, cultural and consumer insights related to issues of equity, inclusivity, and justice can't be compartmentalized and siloed into a separate process. They must be threaded through market and consumer research, strategic goal setting, and planning. If you are a marketing leader spearheading a team, be sure to not only make this integration a priority but also instill and model a cultural intelligence mindset throughout your team's approach to marketing.

Conduct an Impact Forecast and Strategize Ahead!

Cultural intelligence requires a new level of precision, knowledge, and sensitivity to cultural issues, but it doesn't render tried-and-true methods obsolete. Use the S.W.O.T. analysis in conjunction with reception theory to anticipate potential outcomes of cultural alignment. This essentially anticipates how your audience will interpret and respond to your messaging. Reception theory digs into the semiotics and interpretive potential of your brand actions—how they could be read in different ways by different cultural groups. This dual approach allows you to prepare not just for market risks but for cultural receptions that could swing in various directions.

In the S.W.O.T. analysis, internal strengths could refer to the capabilities and resources your brand can use to leverage relevant cultural movements and create cultural impact. Weaknesses could identify areas where your brand might fall short or face criticism. Opportunities might include potential market expansion, increased brand awareness or loyalty with existing customers, and reputation enhancement. Threats could involve anticipated customer responses or any potential misalignment with the brand's identity.

An impact forecast will give you a comprehensive view of likely scenarios. Prepare for the unpredictable. Cultural dynamics are ever-changing, and consumer responses can be varied. Knowing what you will stand for, then, becomes not just part of brand purpose and values but a guiding principle for developing agility in the dynamic cultural marketplace of competing ideologies. Embracing a forward-thinking approach to cultural intelligence in your marketing strategies is as essential for anticipating cultural alignments and potential outcomes as for nurturing adaptability in this ever-changing landscape.

Know What You Are Willing to Stand For

We can cover a variety of techniques and approaches. At the end of the day, though, conviction is what will break or make the long-term potential of an inclusive marketing strategy. When brands know exactly what they stand for, they can go from passively reacting to culture to shaping cultural media. That is the difference between culture-shaping brands and those that struggle to keep up with the cultural rides.

This is particularly pertinent in a world where profit often appears at odds with equity and justice. But fundamentally rethinking what a brand can do in culture pushes against the status quo. This aligns with what we discussed in Chapter 4, where we explored the core tenets of cultural fluency: Subversive storytelling, power-shifting impact, and inclusive innovation.

True conviction means brands need to be willing to disrupt the status quo in order to advance a more inclusive future in which historically marginalized groups are extended the same consideration and dignity. Backlash is often the cost of standing for something significant. The risk of inaction and neutrality—or worse, silent complicity in harm—is far greater.

Revisiting the premise we initially set forward early in this book underscores this point. As producers of media, brands have immense power and tangible influence over culture and society. Choosing inaction out of fear— which is precisely what advertisers did in the 1960s and onwards—is an evasion of social responsibility that advocates of inclusive marketing and researchers wrote about over 50 years ago.

Building an inclusive marketing strategy is for those brands that are ready to commit. Brands that are unwilling or unable to deliver on the commitments to equity and inclusivity they purport to hold are better off stepping back. In today's climate, too many leaders are oblivious to how obvious performative inclusivity is to audiences.

Since the uprising for racial justice in 2020, scrutiny and skepticism have only intensified: Over time, more people realized that brands made promises to change in their respective industries that they did not intend to keep. According to a McKinsey report released in December 2020, between June 2020 and May 2021, over 1,100 organizations collectively pledged

$200 billion toward initiatives focused on racial justice (Fitzhugh et al., 2020). A group of reporters from the *Washington Post* released information concerning financial commitments related to racial justice that were made by 44 of the largest publicly traded companies in the United States in the aftermath of Floyd's killing. These corporations, in total, committed nearly $50 billion (Jan, 2021). Few people know that, according to the *Washington Post*, more than 90 percent of that amount—$45.2 billion—came from financial institutions and "is allocated as loans or investments they could stand to profit from, more than half in the form of mortgages."

At the time of the report, 37 out of the 50 largest companies had distributed just $1.7 billion of the nearly $50 billion they had promised (Harper, 2022). As *Forbes* contributor Shaun Harper notes, companies benefited, at the very least in terms of reputation, and in some cases financially, by publicly declaring their intentions to address the larger structural and systemic issues that were responsible for the police killings of George Floyd and countless other Black Americans. With minimal tangible results to substantiate these promises, an increasing number of individuals are refusing to stay silent on this matter. More than ever, brands that have a sense of conviction and are genuinely committed to enacting change will be the ones able to build trust and credibility in a society that is demanding concrete actions to address racial and social injustice and other systemic inequities.

True conviction necessitates that brands are prepared to risk alienating a small, hateful minority of people holding on to the status quo in order to authentically connect with and resonate with the broader society. It's a conscious choice to stand firmly by the principles of inclusivity, justice, and equity, even in the face of hate.

Conscious marketing is precisely about making deliberate choices that prioritize the inclusion of everyone in society over short-term gains acquired at the expense of those who have historically been excluded, sidelined, and marginalized. Much like advertisers in the 1960s who were confronted with the call for social responsibility, we are faced with a decision today that is entirely ours to make.

A Note From The Author

For her generous insight, I express my profound gratitude to Georgina Gooley, the co-founder of Billie, as well as Catherine Wolpe, the SVP of Brand Marketing at Billie, the rest of Billie's team, and my colleague and cultural strategist Amy Daroukakis, for making the interview in this chapter possible.

In Conversation with Lola Bakare

Lola Bakare is an Anthem Award-winning inclusive marketing strategist, creator of the #responsiblemarketing movement, advisory board member at Sparks & Honey, and founder of be/co, a boutique consultancy that empowers brands and marketing leaders with strategic guidance, coaching, training, and workshops that unleash new levels of success. She was recently named one of Adweek's 2023 Creative 100 *and is a* LinkedIn Top Voice *and* Forbes CMO Network *contributor. Her writing and commentary can be found in major publications, including* Adweek, Harvard Business Review, Marketing Brew, *and* Business Insider, *where she is recognized as one of 13 Top Consultants and Experts helping advertisers with diversity. Lola's first book,* Responsible Marketing: How to Create an Authentic and Inclusive Marketing Strategy, *is in the works with Kogan Page.*

AKG: Lola, in your work, you specifically discuss responsible marketing, which is also the title of your upcoming book. Why should marketers approach inclusivity and social good in marketing from a perspective of responsibility?

LB: I'm passionate about marketers thinking about inclusivity and social good through the lens of responsibility because no other professional function has as much power to shape how people understand and experience the world! At its essence, responsibility is all about the consideration of context.

Responsible marketers consider the context of their work's impact on society to elevate their brand's reputation with the ultimate goal of sustainably maximizing commercial impact on the business they serve. I call this the triple top line flywheel effect. Being a responsible steward of a brand means setting that brand up for long-term success. This can't be done without being accountable to the relevant ways a brand can address the systemic inequities and urgent global challenges that shape how consumers live their lives.

AKG: As a CMO advisor, you surely find yourself in discussions with marketing executives who are eager to get started with increasing their brand's cultural footprint. What are some common challenges that marketing leaders often encounter when embarking on this journey?

LB: How marketers think about risk is the number one mindset shift needed to boldly practice responsible marketing. Far too often, I hear executives mull over the risk of upsetting the status quo, when the bigger risk is contributing to the moral injuries historically excluded consumers are already suffering.

Shouldn't we be more concerned with the risk of missing opportunities to unlock growth by improving lives? When I pose that question to marketers, there's always an "aha" moment. So much opportunity opens up when the risk of inaction becomes the primary concern.

AKG: As a marketing leader, how can one start? What steps do you recommend marketers take to enhance the responsibility of their strategic approach?

LB: I advise marketers to consider three questions to unlock the power of responsible marketing:

- What are your brand's societal debts? Past or present, in what ways has your brand, category, or industry contributed to societal harm?

- What functional benefits and emotional promises can align to meaningfully address relevant societal debts? These are your impact insights.

- How can addressing an impact insight deliver incremental commercial success?

I also advise marketers to focus on four key "responsible marketing moves" when implementing or evaluating their plans. If the work solves real problems, tells real stories, creates real opportunities, or influences real policies in meaningful and measurable ways that deliver long-term societal and commercial impact, you know you're achieving the ultimate goal of every responsible marketer—transcending the performative.

8

What's Next? The Future of Culturally Intelligent Marketing

WHAT TO EXPECT

We began this book by looking back. By this point, we have considered the ins and outs of conducting an audit of a brand's past and the nuances of aligning your brand with cultural movements in the present. Now, it's time to come full circle and consider the future. What lies ahead for cultural fluency in marketing? How can marketers think about the future through the lens of equity, inclusivity, and sustainability? And what values must brands adopt to build a legacy that endures into the future?

We're at a cultural inflection point. Our industry needs to ask such questions more intentionally. The landscape is evolving; those who integrate cultural intelligence into their future strategy will be best positioned to navigate—and thrive—in this uncharted territory. Brands of the future will harness cultural navigation to unlock white spaces of opportunity. This starts with asking tough questions about what kind of future we want to live in. Then, we must ask what we must tackle and resolve to get us there.

In this chapter, we will explore the following questions:

- How can brands maintain integrity in the face of a fast-accelerating future?

- How can brands assess their position within the evolving cultural landscape?

- What role does imagination play in enhancing cultural fluency?
- What does adopting possibility as a paradigm mean, and how do you apply it?
- How can tools of strategic foresight aid marketers in future-proofing brand strategy?
- What actionable steps can brands take to actualize their envisioned future?

Maintaining Brand Integrity Amidst Cultural Change

What lies ahead for culturally inclusive marketing? If there's one takeaway or throughline that stretches across preceding chapters that I hope resonates with you, it's this: The role of power and ideology will be the force that will define the future of sustainable, inclusive brands. In other words, the future of inclusivity in marketing will depend on the willingness of modern-day marketers to wrestle with questions of power, representation, equity, and ideology in marketing. As marketers and brand builders, we have choices to make. Settling for superficial representation is off the table for those of us who believe in the power of brands to positively influence society through the responsible, socially conscious use of media and technology.

Looking forward into the future, something significant will distinguish brands that have the edge to move culture toward more meaningful and transformative outcomes. It's their strategic intent. Culturally intelligent marketing is not merely about how these brands appear in culture or what they offer; it's what determines how brands move, how they resonate within the cultural zeitgeist, and how brands give back to society and the communities with which they engage. Brands that want to successfully show up at the intersection of culture and commerce will need to master two things: Conviction and intentionality.

Intention and Conviction: A Winning Strategy for Cultural Relevance

Intentionality is the difference between success and eventual irrelevance. Especially when it comes to culture, marketers need to make strategic choices at every turn. Being "intentional" with regard to cultural and social has to become an ongoing commitment for brands. Inclusive marketers need to continually ask "why"—why this campaign, why this messaging, why this target audience, and why this cultural issue for this brand—to ensure that every idea, action, and eventual go-to-market strategy is aligned with the brand's values and the overall positioning.

Being fickle doesn't cut it anymore. Too many brands bow under pressure when trying to be socially progressive and culturally relevant. When brands cave in to appease a vocal minority amplified by social media and clickbait content, the brand's identity in culture becomes unclear. Brands appear incoherent when they waver on messaging and fail to take a clear stance. A brand can't build relevance in today's culture by being all things to all people, diluting its cultural messaging and confusing audiences. That is not a sustainable path to inclusive marketing, let alone a solid business strategy. This is a shortcut to becoming obsolete. Brands that will secure the future will learn how to stand for something.

Upholding a brand's intentions through demonstrated conviction sets enduring brands apart. This is evident across sectors in how brands leverage cultural intelligence in their influence to shape social and cultural conversations. As an example, with its 2017 "The President Stole Your Land," Patagonia extended its environmental efforts to educate the public about the decision to reduce the size of two national monuments in Utah. That same year, Airbnb came out with their now-iconic #WeAccept campaign in response to the U.S. travel ban affecting Muslim-majority countries. The brand said it "must stand with those who are affected" and offered free housing to refugees (Gallagher, 2017). And similarly, when in 2018, Colin Kaepernick knelt during the U.S. national anthem as a form of protest against racial injustice, Nike decided to support him. The brand boldly featured Kaepernick in their "Just Do It" 30th anniversary campaign.

Years later, amidst the Black Lives Matter protests in 2020, Ben & Jerry's openly supported the movement and was one of the first brands to use and normalize the term "white supremacy" in its brand communications. Another example is Heineken's "Worlds Apart" social experiment-turned-TV commercial. The brand paired two people with opposing political viewpoints and offered them an opportunity to stay and converse with a Heineken bottle in hand. All of these strategies positioned the product in a way that made sense for the brand or positioned the brand as the "hero" in relation to a particular cultural topic. Their actions weren't just reactive or temporary; they were methodically chosen for lasting impact.

This isn't to say that these brands or campaigns are perfect. These brands aren't beyond scrutiny—far from it. From questions about their supply chain ethics to concerns about their impact on local cultures and sustainability, there's room for critical engagement. For this reason, I advocate for critical engagement as an ongoing element of cultural intelligence.

Today's more inclusive brands aren't and shouldn't be beyond reproach. We can like what a brand does, and we also need to continue to push all businesses to be and do better. Multiple truths can co-exist. The point is, you don't even have to like any of the campaigns I mentioned as examples to recognize that these are the players that are determining the future. Brands like Nike, Patagonia, and Ben & Jerry's set the standard for inclusive marketing in one crucial aspect: Compared to other brands, they have taken a stand and remained committed to it. Enduring brands recognize that avoiding socially charged topics when speaking up works for the brand, and the product is a lost opportunity to innovate against culture. It's not how true innovators think.

Get this right, and you can position your strategy for meaningful impact and long-term success. Maintaining brand integrity and consistency becomes your most valuable asset in future-proofing the brand against cultural volatility. It's your North Star in navigating the complexities of the rapidly evolving cultural landscape. And in the long run, it's this brand integrity and consistency that will separate the contenders from the pretenders.

The Ideology-Representation Nexus: A Matrix for Brand Integrity

The marketplace, of course, is filled with examples of brands trying to get it right. Earlier in the book, we went over several examples of brands that perpetuated stereotypes and harmful tropes but have been forced, through cultural evolution, to shift their strategy. What makes some brands get ahead of others? To truly ask and wrestle with "what's next," we must carefully understand this present-day context: How can we distinguish brands through the lens of cultural fluency? Such a snapshot of the current landscape of brands in culture isn't just a commentary on what individual brands are or aren't doing well. It's a mirror of the cultural ecosystem within which brands operate, a reflection of society's values, norms, and ideologies that shape marketing practices today.

Let's work on refining a more concrete way to understand the nuances of brand integrity. Consider Figure 8.1, in which I share with you one approach

FIGURE 8.1 The Ideology-Representation Matrix

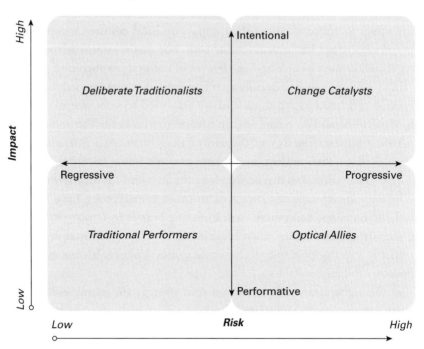

An original framework by Dr. Anastasia Kārkliņa Gabriel.

to understanding what kind of brand you are working on—or aiming to create—in today's cultural landscape. Don't treat this merely as a theoretical tool, though. Theoretical tools become powerful frameworks precisely when we are able to translate them into actionable directives. Take time to think about it as a framework that can help guide your strategy toward the quadrant in this matrix that aligns with ethical imperatives that you aim to embody in your brand or your practice of working with brands.

The Ideology-Representation Nexus presented here is a 2x2 matrix designed to map ideology against representation. As extensively covered in previous chapters, marketers must confront critical questions: a) What ideologies is the brand either reproducing or endorsing through its strategic messaging? b) How are these ideologies communicated to audiences via representation across various brand communications? c) Is it intentional or performative? d) How are inclusive brands negotiating impact and accountability? Let's take a moment to look at other attributes in this matrix more closely.

PERFORMATIVE VS. INTENTIONAL BRANDS

The horizontal axis here represents ideology, extending from regressive on one end to progressive on the other. This spectrum allows us to assess a brand's underlying belief system and how it aligns with cultural values at that point in time. A regressive ideology tends to uphold or revert to traditional stereotypes and cultural norms, potentially perpetuating systemic inequities. For example, this could translate into practice as a brand leveraging gender-normative narratives in its advertising, thereby reinforcing outdated and harmful societal beliefs. Conversely, a progressive ideology aims to disrupt these norms, advocating for inclusivity, social justice, and equitable representation and belonging not only in marketing but in culture at large. Progressive brands might use their platforms to challenge harmful stereotypes and spotlight underrepresented stories.

Then, the vertical axis refers to representation, ranging from performative to intentional. Distinguished along this axis are brands that engage in surface-level diversity efforts—think tokenized casting or performative social media posts during Pride month—and brands that intentionally invest in cultural strategy. These brands don't just hire a diverse cast for a single ad campaign but institutionalize diversity, equity, and inclusion throughout all layers of the organization. Their marketing strategies translate into tangible social impact. Intentional brands embed cultural intelligence into their brand DNA. They craft strategies that resonate with diverse audiences by taking time to understand and reflect genuine lived experiences and values. Intentional brands invest in research and dialogue with the communities they seek to represent, adapting their messaging to be both culturally sensitive and meaningfully impactful.

In contrast, performative brands opt for checkbox diversity, ticking off superficial requirements. They are driven more by market trends and social pressures than by an authentic commitment to social change that translates into a cultural vision that complements brand positioning. The question here is: Is the brand leveraging culture as a commodity exclusively for profit, or is it also contributing to culture as a co-creator of social change? The answer reveals not only the brand's standing in the ideology-representation matrix, but also its potential to make meaningful impact in the cultural marketplace at large.

Change catalysts: Brands in this quadrant are not only progressive in their approach to inclusivity but are also intentional in their actions. They deploy advanced cultural intelligence, leveraging emergent cultural codes to be at the cutting edge. Their marketing is backed by substantive action—think social impact programs, community co-creation, and a genuine commitment to inclusivity that transcends just checking boxes. Change catalysts are brands that do the heavy lifting in shifting paradigms, setting trends rather than just following them.

Optical allies: Brands in this category appear inclusive but lack tangible commitment. They are progressive in rhetoric but performative in practice. While they may adopt the latest buzzwords in diversity, equity, and inclusion, their efforts rarely translate into meaningful action. They're adept at social media campaigns celebrating diversity but don't go beyond marketing efforts nor give back to communities they engage and market to.

Traditional performers: At their core, these brands tap into regressive cultural codes but try to make it appear as if they're still part of the cultural conversation. These brands try to keep up by rolling out an ad campaign featuring a diverse cast but fail to address the deeper systemic issues their industry may perpetuate. A superficial commitment to inclusivity serves more as a smokescreen to deflect criticism than a step toward meaningful change. In the end, traditional performers do more to maintain the status quo than challenge it.

Deliberate traditionalists: Brands in this quadrant are both regressive and intentional. They often cater to a niche audience that shares their more traditional or conservative views and are unapologetic about it. Unlike traditional performers, these brands don't even make a pretense of inclusivity.

Assessing Brand Impact and Risk

Along the matrix, you'll notice two arrows indicating perceived risk and cultural impact, which function as supplementary variables to consider. The arrow labeled "risk" extends from the lower left quadrant, where both ideology and representation are at their most regressive and performative, toward the upper right quadrant, where both are progressive and intentional. The higher you move along this axis, the greater the perceived risk—but also, the greater the potential impact and, thus, the reward.

Engaging in intentional, progressive branding may initially feel like a risky move, given the uncertainty of uncharted territory. However, the payoffs in terms of brand loyalty, consumer engagement, and cultural impact can be significant.

Plus, what's advantageous about this framework is its incremental approach to change. You don't have to make big swings overnight. In fact, that surely is a failing approach to cultural intelligence that requires deep critical reflection. So, what might it mean for your brand to nudge an inch to the right on the ideology axis or inch upward on the representation axis?

Moving an inch to the right, toward a more progressive brand ideology, could be as simple as re-evaluating the imagery in your advertising to ensure it doesn't perpetuate harmful stereotypes. It could mean revising your brand language to be more inclusive, or perhaps supporting a social justice cause relevant to your industry or target audience. It might also mean thinking about your partnerships—what voices, organizations, and communities can your brand start amplifying?

Inching upward toward more intentional representation could involve deeper engagement with your audience or stakeholders. Maybe it starts with investing in user-generated content that showcases more real and genuine perspectives. It could mean auditing your current brand storytelling to evaluate whether it might still be upholding unrealistic standards of beauty or storytelling that does not include the most marginalized people of society. As an example, it might be obvious to point out how a brand in the beauty space doesn't include products for people with darker skin tones or how a clothing brand doesn't accommodate plus-size options.

However, subtler challenges in representation often go unnoticed, especially when they're deeply ingrained in a brand's messaging. Imagine, for instance, a global financial brand that consistently fails to feature dark-skinned individuals in depictions of luxury or financial success, relegating Black models exclusively to middle-class narratives. This may not be overtly performative, but it perpetuates a limited, and limiting, cultural story. Subtle biases in representation still contribute to systemic inequities and require marketers to be vigilant in scrutinizing brand communications to address them effectively.

Depth and Breadth

Think about ideology as the breadth of the brand's inclusivity, and representation as its depth. Ideology as breadth encompasses how widely a brand casts its net—how many different communities, identities, and perspectives it considers. Are you only including the most "convenient" audience to engage with, while leaving other matters of inclusivity behind? Or is the brand genuinely trying to expand its worldview to be inclusive of a broad spectrum of identities—racial, cultural, gender, ability, and so on? Each step you take as a marketer should work toward widening this breadth as your brand moves further along the progressive axis.

On the other hand, representation as depth delves into the quality, rigor, and nuance of how audiences and issues are engaged and represented. Is the brand scratching the surface with tokenistic gestures, or is it investing time, resources, and effort into deepening its approach to representing and engaging with relevant cultural communities?

Depth requires more than just visibility; it demands rigor in research, training, and execution, as well as the co-creation of narratives with the communities involved. Elevating the depth of representation and engagement away from superficial and performative moves the brand upward on the intentional axis.

Navigating this ideology/representation matrix is about expanding the breadth of your efforts in cultural fluency while deepening the substance and the actual impact of your engagement with audiences. This two-dimensional approach—considering the breadth and depths of marketing practices—is what allows inclusive brands to create culturally intelligent strategies with both rigor and impact.

The Only Constant is Change

The matrix is a tool for assessing a brand's current approach to cultural intelligence, social good, and inclusivity, but it's not to suggest that a brand's position with regard to ideology or intentionality is static. Brands can and do move between these categories as they change their strategies and adapt to new realities. These positions are not permanent labels but rather points in a cultural matrix that is constantly shifting and evolving.

For brand strategists who recognize this, the matrix becomes a useful asset. By carefully considering their own relationship to ideology and accountability, brands can make deliberate, strategic decisions that cater to both immediate market needs and wider cultural and social demands. The only constant is change, and brands that both recognize and act on this principle are better positioned to successfully navigate the fluctuating landscape of cultural values.

Cultural Innovation for Commercial Success and Social Impact

For transformation to occur within the industry, rigor, precision, commitment, and impact are imperative. Bringing into being inclusive, sustainable futures demands of us both ingenuity and innovation. That's why innovation is core to cultural intelligence, along with cultural insight and strategy.

What is innovation if not an act of imagining toward the future? Innovation is essentially an imagination of alternative possibilities, solidified into actionable solutions, strategies, or new inventions. Not merely an extension of what already exists, innovation is a kind of break from what is. It is an exercise in creative reimagining of how things could be—better, more efficient and productive, and more sustainable and equitable, for all.

In marketing, we rarely, if ever, talk about the significance of our imaginative capacity to imagine otherwise. Imagination is, perhaps, perceived as too abstract, too removed from the hard metrics that often dictate success in this industry. Imagination is obviously tied to creativity, which underlies brand outputs that take the form of messaging, copy, commercials and advertisements, and marketing campaigns. Imagination is creativity's life force. But imagination has an equal place in strategy, particularly when building an *inclusive* strategy.

Possibility as a Paradigm: A Mindset Shift for Brand Evolution

We only have to look back at the history of inclusivity (or lack thereof!) in advertising and marketing, with which we started this book. What stands out is precisely a crisis of imagination. Marketers and advertisers of the past were too intimidated by the realities of social progress through which they were living. In the 1960s, the demands for inclusive representation seemed too outlandish. In some ways, the case for inclusivity in marketing is still, if not dismissed, then seen as a threat, rather than an opportunity. An opportunity for innovation; for something that might open a new way for business to function and thrive in an increasingly diverse and interconnected world.

The point is this: If we are committed to actualizing a socially conscious future for marketing, we can't underestimate the power of imagination. The challenge, first and foremost, is to recalibrate our imagination of business toward not just what is profitable but what is equitable and sustainable. Then, designing inclusive futures means translating our visions of what could be into actionable steps that businesses can take to bring those futures closer to the present.

But imagination is not a soft skill relegated to the creative department; it's a critical skill for any conscious marketer working toward a better future for business and society. Let's think of it here as "critical imagination," which was the subject of my doctoral dissertation. Critical imagination is a combination of the transformative power of imagination and the discerning, analytical qualities of critical thinking. Critical thinking within the idea of "critical imagination" empowers us not to fantasize aimlessly but to scrutinize existing paradigms precisely in order to envision alternatives. At its core, this is actually what the work of social change and cultural transformation is all about: Recognizing what's not working and daring to imagine boldly what an alternative to the status quo looks like. Then, it means relentlessly pursuing that vision, translating our imagination of the future we want into concrete action that we can follow.

This has *everything* to do with business. If we consider the power and influence that brand-driven businesses have in culture, critical imagination becomes not only an option but a responsibility. We can choose to shift outdated paradigms. We can decide to step into a paradigm shift that helps us recognize the power we have to co-create futures—along with others— that don't only serve the capital but contribute to the betterment of the society that we inhabit.

In the world of marketing, where the search for "the next big thing" often overshadows the need for ethical considerations, critical imagination serves as a compass. It can keep us aligned and oriented toward values that matter, helping to steer marketing practices toward outcomes that elevate not just their market position but also their societal impact.

Dwell in the power of possibility. It's a necessary place to be. This is where marketers don't just observe or react; we have an option to influence, direct, and co-create. In this space of "what could be," you can discover an expansive way of thinking, a mindset free of fear-based limitations and ripe for innovation.

Unlocking Strategic Foresight: Preferred Futures

Thoughtful innovation requires foresight, and foresight is a powerful tool of critical imagination. The objective of foresight is never to predict the future, for that is impossible; it is, however, an effective tool for opening up our thinking to a range of possibilities of what the future might hold. Above all, foresight is about developing agility. Whether you're examining emerging

FIGURE 8.2 Triple-C: Culture, Consumer, Company

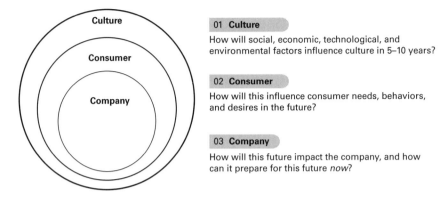

01 **Culture**
How will social, economic, technological, and environmental factors influence culture in 5–10 years?

02 **Consumer**
How will this influence consumer needs, behaviors, and desires in the future?

03 **Company**
How will this future impact the company, and how can it prepare for this future *now*?

Designed by Dr. Anastasia Kārkliņa Gabriel.

technologies or tracking signals in changing public opinions, foresight enables the preparation and adaptability that modern marketing demands. It starts with tracing signals in culture, visualizing scenarios, and working backward to prepare for different scenarios.

Take a moment to consider Figure 8.2. It presents a layered perspective on the future, using concentric circles. The outermost circle represents the macro-cultural landscape, enveloping everything else. Nestled within it is another circle, signifying consumer culture or consumer behavior patterns. Finally, at the core, you'll find the company circle, referencing the brand. This model illustrates how a brand isn't just operating in a vacuum but is deeply interconnected with broader cultural shifts and consumer behaviors. It underscores the imperative for businesses to be responsive to ongoing changes in culture, society, and policy.

This starts by noticing and keeping track of signals. Signals are what futurists call early indicators or precursors to more significant trends or changes that could, over time, substantially change the realities within which the brand operates. Signals can be as trivial as a viral tweet that sparks a sociocultural debate or as significant as a new government policy affecting import tariffs. Signals are easy to ignore as a one-off event, but potentially indicative of an emerging pattern that could lead to a paradigm shift in consumer behavior, cultural movements, technology, or policy. But it's not the size of a signal that matters but the potential impact that it reveals. It's in tracking and decoding these signals and understanding the drivers that push change in this direction that brands can strategically prepare for, or even create, their preferred future.

CONSIDER THIS: SCENARIO PLANNING

You can use the framework above to track and identify trends within culture with an eye toward inclusive marketing. It might be useful to create a practice of tracking signals as you encounter them. Then analyze and take note of possible drivers that are giving rise to these patterns in culture. You can keep a folder with bookmarks in your browser, create an Excel spreadsheet, or utilize other online tools for gathering and storing bits of cultural data. Follow these steps and improvise as needed.

1 Culture/Signal Scouting

- Actively collect and document signals in the cultural landscape without initially considering your brand, client, or company. This could be news stories, memes, trend reports, viral posts, policies, ads, etc.

- Consider organizing the signals you encounter using the STEEP framework: Social, technological, economic, environmental, and political signals.

- Consider asking questions such as:

  o What emerging social norms or behaviors are gaining traction in the public discourse?

  o What are the current economic indicators that may significantly influence the future?

  o Are there technologies emerging that could disrupt existing industries or systems?

  o How is the geopolitical landscape affecting public sentiment and values?

- Now, you can create potential future scenarios. This is called scenario planning. When taken together, what would these signals change in how we operate in culture and society? For example, if you've noticed a rise in environmentally conscious consumer choices along with political movements advocating for sustainability, imagine a scenario where green technologies become the norm, shaping new cultural values around consumer responsibility and ethical production.

2 Consumer/Mapping Behavioral Change

- Now, you're ready to understand how the future might impact the consumer behavior in your category.

- Consider reflecting and asking questions such as:
  - What are the potential consumer pain points that could be exacerbated or alleviated by these emerging cultural trends?
  - How might consumers' purchasing decisions be influenced by shifts in economic or technological landscapes?
  - In what ways could emerging social norms alter consumers' expectations for brand engagement or product features?
- Doing this exercise will help you hypothesize how future scenarios could directly affect consumer behavior, from purchasing habits to brand loyalty and beyond. It's how you can anticipate market needs and stay ahead of the curve in your category.

3. Company/Defining Strategic Intent

- With the insights gathered from cultural signals and consumer behavior, it's time to turn the lens inward to your brand. Understand how these emerging scenarios can affect the environment in which your brand will operate in the future.
- Consider exploring these questions with your team or on your own:
  - What are the organizational vulnerabilities or strengths that these future scenarios expose?
  - What kind of strategic shifts would be necessary to adapt to or capitalize on these emerging trends?
  - How might these changes impact the brand's value proposition, mission, or business strategy in the future?
- For instance, if the future scenarios indicate an increasing emphasis on sustainability and social responsibility, what are the actionable steps your brand can take to align itself with this shift?

Remember, take what is useful and leave the rest. This exercise could be a six-month deep dive to refine your strategy from the ground up, or it could be a 15-minute brainstorming break that allows you to zoom out and refresh your thinking.

The goal here is to equip you with a structured way to engage with an ever-changing cultural landscape. Use it to orient your thinking toward innovation, to preempt challenges, and to incite new ideas for seizing opportunities.

MAPPING PREFERRED FUTURES

How do you prepare for what's to come while working toward what could be? The practice of foresight offers several tangible tools to distinguish realistic scenarios of emerging futures from the kinds of futures we aspire to manifest. Futures thinking is a robust and expansive field. The information presented here offers only a condensed overview; consider consulting additional literature on foresight and futures thinking.

To give you a better idea of this practice, however, below are key categories futurists use to classify different types of futures—these move from more known (possible future) to less known (preferable or potential futures):

- **Possible futures:** The scope here is broad, encompassing anything that isn't impossible. These are any outcomes within the realm of possibility, whether or not they currently seem likely. For example, a technology not yet invented could revolutionize how consumers interact with brands.

- **Plausible futures:** These are a subset of possible futures, narrowed down by what we consider to be more likely based on current data, trends, and insights. Plausible futures are not only possible but also reasonable given today's landscape. For instance, given the focus on sustainability, a plausible future could involve the widespread mass adoption of electric vehicles.

- **Probable futures:** These are even more specific, representing the most likely scenarios based on current trajectories. These futures have strong empirical backing, often supported by years of data. These are our "best bets" based on evidence.

- **Preferable futures:** These are the futures we aim to create, informed by our values, aspirations, and goals. While they may not be the most likely, they capture the vision of what we hope will come to pass.

- **"Wild card":** This refers to a high-impact event that is of low probability. If it occurs, though, it will significantly alter existing trajectories. These events are not highly expected but could have far-reaching implications and consequences.

Mapping different futures is crucial for several reasons, particularly in the context of marketing and cultural strategy. First and foremost, however, this methodological approach leads to informed decision making. It ensures that a brand develops a long-term vision for business strategy, one that allows organizations to become more agile in strategic planning but also more visionary in enacting changes based in ethical considerations.

Plotting out diverse future scenarios gives businesses the tools to withstand unpredictability. Investigating a spectrum of potential outcomes, from the most favorable to the direst, enables brands to uncover both hidden risks and untapped opportunities that might otherwise go unnoticed in daily business activities. This forward-thinking strategy primes marketers to think and adapt when the landscape inevitably shifts.

PRO TIP

Another useful tool you might wish to look up is the Three Horizons Framework. It was originally created by Bill Sharpe and the team at the International Futures Forum. The framework has since been widely used for futures studies, strategic planning, and innovation across sectors. This method divides the future into three distinct horizons based on the lifecycle of practices and trends. It is similar to the Residual-Dominant-Emergent framework but focused on the future with an eye toward innovation:

- The "first horizon" represents the current dominant practices that are gradually receding. This is the space most traditional brands occupy, and their challenge is to innovate before becoming obsolete.

- The "second horizon" is a space of transition: Emergent ideas co-exist with dominant practices, using disruption and a break away from the status quo. This stage is occupied by forward-thinking brands that are leveraging cultural currents to harness innovation.

- The so-called "third horizon" is an aspirational future state that embodies the possibilities of long-term systemic change. This stage is a space of exploration. The "third horizon" is made up of entirely new possibilities: Radically new paradigms, innovations, technologies, and practices.

In strategic planning, the "third horizon" is crucial for backcasting: A method of defining a preferable future and then working backward to identify practices, policies, shifts, and actions that the organization needs to reach that future state.

BACKCASTING: CRAFTING VISION-DRIVEN STRATEGY WITH THE END IN MIND

While scenario planning helps us understand the spectrum of possible futures based on current signals, it can sometimes leave us constrained by the limits of what we know today. Preparing for the future, which could often be rather grim, doesn't address how to evolve the current status quo toward a more liberatory future, in which equity and abundance, and not marginalization and scarcity, are the operating models for how we organize society. Backcasting is particularly useful for breaking out of this restrictive box.

Backcasting can be a critical asset in developing your cultural strategy. As a practice, backcasting begins with an ideal endpoint and then reverse-engineers the steps needed to achieve it. It's not just about predicting a future shaped by existing trends, however, but about actively co-creating a future that embodies the visions of inclusive and equitable possibilities we should aim for.

In the context of inclusivity, this means starting with an ideal or preferred vision of a future society. From there, you can work backward to map out the policies, shifts, and initiatives that the brand can activate upon to bring that future closer to existence. This makes it an invaluable tool for marketers who are committed to not merely reacting or responding to change but actively advancing the industry toward a better, more inclusive, and sustainable tomorrow.

Take a moment and imagine your brand or—if you work independently or support various clients in your role—the future of marketing between 5 and 10 years from now. Start with the end in mind, reflecting on the core values the brand upholds, the kind of impact it has on society, and how it's perceived by various consumer segments, community partners, and stakeholders. Then, work backward.

Map out key milestones, necessary innovations, internal policies, and strategic partnerships needed to make this ideal future a reality.

Spend time identifying the barriers to this future. Are there regulatory, technological, or market challenges? What are the potential cultural or societal barriers? For each barrier, brainstorm possible solutions or workarounds. Obviously, your brand cannot fix the entirety of social issues. But consider what the brand can do to influence public opinion. Could partnerships or specific initiatives move the needle forward, if only an inch?

Depending on how mature the brand's cultural strategy is, you can continue with this activity to create a strategic plan. For most brands, this will mean using this exercise to begin developing a more inclusive and forward-thinking outlook on culture and the brand's role within it.

When asking "what's next," our reflex can often turn to experts for an answer. What I hope this chapter reminds you of is that we all have the opportunity to imagine, envision, and strategize toward a future that *we* want to bring into being. Certainly, experts are excellent sources of knowledge. But our responsibility for the state of the industry cannot be conveniently passed on to someone else. That's why the idea of critical imagination as a form of agency is so important: We all have the capacity for it.

And not just the capacity, but the imperative. Critical imagination isn't merely an intellectual exercise; in some ways, it's a form of civic engagement. It compels us to question, to challenge the status quo, and most importantly, to act. It offers a dual lens, one that deconstructs existing paradigms and another that projects new possibilities forward. In a world often characterized by systemic inertia—be it social, economic, or political—critical imagination serves as a counterweight to the status quo.

In this sense, critical imagination, along with foresight tools and futures thinking, is an asset not only for researching potential future scenarios but also for taking concrete actions to expedite the realization of our preferred futures. We must embrace our responsibility in shaping them. In leveraging critical imagination, we don't just forecast the future, we shape it. We go from being passive consumers of expert opinion to becoming active co-creators of culture. This agency resides in each of us, fueled by our ability to imagine a world not just as it is but as it could be.

The next time someone asks, "What's next?" for the marketing industry, don't just ponder the question—be the answer. "What's next" depends on us, as marketers, practitioners, and leaders with the inherent capacity to imagine and enact the change we want to see in the world. What vision will you create for the future you wish to live in?

In Conversation with Leading Voices
for Social Impact in Business

We are now nearing the end of this journey. As we conclude this book, I asked the leading voices at the forefront of inclusive marketing and social good in business about their own visions of the future: What's next for the future of marketing? Where do we need to go as an industry, and what kind of changes do we need to bring forth? Here are some of the insights that they shared.

Lola Bakare: As an industry, we need to think less about extracting value from historically excluded audiences and more about meaningfully solving their problems in ways that deepen emotional connections with them. The shift from "extraction" to "problem solving" is how I define the necessary shift from overly segmented "multicultural marketing" to inclusively impactful "responsible marketing."

Brand-driven businesses should examine their own societal debts. What cultural problems are theirs to solve? Identifying these reveals new levers of growth. Think about examples like Citi's "Action For Racial Equity" and Mastercard's "True Name" and "Touch Card" features. By solving real problems for historically excluded consumers in brand-relevant ways, they harness the power of responsible marketing to do well for the business by doing good for the world.

Reema Mitra: As more people get clued in on how marketing works, it's hard to distinguish whether or not you're actually just borrowing from culture or whether you're aiming to change it or aiming to build something for the culture in whatever way that means. I would love to see us push the envelope even further.

We need to start hiring people who are not the typical college graduate or people who have had a very straight line into marketing from college to internships. It's a very privileged field to be in. You don't get insights and interesting perspectives from the same people over and over again. We need to hire differently. We need to be able to bring in people who have been in jail or single mothers or people who have had lives and who've lived a life different from ours.

That's the only way that we move forward, beyond having a dedicated function that works on cultural intelligence.

Coco Videla: To add to that, I still join a lot of Zoom meetings that don't represent the diversity of who we are. I really wish there was a mechanism to have advertising become more diverse. The people that come into advertising need to be more diverse. The industry is still predominantly white—I don't know what we can do to encourage more diversity from the inside out, but that is where it all starts.

Tameka Linnell: And it's not just about hiring more people of color; it's about bringing forth a profound structural change. That's what I'd like to see change.

What I'd also love to see is more honest conversations! I can have professional conversations and say things the way they need to be said in meetings. But what I don't like is when we all sit in a room, smile, agree with everything, and nothing happens. Let's just call it what it is. Because it's very obvious when you're not getting the support. This makes it harder for the people that are trying to do the work. Let's have honest conversations about where we stand, and what we want to do. I'd rather have that conversation and know where I stand and what needs to happen versus putting a veil over it. Honesty makes the work more meaningful and actionable, rather than just spinning wheels. We don't have to agree; our values don't have to align. We can still benefit people, your consumer, your customer, your brand, and your business. Even a tiny step is okay.

Ambika Pai: The industry seems to be drifting further away from addressing humanity's real problems and becoming increasingly focused on the bottom line. I anticipate a return to small strategy consultancies or accelerators collaborating with creative agencies. Creative agencies seem to be drifting toward an intense focus on profitability, the bottom line, performance, and media optimization, moving away from impacting business and capitalist structures from the top down.

As a strategist, I firmly believe that we possess the curiosity, research skills, and innovative thinking to tackle almost any challenge. We can approach problems holistically, considering business, culture, categories, and people. Thinking back to the 2010s, we were creating remarkable advertising, like "Dear Sophie" and Google's collaboration with Lady Gaga. More recently, agencies like Mekanism worked on projects such as MedMen, which aimed to destigmatize marijuana use, connecting it to criminal justice reform.

All of this is still strategy to me. Strategy must maintain its ambition to ask unconventional questions and seek answers others haven't considered. Since strategy is the first step in any creative endeavor, it's crucial for strategists to remain committed to the truth and to ensure the truth is reflected in our work.

Conclusion

Becoming a Catalyst for Inclusive Marketing

As we come to the end of this book, it is my hope that this last chapter will not mark the end of your journey toward cultural intelligence. Rather, I hope that reading *Cultural Intelligence for Marketers* has opened a new framework for you to explore and that you can, in time, build upon this conversation in ways that are meaningful to the specific work that you do. Consider this book a launching pad from which you can delve deeper into the interconnected worlds of culture and marketing as they relate to your brand or the clients you work with.

As the intersection of culture and commerce continues to evolve, your growing expertise in this subject matter will enable you to lead your brand— or your roster of clients—toward a vision of marketing strategy that is not only more efficient and profitable but also more socially conscious, inclusive, and sustainable. The work of decoding and leveraging advanced cultural insight for both commerce and social good doesn't end with this book; it is where it begins.

No one book, of course, can cover every aspect of a topic that is so vast and complex. But more than that, it certainly cannot be a substitute for continued learning, earnest introspection, and ongoing critical engagement with questions of culture, ideology, and power and ongoing inequities in this industry and society at large. Because while "theory" is essential, theory without actual practice is as limited as practice without a solid theory of culture. By "theory" I don't just mean theoretical musings for the sake of some kind of intellectual edification; rather, I want to suggest that marketing urgently needs a "theory of culture" because it offers us necessary knowledge into how things in culture work—and why. Actions divested from this foundation end up lacking in crucial attributes that inclusive marketers are called to practice consistently: intentionality, foresight, and critical thinking, all of which lead to a more nuanced understanding of how culture evolves over time.

Without critical thought, what we are left with are performative actions that only seek immediate applause. But this is not how this works. In the context of cultural intelligence specifically, uninformed practices can lead to missed opportunities and preventable mistakes that alienate audiences, perpetuate harmful narratives, and eventually, harm brand credibility.

This is why our ongoing commitment to critical thinking is so essential: It is certainly crucial to any forward-thinking brand aiming to embed ethics, responsibility, and integrity alongside market sustainability into cultural strategy. Those who invest in building a foundation rooted in both theoretical understanding *and* conscientious marketing practice understand that intellectual humility and long-term commitment are the cornerstones of sustainable change.

This combination of cultural knowledge and intentional practice is what ultimately sets apart genuinely engaged efforts that have the potential to be truly meaningful and socially impactful from mere performativity and superficial actions.

Just as culture is never static, so, of course, our conceptual maps must be continually reconsidered and redrawn to account for cultural evolution with its shifting values, ideological struggles, and emergent narratives. Agility and resilience in the face of constant change is not just a choice but a necessity for a sound brand strategy in the fast-accelerating cultural ecosystem that we inhabit. And yet, there must be something more tangible to anchor us in this practice.

A shared language and ethical direction are urgently needed to chart a course forward. Without them, we risk repeating the same mistakes of the past, reproducing an industry landscape where intention gets muddled, inclusivity is replaced by tokenism, and the power structures we aim to confront, challenge, and transform remain opaque. We can't change what we don't understand.

This book aims to provide that foundational understanding of where culture and marketing intersect, one that pushes against efforts to silo inclusivity and equity as a nice-to-have afterthought within marketing processes. Instead, I wanted to share with you a vision of cultural fluency in the world of brands that positions these concepts as integral components of developing culturally resonant and ethical marketing strategies.

Without it, the future of marketing in a globalized world, where media and technology hold such immense influence on culture and society, is ethically untenable. The principles outlined in the preceding chapters are designed to direct you toward a vision for brand marketing that does not just capitalize on culture but looks for ways to enrich it.

Cultural Intelligence for Marketers: Key Lessons to Remember

Whether you're a seasoned marketer or an aspiring brand strategist, the takeaways below will help you develop a compass that is both inclusive and rooted in social consciousness and ethical rigor. Consider this your actionable roadmap for getting started. Now, let's recap what we covered in this book.

#1: The era of evading social responsibility in marketing is over. Building on half a century of conversations about representation, it is now imperative to recalibrate how the industry influences, engages with, and contributes to culture.

We no longer have the privilege of asking *if* brands should be inclusive and socially responsible. The history record is clear: it's been too long, and change is overdue. The question of the "social responsibility" of advertisers has been raised by researchers, scholars, and activists since the 1960s, shaping conversations—but not always actions. The conversation in the industry must evolve into the question of *how*.

Today, the charge is clear. The current sociocultural moment calls for a complete overhaul; a new beginning, if you will. Representation can no longer be just a checkbox to tick off or a merely perfunctory nod to "diversity." Cursory attempts at enacting change no longer cut it—or at least, they shouldn't. Now, it's *our* mandate to recalibrate how marketers and advertisers engage, contribute to, and influence culture.

Contemporary marketers are tasked with developing an understanding of representation in culture as an intricate, ideologically complex system that demands ongoing responsibility from industry leaders, marketers, advertisers, strategists, and creatives. To this end, organizations and brand-driven businesses must begin to build sustainable practices that support and empower marketers in developing social consciousness that will enable brands to continually reassess and update their understanding of culture—and then act on it in ways that advance us forward, not pull us back.

Inaction is precisely why harmful tropes, outdated narratives, and stereo-typical depictions of historically marginalized groups have persisted in marketing and advertising for so long. Overlooking the ways in which marketing media may perpetuate various forms of oppression—be it racism, sexism, heteronormativity, classism, ableism, or unrealistic beauty stand-ards—leads to brand narratives that not only sustain the status quo but also miss the transformative potential of cultural innovation.

When brands merely steer clear of the most egregious stereotypes with-out grasping the nuances of culture, ideology, and representation, they end up putting out marketing messages that still prioritize and center dominant social groups. While a step in the right direction, this kind of marketing can't be considered genuinely inclusive and equitable. Brands may purport to practice "intersectional" marketing and integrate diverse representation, but a superficial understanding of historical power dynamics often results in brand storytelling that harbors subtler biases, such as a preference for light-skinned actors, ageism, or a skewed emphasis on thinness. This is not only a setback for culture but a missed opportunity for commercial advantage.

The time for passive observation is over. Staying on the sidelines might feel safe in the moment, but it carries a long-term business risk in a market-place that increasingly demands that brands evolve toward cultural fluency. In the future of marketing, cultural intelligence is essential. Cultural intelli-gence is the difference between superficial representation and accurate storytelling that amplifies voices, challenges assumptions, and reflects the complexity of human experience. Brands that embed cultural fluency and social consciousness at the core of cultural strategy future-proof their success and secure their long-term cultural legacy.

#2: To execute culturally fluent marketing successfully, brands must embed inclusive innovation alongside cultural intelligence. This not only enriches marketing strategies but also mitigates long-term business risks in a fast-accelerating cultural climate.

Brands need innovation to maintain cultural relevance. Innovation is the lifeblood of competitive advantage. But it gains a new dimension when looked at through the lens of cultural intelligence that is intentionally atten-tive to questions of inclusivity and equity in the marketplace. In engaging with culture, innovation, then, is not just about creating the next ground-breaking product or service; it's about fundamentally reimagining how brands interact with increasingly diversified cultural ecosystems. Innovation rooted in cultural intelligence is how businesses can prevent creating products that are rooted in racial and gender bias. Some forward-thinking brands are acting on this, from Microsoft's Xbox Adaptive Controller, designed to make gaming accessible to people with limited mobility, to algorithms on Pinterest now being developed to consider differences in hair texture and body size.

The need for innovation to be integrated with cultural intelligence becomes especially pressing when we consider the rapid pace at which societal norms, values, and expectations are evolving—innovation without cultural sensitivity risks not only irrelevance but also preventable damage to brand equity.

Brands have the opportunity to engage in a form of "responsive innovation," where market research isn't only focused on consumer preferences or market demands but also tracks and harnesses insights about deeper cultural movements and societal shifts. Cultural intelligence not only enriches innovation but also acts as a safeguard, mitigating the risks that marketers fear when venturing into new cultural territories. Not to say that mistakes don't happen, but it's much harder to mess up when you're operating with a deep and nuanced understanding of the cultural dynamics at play.

In this sense, cultural intelligence is more than a methodology; it is a framework and an approach to doing cultural strategy in a way that's socially conscious, responsible, and agile. It empowers brands to go beyond "keeping up" with culture. Culturally fluent brands participate and contribute to cultural evolution instead of merely extracting knowledge and insight for commercial gain.

#3: Conscious marketers recognize the power that brands hold in actively shaping and driving culture forward and deploy cultural intelligence to navigate culture thoughtfully. Forward-thinking brands develop analytical capabilities that allow them to leverage advanced cultural insights to execute socially responsible communications; inclusive brands do this in a way that is critically conscious and grounded in reciprocal principles of accountability and co-creation.

Historically, the prevailing notion in brand marketing has been simple: Marketers sell products by strategically tapping into emotional registers and leveraging cultural codes to drive purchase behavior at a profit. In short, the marketer's job is to persuade. But increasingly, we ask—at what cost? And might there be another more conscientious and responsible way to move people?

Consumers increasingly expect businesses to exhibit an understanding of the significant societal influence that brand-driven businesses wield in society. In a hyper-connected, media-saturated world, where marketing accounts for a significant portion of mass media consumed by people, brands don't just compete for market share. By distributing paid media and participating in storytelling at scale, brands are shaping how people perceive and engage with the world. The influence of brands extends far beyond driving commercial objectives.

For inclusive marketers, the business challenge, then, lies in acknowledging and harnessing this capacity for cultural influence in a manner that is both ethically sound and commercially viable. In this sense, marketers have an opportunity to be vanguards of positive change—for business and society—advancing conversations in culture rather than merely echoing them.

This starts with unlocking the power of cultural intelligence. Inclusive brands first learn to decode culture and leverage advanced cultural insights to thoughtfully strategize brand communications and anticipate audience reception. Then, brands do due diligence to ensure that strategic outputs integrate critical consciousness to evaluate the saliency of the work. Finally, the execution of strategy requires that brands pay attention to the cultural communities they are speaking to and about. Co-creation is the new community engagement model that invites marketers to consider the nuances of brand accountability and social impact.

#4: Marketing messages can either reinforce existing beliefs or challenge them. Conscious marketers must be intentional about the impact of their messaging on society.

At its core, marketing is a communicative practice. The impact marketers have can go far beyond driving results up and down the funnel. It is critical that marketers grasp the gravity of the words, images, and narratives that brands disseminate in culture and society. The imperative for intentional, socially conscious messaging becomes even more pressing in a rapidly evolving sociocultural environment, where a single misstep can trigger a tidal wave of reaction, and a campaign can ignite a societal debate. This is not, however, a reason not to engage with contentious or complex issues. Rather, it amplifies the necessity for marketers to invest in developing a nuanced understanding of cultural contexts and implications, enabling them to participate meaningfully in societal conversations without perpetuating stereotypes or perpetuating past harms.

Marketing messages can either uphold prevailing ideologies or question dominant ones. This ethical responsibility demands that marketers don't merely echo the status quo but engage with cultural issues critically, offering counter-hegemonic, nuanced perspectives that challenge dominant narratives and embed meaningful representation. Avoiding this responsibility is not an option in a consumer culture in which expectations for cultural fluency are at an all-time high, and where the social, economic, and reputational stakes for getting it wrong are increasingly severe.

#5: Conscious marketers work to understand their audience's perspectives to prevent misinterpretation of messages and ensure conscious, culturally sensitive, and responsible communication across media.

Conscious marketers engage in a rigorous process of audience analysis not just to target more effectively but to communicate more responsibly. Inclusive brands understand that in the act of messaging, they're participating in a larger cultural dialogue, one fraught with power dynamics, histories, and social contexts that they must navigate with care. By sharpening cultural intelligence on how messages resonate within various cultural communities and demographic groups, marketers can create campaigns that are not just effective but also culturally sensitive and socially responsible.

The task for culturally fluent brands isn't merely to convey a message but to ensure its accurate transmission. Investing in cultural intelligence safeguards brands against the risk of audiences misinterpreting their message; advanced cultural insights, in turn, enable brands to produce more culturally sensitive storytelling. To this end, it's crucial for marketers to remember that interpretation is an active process, one shaped by the cultural, social, and even historical context of the receiver. Cultural intelligence as a set of analytical skills requires marketers to intentionally understand the range of possible interpretations among audience segments. Put simply, the focus isn't just on what the brand wants to say but on how it will be heard, decoded, and internalized across multiple cultural touchpoints.

This calls for an investment in cultural analysis that goes beyond traditional market research or social listening tools. Cultural analysis invites an interdisciplinary approach to the marketing strategy, one that leans into learnings from cultural studies, sociology, media studies, and even psychology to gain a thorough understanding of the numerous ways a message might be received in present-day culture. This isn't just about tuning into the likes and dislikes of an audience as much as it is being attuned to how cultural messaging influences consumer perception.

Various factors that shape lived experiences, individual subjectivities, and perceptions—like race, gender, socioeconomic status, cultural affiliation, and geographic location—can significantly alter how an audience perceives a message. Conscious marketers acknowledge these nuances and strive to tailor their messages to be inclusive and accessible. By actively seeking to understand and reflect the lived experiences of marginalized communities, socially conscious marketers aim to craft messages that resonate without alienating, that engage without exploiting, and that inspire without appropriating.

#6: To be an intersectional marketer means to engage directly with the dynamics of power and oppression. Practicing intersectionality, as it was originally conceived in Black feminist thought, calls for marketers to adopt a critical approach that actively considers systems of marginalization and brands' role as corporate entities within this context.

The term "intersectionality," originally coined by Dr. Kimberlé Crenshaw, has been depoliticized in the business world. Initially an analytical prism for identifying how multiple systems of oppression intersect, it's been diluted to simply signify diverse identities. Our "differences" are not what perpetuates inequality; it's systems of oppression that manipulate these differences to create hierarchies. In its initial formulation, it served as an analytical framework for understanding the intersection of various systems of oppression. In commercial marketing, deploying intersectionality demands more—it necessitates a critical interrogation of the power structures that both inform consumer behavior and pervade the societal fabric. In the context of marketing, utilizing intersectionality involves a critical examination of the power dynamics and marginalizing forces that influence both consumer behavior and broader societal patterns.

Within marketing practice, intersectionality requires more than segmenting markets by identity and then seeking to understand or empathize with their values or perspectives. The objective is not merely to reflect diverse identities in marketing material but to contextualize these identities within the larger sociopolitical landscape. This means that marketers have to wrestle with the asymmetries of power that exist in society, which in turn shape people's lived experiences, needs, problems, and expectations.

Don't just acknowledge identities but recognize that people operate within intersecting oppressive systems; their experiences and needs as users are shaped by the real-life impact of racism, heterosexism, classism, ableism, and other forces that affect how people experience the world.

Returning to intersectionality's original focus on challenging power structures and systemic oppression sets apart tokenistic efforts from genuinely responsible and critically informed marketing campaigns. Campaign strategies must be designed not only with a nuanced awareness of intersecting identities but with a critical understanding of how brands can help solve problems relevant to them. And further, to practice truly intersectional marketing, brands must first examine their own relationship to societal power dynamics and the harmful role that brands can themselves have in society when extracting cultural value solely for the sake of profit-making.

This self-scrutiny is necessary to identify how the brand is implicated in past harms. Candid audits of the brand's past provide actionable direction for where it is most meaningful for a brand to lean in within culture. But it also future-proofs the business. Unresolved or unacknowledged issues can resurface, particularly when consumers can easily excavate a brand's history and hold it publicly accountable. Recognizing past harms is the first step toward reparative actions *and* future-forward business strategy.

#7: The paradigm for engaging cultural communities, marginalized groups, and subcultures must move from extraction to co-creation. Cultural strategy is only truly ethical when businesses seek out ways to contribute to communities which they engage and to whom they market.

Traditionally, marketing and advertising industries have engaged with cultural communities, marginalized groups, and subcultures in a manner that is essentially extractive. Brands have repeatedly lifted aesthetic elements, language, artifacts and cultural symbols from these communities without offering anything in return. This dynamic isn't just unsustainable, it's ethically fraught.

Unconscious marketing actions perpetuate cultural appropriation, dilute genuine narratives, and uphold systemic imbalances that favor corporate profit over cultural integrity. Brands should not merely draw from these communities for consumer insights and cultural capital; brands must also reinvest, contributing tangible value and resources back into the communities they engage with and market to.

What's the way forward? Shift from a model of extraction to one of co-creation. Co-creation necessitates a move toward long-term, reciprocal, and mutually beneficial relationships between brands and cultural communities. It underscores the importance of shared agency, where audiences are sought out to provide feedback that shapes the decision-making processes about how cultural communities are represented and engaged.

It begins with economic reciprocity. If a brand-driven business is directly profiting from a community's cultural capital, it has a responsibility to reinvest back into the community. It's not just about financial transactions or dumping money into initiatives for the sake of looking good to consumers;

it's about modeling a more reciprocal relationship in which compensating communities is more normalized in our profit-driven culture.

But resource sharing also extends beyond capital. Brands have access to influential media platforms in a culture where historically marginalized groups advocating for change do not. Distributing these resources can amplify established initiatives and grassroots leaders while providing a platform for causes focused on uplifting marginalized communities. In doing so, brands not only solidify their social license to operate but also leverage and redirect their extensive resources to pave the way for a more equitable and inclusive future.

#8: Chasing cultural trends is short-sighted. Brands looking for longevity need to be futurists, not opportunists. Adopting a future-oriented mindset, grounded in strategic foresight and critical imagination, is necessary for long-term ethical and sustainable impact.

Brands must extend their vision beyond the immediate, considering the far-reaching implications of their actions today on the future landscape of culture and society. Developing strategic foresight involves a nuanced understanding of societal shifts, technological advancements, and emergent cultural dynamics. Forward-thinking brands recognize strategic foresight and cultural innovation as the cornerstones of a long-term business strategy.

Don't just understand the zeitgeist—anticipate the next one. This requires that brands develop a practice that enables them to dive deep into societal shifts, technological leaps, and emergent cultural currents. Brands that invest in this kind of critical cultural foresight aren't just better positioned for the future; they're well positioned to start shaping it. This transcends corporate social responsibility as a mere afterthought; it centers ethical integrity as the cornerstone of conscious marketing. By this point, the choice should be evident: Brands can either remain peripheral and merely respond to passing cultural moments or choose to play an active role in shaping what comes next.

Where to Start: Expand Your Point of Reference

As you close this book, start by expanding your point of reference. Let it be your first step toward becoming a conscious marketer or a leader of a culturally fluent brand. This isn't just about reading more books or consuming more content; it's about a strategic shift in how you engage with the world and your own work.

The cultural narratives that dominate mainstream business spaces are often too narrow to capture the intricacies of social change and the nuances of cultural communities that marketers speak to. By broadening the scope of information you absorb—whether through academic scholarship, independent journalism, or firsthand accounts of lived experiences from a range of cultural communities—you're doing more than just amassing cultural data. You're actively redefining your criteria for what constitutes valuable and valid knowledge. This isn't merely about gathering information; it's about reshaping your intellectual framework to appreciate a wider array of perspectives, worldviews, and lived experiences other than your own.

The goal is to burst through the industry bubble and achieve a multidimensional understanding that recognizes intersecting forms of power, privilege, and oppression in the wider cultural context. It's more than just "staying updated," too. If we want to expand our practice of inclusivity and cultural intelligence, we must fundamentally reorient how we interpret the signals in the culture around us. What do we pay attention to? Who do we see as an authority? Who captures our attention? Take this broader point of reference into your professional life. Integrate this expansive lens into your strategies, campaigns, and organizational culture. With a broader, more nuanced point of reference, you'll be better equipped not only to interpret the world but to integrate cultural insights into your work in a truly meaningful way.

The path forward is less about taking a single first step and more about developing a more nuanced approach to cultural literacy in marketing altogether. Your journey begins with the acquisition of knowledge—a foundational layer you can build through a wide range of readings, podcasts, and engagement with alternative media sources. But the next crucial component is transitioning from passively consuming information to proactively sharing knowledge within your professional network, organization, and team. Here are some specific suggestions to consider after you close this book:

1 **Integrate marginalized perspectives in decision making:** This is something that your team can start doing tomorrow. Encourage a culture of questioning and critical thinking. Probe assumptions and keep yourself accountable to interrogate your own biases and gaps in knowledge. Thoughtfully engage with and include perspectives from marginalized

cultures to enrich your understanding and inform your decision making. Encourage team members and collaborators to seek out, compensate, and incorporate various forms of formal and organic knowledge from marginalized communities. Historically overlooked perspectives on culture, business, and society contain invaluable insight that can challenge mainstream narratives and inform your strategy to be more socially conscious and inclusive. It's the cornerstone of creativity and innovation. Above all, hire relevant talent and invest in their access to positions of leadership.

2 **Engage external thought leaders:** Proactively invite and compensate speakers, consultants, or subject matter experts who specialize in critical analysis, identity studies, and equity and inclusion. Whenever possible, bring them into your organization to offer workshops, deliver seminars, or consult on specific projects. Their external viewpoints can serve as a catalyst for internal change, challenging ingrained biases and broadening your collective understanding of culture, power dynamics, and social issues. This not only enhances the depth of your organizational knowledge but also helps actualize more socially conscious and inclusive practices at the company level.

3 **Conduct an organizational audit and establish objectives:** Initiate an internal audit to evaluate existing levels of cultural literacy and inclusivity across research, strategy, and creative teams. Too often, inclusivity training focuses on workplace dynamics; rarely if ever do brand-driven businesses focus on continued education across brand marketing functions in the organization. Cultural intelligence is key to inclusive storytelling, so brands' commitments to creating a culture of equity and inclusion cannot be solely relegated to human resources or business management. Interrogate how social consciousness as a mindset is incorporated into approaches to research design, methodologies, insights generation, strategy, communications, copywriting, creative direction, and casting. Use the audit's findings to establish measurable objectives that align with your brand's long-term business strategy. These objectives should be designed to directly address any gaps in cultural literacy or inclusivity that are identified in the audit. In this way, cultural intelligence is not an afterthought but a central component on the journey to evolving into a culturally fluent brand.

SUGGESTIONS FOR FURTHER READING

On Culture, Media, and Representation

- *Representation: Cultural representations and signifying practices* by Stuart Hall (1997)
- *Practices of Looking: An introduction to visual culture* by Marita Sturken and Lisa Cartwright (2017)
- *Ideology: An introduction* by Terry Eagleton (1993)
- *The Culture Industry: Selected essays on mass culture* by Theodor W. Adorno (2001)
- "Encoding and Decoding in the Television Discourse" by Stuart Hall (1973)
- *The Society of the Spectacle* by Guy Debord (1967)
- *Television: Technology and cultural form* by Raymond Williams (1974)
- *Subculture: The meaning of style* by Dick Hebdige (1979)

On Race, Gender, and Social Identity

- *Black Feminist Thought: Knowledge, consciousness, and the politics of empowerment* by Patricia Hill Collins (1990)
- "Mapping the Margins: Intersectionality, Identity Politics, and Violence against Women of Color" by Kimberlé Crenshaw (1991)
- *Intersectionality: An intellectual history* by Ange-Marie Hancock (2016)
- *Ain't I a Woman: Black women and feminism* by bell hooks (1981)
- *Sister Outsider: Essays and speeches* by Audre Lorde (1984)
- *Black Looks: Race and representation* by bell hooks (1992)
- *Women, Culture, and Politics* by Angela Y. Davis (1989)
- The Combahee River Collective Statement by Combahee River Collective (1977)
- *Critical Race Theory: An introduction* by Richard Delgado and Jean Stefancic (2001)
- *This Bridge Called My Back: Writings by radical women of color* edited by Cherríe Moraga and Gloria Anzaldúa (1981)
- *Black Disability Politics* by Sami Schalk (2022)
- *Living a Feminist Life* by Sara Ahmed (2017)

- *Transgender History* by Susan Stryker (2017)
- *Black on Both Sides: A racial history of trans identity* by C. Riley Snorton (2017)
- *Fearing the Black Body: The racial origins of fat phobia* by Sabrina Strings (2019)

On the Cultural History of Advertising

- *Gender Advertisements* by Erving Goffman (1979)
- *Provocateur: Images of women and minorities in advertising* by Anthony J. Cortese (1999)
- *Madison Avenue and the Color Line: African Americans in the advertising industry* by Jason Chambers (2009)
- *Aunt Jemima, Uncle Ben, and Rastus: Blacks in advertising, yesterday, today, and tomorrow* by Marilyn Kern Foxworth (1994)
- *Pioneering African-American Women in the Advertising Business: Biographies of MAD Black WOMEN* by Judy Foster Davis (2016)
- *Desegregating the Dollar: African American consumerism in the twentieth century* by Robert E. Weems Jr. (1998)
- *Advertising Diversity: Ad agencies and the creation of Asian American consumers* by Shalini Shankar (2015)
- *Latino Spin: Public image and the whitewashing of race* by Arlene Dávila (2008)

On Brands and Media

- *The Reality of the Mass Media* by Niklas Luhmann (1995)
- *How Brands Become Icons: The principles of cultural branding* by Douglas Holt (2004)
- *Cultural Strategy: Using innovative ideologies to build breakthrough brands* by Douglas Holt and Douglas Cameron (2012)
- *For the Culture: The power behind the world's most successful brands, from Apple to Beyoncé* by Marcus Collins (2023)
- *The Image Factory: Consumer culture, photography, and the visual content industry* by Paul Frosh (2003)
- *No Logo* by Naomi Klein (1999)

Final Words: Cyclical Struggles, Endurance, and the Future of Inclusive Marketing

To face evolving challenges of the future, we must take stock of the current moment we are in. Too often, the business world sees histories of activist resistance as irrelevant to the professional world. But there is a reason why we started this book with an overview of the history of representation in marketing and advertising. We need to understand where we have come from in order to know where we need to go.

This isn't just an intellectual exercise—applying a critical lens on the industry's history and present-day culture prepares us to better understand how to confront the challenges of the present moment. Recognizing that equity and commerce are not separate but entwined, we cannot afford to neglect the history of marketing and advertising as an inconsequential footnote; this kind of cultural knowledge is, in fact, the building block of any strategy aimed at dismantling logics that continue to perpetuate inequity in representation today. More than that, taking this cultural history seriously begs the question: Why hasn't substantial change happened after all these years?

The answer is as instructive as it is cautionary. Remember this: Social change is cyclical, and so is the struggle to confront and dismantle oppressive power. As the legendary abolitionist Frederick Douglass once proclaimed in 1857, "Power concedes nothing without a demand. It never did, and it never will" (Foner and Taylor, 2000). Students of history recognize that the impediments to societal transformation are deeply embedded in our cultural ecosystems. Each wave of activism, each surge of social awakening, echoes past movements while exposing both new challenges and asserting evolved demands. This isn't an excuse for how things are; recognizing this reality, as much as we wish it to be different, is an essential step for formulating targeted, impactful interventions. It's the premise of this entire book: We have to know how culture works in order to transform it.

This starts with understanding that we are always already in struggle over meaning. Movements for justice and inclusivity begin on the peripheries of society and public discourse, gaining momentum when new ideas get past the walls of the mainstream—the ideologies that make the status quo seem immutable. It's at these margins where movements against oppression are nurtured by radical activists, visionary thinkers, and grassroots organizers who fight on the frontlines of social change. Once these emerging perspectives infiltrate mainstream consciousness, they begin to shift the cultural landscape, reconfiguring power dynamics and forcing brands, institutions, and individuals to reckon with newly articulated norms, values, and expectations. Over time, activists, advocates, and movement leaders manage to create enough pressure to push these issues from the peripheries into the heart of public debate. Sometimes, a shocking event acts as a catalyst, breaking through the general inertia to force a collective reckoning. The Black Lives Matter protests that shocked the industry in 2020 are a case in point. But understanding what happens next is instructive for our purposes.

What usually follows is a complex and fraught negotiation between radical ideas and mainstream acceptance. As these conversations become more mainstream, they often undergo a transformation—too often, anti-oppressive ideas are depoliticized and co-opted. The risk of dilution and co-optation looms large now in a media-saturated landscape, where appearing to be inclusive becomes a social currency.

But once transformative, visionary concepts become buzzwords, they are stripped of their incisive critiques. This process of absorbing anti-oppressive visions of the future into the mainstream is not just a failure of translating activist concepts into the mainstream but a systematic re-engineering of the discourse itself; a way to absorb the language of change without committing to its implications—and actions that are expected to follow. The whitewashing of intersectionality serves as a prime example of this that we explored in the book. What began as a radical framework for understanding complex, interwoven, oppressive systems has been diluted into a mere catchphrase in corporate diversity seminars.

Consider also how the Civil Rights Movement catapulted inclusivity issues onto the advertising industry's agenda in the sixties. As I wanted to demonstrate in this book, there is plenty of evidence to suggest that the language of brands' social responsibility was, indeed, a part of the marketing discourse as early as 1969, when people like Dr. Harold Kassarjian wrote about the pressures advertisers faced to accept their social responsibility in culture. However, the vision was merely drawn, not followed, as structural inequities remained relatively unchallenged.

Fast-forward to the second-wave feminist movements, where advertisers felt the heat again, but the transformations were more superficial than systemic. Now, yet again, the call for inclusivity and equity is back on the table. And still, looking back at the last several years, it's hard to argue that changes are anything but perfunctory, at best. Most brands and agencies never fulfilled the commitments they claimed to make.

The way that the corporate industry intermittently flirts with inclusivity without committing to systemic change makes the pattern clear: Revolutionary demands are too often sanitized to fit comfortably within existing power structures. The cycle of struggle for change begins again. The cycle renews not because change is unwelcome, but because a deeper, transformative shift would mean unsettling the very foundations upon which these corporate structures rest.

At the core of this book's argument is the idea that culture is a constant site of negotiation where dominant ideology is contested, negotiated, and challenged. In this sense, the repetitive cycles of marginalization, activism and advocacy, and eventual co-optation are not accidental glitches but systemic features. When we ask why change hasn't happened fast enough, we are called to interrogate the resilience of oppressive structures and the ingenuity with which they adapt to accommodate the appearance of progress, all while resisting the substance of the demands.

Acknowledging this pattern offers more than a sobering reflection on our past—it offers strategic insight for those committed to breaking this cyclical pattern. And it further underscores the necessity for endurance, critical thinking, and innovation in the ongoing struggle for substantial and sustainable change in the industry and beyond.

Reflecting on my time in grassroots activist organizing, this cycle is not new or shocking. I've seen this happen over and over again. I've seen movements crushed; I was part of many soul-crushing setbacks myself. And yet, amidst defeat and a seductive sense of hopelessness, I've also seen the resilience that emerges from these fractures: People who refuse to settle for the world we have inherited, people who are fired up about the possibilities of bringing forth a radically different new world. It's a cycle of victories and defeats that every preceding movement has endured; a challenge that our predecessors inherited from those who had come before them—and those who had come before them. As much as we might wish otherwise, this is the reality we confront. Transformation is never an avalanche of overnight changes; it's a painfully slow drip. No tipping points, only tipping scales.

This hindsight is our power, though; this isn't cause for despair but a call for strategic action. It confronts us with a question: How do we stay steady when a sense of change is perpetually elusive? How do we endure when despair and disappointment seem like rational reactions to systems that refuse to bend? How do we maintain our sense of purpose? How do we protect the motivation to keep pushing for radical change when we recognize that exclusion is built into the very fabric of the organizations we are part of; that they operate exactly as designed?

Our biggest mistake would be to wait for some cataclysmic event to come and save us. It would be an error on our part to stall, waiting for another culture-shattering moment to galvanize sweeping change at last. It might be tempting to think of radical systemic change as a defining event—a singular moment in time that alters the entire culture. But, if history is any guide, this is not how change comes to be.

The tendency to retrospectively streamline history into a series of iconic moments and figures is pervasive. We lionize historic milestones while over-looking the tireless efforts of activists and changemakers that brought us to those points in history. It's a common oversight; many don't realize, for example, that the Civil Rights Movement in the United States began in the mid-1950s. I will never forget the lecture where, as a college student, I first heard that historians consider the Civil Rights Movement to have spanned 13 years—a timespan that, interestingly enough, mirrors the duration of the Haitian Revolution. Waiting for a tectonic cultural shift would mean miss-ing the subtler, yet equally significant, opportunities to effect meaningful transformation day to day. Waiting also means becoming an observer rather than a participant in the unfolding narrative of social change; it breeds complicity.

The true challenge for us, then, lies in recognizing that significant change comes in a sequence of smaller yet impactful actions. Methodical work rooted in endurance and commitment lays the groundwork for any substan-tial shift in cultural practices, norms, policies, and societal attitudes. Neither business nor marketing and advertising are an exception.

Turning the final pages of this book, reflect on this sobering reality. In a media-dense landscape desperate for meaningful social change, we are more than just custodians of brands, products, or services; marketers are interme-diaries that transmit meaning into culture through media. Brands are not simply commodities either, but influential cultural actors that reflect and drive culture forward.

With that comes responsibility. So, learn to be steady. And stay the course. Steadiness comes from maintaining an unwavering commitment to bringing forth the future we wish to see through into existence. It demands that we move with accountability, integrity, and moral courage, even when the path of least resistance is more convenient, popular, beneficial, and safe. Change requires discipline.

As you digest these ideas, it's critical also to do the internal work—understand your role and stake in the system. Knowledge without introspection and practical application is inert. Expand your point of reference. Absorb other voices, engage with new perspectives, and confront inconvenient truths. Don't just ask yourself if you're up for the challenge; probe deeper. Why are you in this work? What specific cultural, social, or systemic practices within your organization are you aiming to transform, and to what end? What are you willing to commit to? Importantly, what's at stake for you personally?

Don't rush past these questions. Your answers will shape your role as a conscious marketer in the continuous push toward equity and inclusion in marketing, advertising, and beyond. Knowing your "why" is what helps ensure accountability, which is essential for sustained commitment. It helps keep us committed for the long run. When your actions stem from a well-defined sense of purpose, they take on a new dimension. That new dimension of purpose-driven action is precisely what we so urgently need.

As we conclude this final chapter, remember that unlocking cultural fluency takes time and practice; the more you sharpen your analytical skills, the more incisive your view of culture will become. Cultural intelligence isn't just about collecting data points; it's about embedding an entirely new cultural outlook into the core of your marketing approach. This is the only way to move beyond performative gestures and tap into the cultural potential of genuinely inclusive and socially conscious marketing.

Cultural Intelligence for Marketers is an invitation to start where you are but refuse to stay there. This book may end here, but the transformation it hopes to inspire—that's on all of us to carry on.

REFERENCES AND FURTHER READING

Foreword

Avery, J. (2010) *Saving Face by Making Meaning: The negative effects of consumers' self-serving response to brand extension*, Cambridge, MA: Harvard University Press

De Mooij, M. (2001) The future is predictable for international marketers: converging incomes lead to diverging consumer behavior, *International Marketing Review*, **17** (2), pp. 103–13

McCracken, G.D. (1990) *Culture and Consumption: New approaches to the symbolic character of consumer goods and activities*, United States: Indiana University Press

Introduction

Amazon Ads (2022) The importance of diversity and inclusion in marketing and advertising, https://advertising.amazon.com/library/guides/inclusive-marketing (archived at https://perma.cc/F7FV-ZKQB)

Barthel, D. (1988) *Putting on appearances: Gender and advertising*, Temple University Press

Behnken, B.D. and Smithers, G.D. (2015) *Racism in American Popular Media: From Aunt Jemima to the Frito Bandito*, ABC-CLIO

Boyenton, W.H. (1965) The Negro Turns to Advertising, *Journalism Quarterly*, **42** (2), pp. 227–35

Chambers, J. (2011) *Madison Avenue and the Color Line: African Americans in the advertising industry*, University of Pennsylvania Press

Cohen, D. (1970) Advertising and the Black Community, *Journal of Marketing*, 34 (4), pp. 3–11

Colby, T. (2012) Mad Men's handling of race has been brave—and painfully accurate, *Slate*, https://slate.com/culture/2012/03/mad-men-and-race-the-series-handling-of-race-has-been-painfully-accurate.html (archived at https://perma.cc/W675-MQY3)

Collins, M. (2023) *For the Culture: The Power behind the world's most successful brands, from Apple to Beyoncé*, New York: PublicAffairs

DePalma, M.J. (2020) The Psychology of Inclusion and the Effects in Advertising, Microsoft Advertising, https://about.ads.microsoft.com/en-us/blog/post/july-2020/the-psychology-of-inclusion-and-the-effects-in-advertising (archived at https://perma.cc/5JKN-RGL5)

Ferretti, F. (1970) N.A.A.C.P. Says TV Uses Few Blacks in Ads, *The New York Times*, www.nytimes.com/1970/10/07/archives/naacp-says-tv-uses-few-blacks-in-ads-survey-discloses-patterns-here.html (archived at https://perma.cc/N9TU-W2G6)

Floyd, G. (2020) Obituary: George Perry Floyd, Jr, *Buies Funeral Home*, www.buiesfuneralhome.com/obituary/George-FloydJr (archived at https://perma.cc/F5AG-53XJ)

Fox, M. (2014) Judy Protas, writer of slogan for Levy's Real Jewish Rye, dies at 91, *The New York Times*, www.nytimes.com/2014/01/12/business/judy-protas-writer-of-slogan-for-levys-real-jewish-rye-dies-at-91.html (archived at https://perma.cc/MSR4-SLYB)

Google/Ipsos (2019) How inclusive marketing affects behavior, Think with Google, www.thinkwithgoogle.com/future-of-marketing/management-and-culture/diversity-and-inclusion/inclusive-marketing-consumer-data (archived at https://perma.cc/3CSG-W6DQ)

Hall, S. (1977) Culture, the media and the "Ideological Effect", in J. Curran, M. Gurevitch and J. Wollacott (eds), *Mass Communication and Society*, London: Edward Arnold

Helmore, E. (2023) Gen Z will be last generation with white majority in US, study finds, *The Guardian*, www.theguardian.com/us-news/2023/aug/08/gen-z-americans-white-majority-study (archived at https://perma.cc/4K5E-48LW)

Herman, R. and Johnston, L. (1983) New York Day by day, *The New York Times*, www.nytimes.com/1983/02/25/nyregion/new-york-day-by-day-254551.html (archived at https://perma.cc/RSR9-7XFH)

Hymson, L. (2011) *The Company that Taught the World to Sing: Coca-Cola, globalization, and the cultural politics of branding in the twentieth century*, The University of Michigan Library, https://deepblue.lib.umich.edu/handle/2027.42/86471 (archived at https://perma.cc/UL7D-EZHS)

Kassarjian, H.H. (1969) The Negro and American Advertising, 1946–1965, *Journal of Marketing Research*, 6 (1), pp. 29–39

Kassarjian, H.H. (1971) Blacks in Advertising: A Further Comment, *Journal of Marketing Research*, 8 (3), pp. 392–393

New York Times (1964) All except profits are big in advertising; changes, problems and acquisitions on large scale; but rise in volume fails to come up to forecasts, www.nytimes.com/1964/01/06/archives/all-except-profits-are-big-in-advertising-changes-problems-and.html (archived at https://perma.cc/8W44-CWV6)

Reilly, K. et al. (1983) Women Against Pornography, *Women Against Pornography*, 5 (1), https://jstor.org/stable/community.28046787 (archived at https://perma.cc/96J7-LRLC)

Sivulka, J. (1998) *Soap, Sex, and Cigarettes: A cultural history of American advertising*, Belmont, CA: Wadsworth sparks & honey (n.d.) Culture in five: building brand loyalty with inclusivity, www.sparksandhoney.com/reports-list/2022/10/26/building-brand-loyalty-with-inclusivity (archived at https://perma.cc/WCE8-N6UU)

Telford, T. (2023) How queer went corporate: The 50-year evolution of LGBTQ+ marketing, *The Washington Post*, www.washingtonpost.com/business/2023/06/16/lgbt-marketing-advertising-history-pride-month/ (archived at https://perma.cc/HRW8-VP6M)

Williams, J.D., Lee, W.-N. and Haugtvedt, C.P. (2015) *Diversity in Advertising: Broadening the scope of Research Directions*, New York: Psychology Press

Chapter 1: Redefining Brand Success

Ang, S., Van Dyne, L. and Tan, M. (2011) Cultural Intelligence. In R. Sternberg and S. Kaufman (Eds.), *The Cambridge Handbook of Intelligence* (Cambridge Handbooks in Psychology, pp. 582–602) Cambridge: Cambridge University Press

Bakare, L. (2023) Cultural literacy belongs in every advertising classroom, *AdWeek*, www.adweek.com/creativity/cultural-literacy-belongs-in-every-advertising-classroom/ (archived at https://perma.cc/CCR9-JWRE)

Bennett, C. (2015) Victoria's Secret shows are modern sexism uncovered, *The Guardian*, www.theguardian.com/commentisfree/2015/nov/15/victorias-secrets-feminism-women-sexuality (archived at https://perma.cc/U5KZ-UTJB)

Craig, S. (1999) Torches of freedom: Themes of women's liberation in American cigarette advertising. A paper presented to the gender studies division Southwest/Texas Popular Culture Association, https://irl.umsl.edu/cgi/viewcontent.cgi?article=1111&context=urs (archived at https://perma.cc/4DTH-TF8X)

D'Innocenzio, A. (2023) Victoria's Secret overhauls its fashion show in its latest move to be more inclusive, *AP News*, https://apnews.com/article/victorias-secret-lingerie-marketing-supermodel-325baab972da88138f604d521a39e6da (archived at https://perma.cc/Z2CR-BHFJ)

Debia, A., Baladda-Brenas C., Rougier, L., Sandro Kaulartz and Roy, R. (2022) Cultural Intelligence: How can brands and communication travel across cultures? Ipsos, www.ipsos.com/en/cultural-intelligence-how-can-brands-and-communication-travel-across-cultures (archived at https://perma.cc/6RYM-Y8FK)

Earley, P. and Ang, S. (2003) *Cultural Intelligence: Individual interactions across cultures*, Stanford, Calif: Stanford University Press

Embry, S. (2023) To build a brand that lasts, dedicate time to cultural intelligence now, The Diversity Marketing Consortium, www.diversitymarketingconsortium.com/blog/to-build-a-brand-that-lasts-dedicate-time-to-cultural-intelligence-now (archived at https://perma.cc/XTE9-4EPC)

Evans, D. (2023) Future-proof your brand with cultural fluency, The Collage Group, www.collagegroup.com/2023/06/14/future-proof-your-brand-with-cultural-fluency/ (archived at https://perma.cc/B6SB-CWN9)

Ferretti, F. (1970) N.A.A.C.P. says TV uses few blacks in ads, *The New York Times*, www.nytimes.com/1970/10/07/archives/naacp-says-tv-uses-few-blacks-in-ads-survey-discloses-patterns-here.html (archived at https://perma.cc/3XQC-DZSV)

Freire, P. (1973) *Education for Critical Consciousness*, New York: Seabury Press

Freire, P. (1985) Reading the world and reading the word: an interview with Paulo Freire, *Language Arts*, **62** (1), pp. 15–21

Freire, P. (2017) *Pedagogy of the Oppressed*, Penguin Modern Classics, London

Friedman V. and Maheshwari, S. (2021) Victoria's Secret swaps Angels for 'What Women Want.' Will they buy it? *The New York Times*, www.nytimes.com/2021/06/16/business/victorias-secret-collective-megan-rapinoe.html (archived at https://perma.cc/L5ZB-2MFG)

Holt, D. and Cameron, D. (2012) *Cultural Strategy: Using innovative ideologies to build breakthrough brands*, Oxford University Press

Kassarjian, H.H. (1969) The Negro and American Advertising, 1946–1965, *Journal of Marketing Research*, **6** (1), pp. 29–39

McManis, S. (2007) Amusing or offensive, Axe ads show that sexism sells, *The Seattle Times*, www.seattletimes.com/life/lifestyle/amusing-or-offensive-axe-ads-show-that-sexism-sells/ (archived at https://perma.cc/JTZ4-ZJTG)

Miller, K. (2016) Confessions of an anonymous Victoria's Secret photoshopper, Refinery29.com, www.refinery29.com/en-us/2016/07/117242/victoria-secret-photoshopping-tricks-interview (archived at https://perma.cc/TJ2X-KRCG)

Millman, D. (2019) How symbols and brands shape our humanity, TED Talk, www.ted.com/talks/debbie_millman_how_symbols_and_brands_shape_our_humanity?language=en (archived at https://perma.cc/FN5V-86AT)

Oakenfull, G. (2021) Marketing with cultural intelligence for growth and good, Forbes, www.forbes.com/sites/gillianoakenfull/2021/04/07/pg-brands-lead-with-cultural-intelligence (archived at https://perma.cc/J7YQ-HPD3)

Procter, J. (2004) *Stuart Hall*, London: Routledge

Schlossberg, M. (2016) Victoria's Secret is ignoring a massive shift in the lingerie industry, and it could be costing it tons of money, Yahoo Sports, http://sports.yahoo.com/news/victorias-secret-ignoring-massive-shift-200800240.html? (archived at https://perma.cc/YN62-6AS4)

Sivulka, J. (1998) *Soap, Sex, and Cigarettes: A cultural history of American advertising*, Belmont, CA: Wadsworth

Smith, M.D. (2002) Decoding Victoria's Secret: The marketing of sexual beauty and ambivalence, *Studies in Popular Culture*, **25** (1), pp. 39–47, http://www.jstor.org/stable/23415007 (archived at https://perma.cc/KK4L-GUWB)

Sturken, M. and Cartwright, L. (2001) *Practices of Looking: An introduction to visual culture*, Oxford University Press

Tetrick, K. (2023) Cultural intelligence unlocks campaign strategies to support brand-led culture change, *Sustainable Brands*, https://sustainablebrands.com/read/behavior-change/cultural-intelligence-unlocks-campaign-strategies-to-support-brand-led-culture-change (archived at https://perma.cc/4KCQ-3BXY)

Williams, J.D., Lee, W.-N. and Haugtvedt, C.P. (Eds.) (2004) *Diversity in Advertising: Broadening the scope of research directions*, Lawrence Erlbaum Associates Publishers

Zalis, S. (2022) Busting gender stereotypes: the pink versus blue phenomenon, Forbes, www.forbes.com/sites/shelleyzalis/2019/09/05/busting-gender-stereotypes-the-pink-versus-blue-phenomenon/?sh=4fc774e32764 (archived at https://perma.cc/2C92-HAZN)

Chapter 2: Unlocking the 4Cs of Cultural Intelligence

Diemer, M.A., Rapa, L.J., Park, C.J. and Perry, J.C. (2017) Development and validation of the critical consciousness scale, *Youth & Society*, **49** (4), pp. 461–83

Chapter 3: Culture

Hall, S. (2016) *Cultural Studies 1983: A theoretical history*, Duke University Press

Williams, R. (1977) *Marxism and literature, Vol. 392*, Oxford Paperbacks, Oxford University Press

Chapter 4: Communication

Advil.com (2023) The Advil Pain Equity Project, www.advil.com/thepainequityproject (archived at https://perma.cc/4T9X-TDUU)

Adweek (2023) Why Inclusivity Matters, www.adweek.com/sponsored/why-inclusivity-matters (archived at https://perma.cc/AC87-NQND)

Chen, C. (2023) Why Telfar's new pricing model matters, *The Business of Fashion*, www.businessoffashion.com/briefings/retail/why-telfars-new-pricing-model-matters (archived at https://perma.cc/BG4A-JX8J)

Durkin, E. (2019) New Gillette ad shows father helping transgender son to shave, *Guardian*, www.theguardian.com/world/2019/may/28/gillette-ad-shaving-transgender-son-samson-bonkeabanut-brown (archived at https://perma.cc/E2GK-YUJF)

Hall, S. (1973/2000) 'Encoding/decoding', in Marris, P. and Thornham, S. (eds.) *Media Studies: A Reader*, 2nd edn, Edinburgh University Press, pp. 51–61

Microsoft (2023) Commemorating the impact of The King legacy, Microsoft Education Blog, https://educationblog.microsoft.com/en-us/2023/01/commemorating-the-impact-of-the-king-legacy (archived at https://perma.cc/WR7D-3ZRF)

Pauly, A. (2023) Telfar's live pricing model ≠ more expensive clothes, High Snobiety, www.highsnobiety.com/p/telfar-live-pricing-model/ (archived at https://perma.cc/85UV-DN23)

Payton, L.T. (2023) 83% of Black Americans have had a negative experience when seeking help for managing pain. A new equity project aims to change that, Fortune Well, https://fortune.com/well/2023/09/12/pain-equity-project-advil-morehouse-medical-school/ (archived at https://perma.cc/SC8C-WVNA)

Chapter 5: Consciousness

Coaston, J. (2019) Intersectionality, explained: meet Kimberlé Crenshaw, who coined the term, *Vox*, www.vox.com/the-highlight/2019/5/20/18542843/intersectionality-conservatism-law-race-gender-discrimination (archived at https://perma.cc/SE6V-UMRT)

Crenshaw, K. (1989) Demarginalizing the Intersection of Race and Sex: A Black Feminist Critique of Antidiscrimination Doctrine, Feminist Theory and Antiracist Politics, *University of Chicago Legal Forum*: Vol. 1989, Article 8, https://chicagounbound.uchicago.edu/uclf/vol1989/iss1/8/ (archived at https://perma.cc/865E-BJCP)

Google Trends (2020) Intersectionality 5/24/2020-5/31/2020

Krishnan, M., Madgavkar, A. Ellingrud, K., Yee, L., Hunt, V., White, O. and Mahajan, D. (2020) Ten things to know about gender equality, McKinsey & Company, www.mckinsey.com/featured-insights/diversity-and-inclusion/ten-things-to-know-about-gender-equality (archived at https://perma.cc/BX6N-D9QW)

REI (2023) REI Cooperative Action Fund invests $4 million in nonprofits working to create a more equitable outdoors, www.rei.com/newsroom/article/rei-cooperative-action-fund-invests-4-million-in-nonprofits-working-to-create-a-more-equitable-outdoors (archived at https://perma.cc/R8U3-PEAV)

Chapter 6: Community

Aten, J. (2023) I can't stop thinking about how awkward Apple's 'Mother Nature' ad was, and I finally figured out why, Inc.com, www.inc.com/jason-aten/i-cant-stop-thinking-about-how-awkward-apples-mother-nature-ad-was-i-finally-figured-out-why.html (archived at https://perma.cc/K4GJ-BZXV)

Atske, S. (2019) In their own words: behind Americans' views of 'socialism' and 'capitalism', Pew Research Center—U.S. Politics & Policy, www.pewresearch.org/politics/2019/10/07/in-their-own-words-behind-americans-views-of-socialism-and-capitalism/ (archived at https://perma.cc/ZRP6-AAPQ)

Barth, M. (2023) Gen Zers are turning to 'radical rest,' delusional thinking, and self-indulgence as they struggle to cope with late-stage capitalism, *Fortune*, https://fortune.com/2023/06/27/gen-zers-turning-to-radical-rest-delusional-thinking-self-indulgence-late-stage-capitalism-molly-barth/ (archived at https://perma.cc/VDD2-SYBD)

Begoun, E. (2021) Why the natural products industry should drop the term 'consumer', Newhope.com, www.newhope.com/business-management/why-the-natural-products-industry-should-drop-the-term-consumer- (archived at https://perma.cc/ZU7L-GDYA)

Edelman (2023) 2023 Edelman Trust Barometer, www.edelman.com/trust/2023/trust-barometer (archived at https://perma.cc/F54Z-2W9C)

Edwards, K. (2023) Black Americans view capitalism more negatively than positively but express hope in Black businesses, Pew Research Center, www.pewresearch.org/short-reads/2023/03/08/black-americans-view-capitalism-more-negatively-than-positively-but-express-hope-in-black-businesses (archived at https://perma.cc/22K9-D6Y4)

Elson, C. and King, K. (2023) Millennial and Gen Z views of free markets, social issues, and the workplace, Center for the Study of Capitalism, Wake Forest University, https://capitalism.wfu.edu/wp-content/uploads/2023/01/SocialIssuesWorkplace_ElsonKing.pdf (archived at https://perma.cc/6XPK-WFQ5)

Harvey, D. (1982/2005) *The New Imperialism*, Oxford University Press, Oxford

Hiebert, P. (2023) Infographic: When brands speak out, many consumers are skeptical, Adweek.com, www.adweek.com/brand-marketing/infographic-when-brands-speak-out-many-consumers-are-skeptical/ (archived at https://perma.cc/94EK-7E4X)

Hodson, L. (2023) Engaging with the gen Z community: a strategic guide for global brands, *The Drum*, www.thedrum.com/opinion/2023/08/10/engaging-with-the-gen-z-community-strategic-guide-global-brands (archived at https://perma.cc/RC93-LV67)

Holt, B. (2023) How luxury fashion has appropriated Black fashion and streetwear, *Insider*, www.insider.com/luxury-fashion-cultural-appropriation-black-streetwear-style-2023-8 (archived at https://perma.cc/H549-45L5)

Hyken, S. (2023) Belonging to the brand: how community is reshaping the marketing landscape, *Forbes*, 20 Feb, www.forbes.com/sites/shephyken/2023/02/19/belonging-to-the-brand-how-community-is-reshaping-the-marketing-landscape/?sh=964d88e2fb76 (archived at https://perma.cc/GH3H-926S)

Laneri, R. and Wang, C. (2014) Ralph Lauren runs an assimilation-themed campaign, Refinery29.com, www.refinery29.com/en-us/ralph-lauren-native-appropriation (archived at https://perma.cc/FYA4-BVSA)

Microsoft (2023) Commemorating the impact of The King legacy, Microsoft Education Blog, https://educationblog.microsoft.com/en-us/2023/01/commemorating-the-impact-of-the-king-legacy (archived at https://perma.cc/4QB7-WN84)

Mordecai (2020) Why every brand should be anti-capitalist, *The Drum*, www.thedrum.com/opinion/2020/10/12/why-every-brand-should-be-anti-capitalist (archived at https://perma.cc/XSW7-UAUZ)

Nadeem, R. (2022) Modest declines in positive views of 'socialism' and 'capitalism' in U.S., Pew Research Center—U.S. Politics & Policy, www.pewresearch.org/politics/2022/09/19/modest-declines-in-positive-views-of-socialism-and-capitalism-in-u-s/ (archived at https://perma.cc/HXJ3-WCEU)

Schafer, M. (2023) *Belonging to the Brand: Why community is the last great marketing strategy*, Schaefer Marketing Solutions

Schroeder, R. (2021) The beauty brands placing cultural appreciation over appropriation, *Harper's Bazaar*, www.harpersbazaar.com/uk/beauty/a35613683/best-niche-beauty-brands/ (archived at https://perma.cc/BJ6B-3VL4)

Sprout Social (2019) Stand Up, Stand Aside, https://media.sproutsocial.com/uploads/SproutSocial-BrandsGetReal-StandUp-StandAside.pdf (archived at https://perma.cc/T2G6-SEGG)

Wallerstein, I. (1974) *The Modern World-System I: Capitalist agriculture and the origins of the european world-economy in the sixteenth century*, Academic Press, New York

Wronski, L. (2021) Axios/Momentive poll: Capitalism and socialism, www.surveymonkey.com/curiosity/axios-capitalism-update (archived at https://perma.cc/Z858-D8H7)

Chapter 7: Now What?

Bhattarai, A. (2021) Sephora's plan to combat racial bias: Fewer security guards, more black-owned brands and New Protocols, *The Washington Post*, www.washingtonpost.com/business/2021/01/13/sephora-race-bias-discrimination/ (archived at https://perma.cc/9KE4-7CSY)

Breen, A. (2023) The viral brand behind soaring searches for 'female body hair' still gets up close and personal after its $310 million sale, *Entrepreneur*, www.entrepreneur.com/leadership/the-viral-brand-that-sold-for-310-million-isnt-afraid-of/446564 (archived at https://perma.cc/G7GJ-GG7R)

Dockterman, E. (2023) Every single Barbie partnership that we could find, *TIME*, https://time.com/6294123/barbie-partnerships-crocs-burger-king (archived at https://perma.cc/L96S-TKHF)

Driver, G. (2019) Shaving brand Billie invited me to join Movember and to shed my body hair insecurities, *Elle*, www.elle.com/uk/beauty/body-and-physical-health/a29633589/shaving-brand-billie-women-movember/ (archived at https://perma.cc/5GSC-CJH4)

Feingold, S. (2022) What is the 'pink tax' and how does it hinder women? World Economic Forum, www.weforum.org/agenda/2022/07/what-is-the-pink-tax-and-how-does-it-hinder-women/ (archived at https://perma.cc/36UH-6PPY)

Fitzhugh, E., Julien, J., Noel, N. and Stewart, S. (2020) It's time for a new approach to racial equity, McKinsey & Company, www.mckinsey.com/bem/our-insights/its-time-for-a-new-approach-to-racial-equity (archived at https://perma.cc/74U9-2H93)

Harper, S. (2022) Where is the $200 billion companies promised after George Floyd's murder? *Forbes*, 18 Oct, www.forbes.com/sites/shaunharper/2022/10/17/where-is-the-200-billion-companies-promised-after-george-floyds-murder/?sh=4df18e544507 (archived at https://perma.cc/4QUL-4ACG)

Jan, T. (2021) After George Floyd's death, big business pledged nearly $50 billion for racial justice. This is where the money is going, *Washington Post*, www.washingtonpost.com/business/interactive/2021/george-floyd-corporate-america-racial-justice/ (archived at https://perma.cc/2T25-W3MD)

Klein, M. (2023) Trends have lost all meaning, *Contagious*, www.contagious.com/news-and-views/trends-have-lost-all-meaning (archived at https://perma.cc/XTL5-B5YG)

Lobad, N. (2023) Billie takes aim at double standards for women with board game launch, *Women's Wear Daily* (WWD), https://wwd.com/beauty-industry-news/beauty-features/billie-takes-aim-at-the-double-standards-for-women-with-board-game-launch-1235759362/ (archived at https://perma.cc/S23N-UFTZ)

Nelson, S. (2023) Eos tackles toxic masculinity as it expands into men's shaving, *AdWeek*, www.adweek.com/creativity/eos-tackles-toxic-masculinity-as-it-expands-into-mens-shaving/ (archived at https://perma.cc/2BK3-PKDE)

Shu, C. (2018) Billie, which wants to eliminate the "pink tax," closes a $6M seed round for its razor subscription service, *TechCrunch*, https://techcrunch.com/2018/04/12/billie-which-wants-to-destroy-the-pink-tax-closes-a-6m-seed-round-for-its-razor-subscription-service/ (archived at https://perma.cc/C3QN-5BWJ)

Solé, E. (2019) People are grossed out by razor company telling women they don't have to shave: 'It's just tacky,' *Yahoo!*, https://ca.style.yahoo.com/people-are-grossed-out-by-razor-company-telling-women-they-dont-have-to-shave-005733384.html (archived at https://perma.cc/2JKQ-UU9R)

Chapter 8: What's Next?

Gallagher, L. (2017) President Trump wants to keep them out. Airbnb is inviting them in, *Fortune*, https://fortune.com/2017/01/29/donald-trump-muslim-ban-airbnb/ (archived at https://perma.cc/QH8B-XTDG)

Conclusion

Foner, P.S. and Taylor, Y. (Eds.) (2000) *Frederick Douglass: Selected speeches and writings*, Chicago Review Press

INDEX

The index is filed in alphabetical, word-by-word order. Numbers in main headings and "+" are filed as spelt out in full. Acronyms and "Mc" are filed as presented. Hashtags (#) are ignored for filing purposes. Page locators in *italics* denote information contained within a table or figure; those in roman numeral denote information within the foreword.

Looking for another book?

Explore our award-winning
books from global business
experts in Marketing and Sales

Scan the code to browse

www.koganpage.com/marketing

More books on Brand Strategy from Kogan Page

Second Edition

Using Semiotics in Marketing

How to achieve consumer insight for brand growth and profits

RACHEL LAWES

ISBN: 9781398607644

BRAND LOVE

Building Strong Consumer-Brand Connections

Lydia Michael

ISBN: 9781398611276